GO QUIETLY

... or else

GO QUIETLY

. . . or else

Spiro T. Agnew

WILLIAM MORROW AND COMPANY, INC.

New York   *1980*

Library of Congress Catalog Card Number 80-80399

ISBN 0-688-03668-6

Printed in the United States of America

First Edition

1   2   3   4   5   6   7   8   9   10

Book Design by Michael Mauceri

To Frank Sinatra

CONTENTS

PROLOGUE

I am writing this book because I am innocent of the allegations against me which compelled me to resign from the vice-presidency of the United States in 1973.

This is not to say I have not made mistakes, or failed to do things I ought to have done, or done things I ought not to have done. I am human, and my conduct has been no better and no worse than that of other officeholders in these United States. But I am innocent of the charges of bribery and extortion which are detailed in the Exposition of Evidence filed against me by the prosecutors in the United States District Court of Maryland. I categorically denied these allegations in open court, and I continue to deny them to this day.

It has taken me a long time to confront squarely the immutable reality that this book cannot further be delayed. During the past six years, I have found many reasons to put off the detailed re-visitation of the most unpleasant days of my life. Some of the reasons were good ones, and others were simply defensive. For me, the writing of this book has reopened old wounds, as I knew it would. There is little doubt that its discussion will bring more pain. There is no hell quite like being dissected before an audience of millions. But the story must be told to complete the historical record—even if it changes few opinions.

I am not so naïve as to think that even if I could *prove* my innocence beyond any reasonable doubt there would not still be many people—some of much influence and even of fair-mindedness—who would disbelieve me.

I have made many enemies in my political life. I believe this happened mainly because I was an outspoken advocate of unpopular stands—stands which I believed were correct and still believe to be correct. I was a conservative at a time when liberals

9

captured the imagination and sympathy of the communications media. I took a tough line when those who had the attention of the nation wanted a weak line. I staunchly and loyally supported a President who eventually left office against his will and in disgrace. I challenged some of the myths of the liberal establishment. And perhaps more dangerous politically to myself than any other factor, I antagonized the press of this nation.

I turned on them—the newspapers, the newsmagazines, the radio and television people—the same glaring light of examination that they so indiscriminately, and sometimes so recklessly, turn on those in public office. I believe in a free press, not an irresponsible press, and because of that belief I was reviled and damned.

Friends have warned that this book will goad my enemies to further efforts to destroy me, and that new accusations and revelations from "reliable sources" will plague my peace. That is probably true, but hardly a valid reason for silence. Agnewphobes have never held back in the past.

Other friends have positively hungered for this book. They say that covering up in a corner and taking the blows without any defense is alien to my nature. They too are correct.

In any event, I am glad I waited. The passage of time has revealed a great deal that was hidden on October 10, 1973, the day I resigned. Details dredged by those who used the Freedom of Information Act to seek undisclosed Agnew wrongdoing have proved helpful, rather than harmful. Braggadocian struttings by the celebrated prosecutorial giant-killers have given great insight into their motivations and machinations. Best of all, the ultimate payment to the witnesses against me, a quid pro quo that the Justice Department still denies having made, is now naked for all to see. Three of the four government witnesses who admitted to serious crimes in the Exposition of Evidence have walked away scot-free—no imprisonments, no fines, no convictions to mar their futures. The fourth went to jail for a few months, but not for any offense related to my case.

But in spite of all this, no easy, clear-cut proof of my innocence is available to me. I am a man who was judged out of court on the basis of false testimony abetted by those who sought my political ruin. So eager were my enemies to convict me, not one questioned the fact there was no corroboration that I had committed the alleged crimes. Nor could there have been any corroboration.

As a man I once knew often said, let me make one thing perfectly clear. This is not an autobiography; it is not intended to be a chronological account of my life. Primarily, it covers the events leading to my resignation. Secondarily, it reflects a little of my philosophy and my thoughts on the course of our country. Finally, it tells in part what my life has been like after leaving public office under the label "disgraced former Vice-President and convicted felon."

Because this is not a complete memoir, I have made no attempt to express here my appreciation to many, many people who have, at one time or another, touched and lighted my life. Someday in the future I may write a complete autobiography and will then have an opportunity to thank them adequately. Meanwhile, I would be remiss if I failed to acknowledge the invaluable help of the former and present members of my staff who accumulated and correlated much of the record upon which this book is based. I am also grateful to my lawyers and the members of my former Secret Service details for their recollections and assistance. But most of all, I am indebted to my family and friends, whose loyalty and faith sustained me during some very dark days.

SPIRO T. AGNEW

THE NUMBER OF THOSE WHO UN-
DERGO THE FATIGUE OF JUDGING
FOR THEMSELVES IS VERY SMALL IN-
DEED.

—RICHARD SHERIDAN
1777

CHAPTER ONE

PLAY THE PART WELL

It was four minutes past 2:00 P.M., October 10, 1973, when the bailiff intoned the ancient litany; the judge was approaching.

Background noise from the crowded room abated, except for the voices of the few who never quiet immediately on instruction. Everyone rose as directed, eyes on the black-robed, stocky figure quickly mounting the few steps to the bench.

I was conscious only of the ritual. It seemed very important to play the part well—to stand erect, to be calm, to retain dignity, to speak clearly and firmly.

There was a rustle of clothing as, again on signal, we sat. I felt the presence of my New York trial counsel—Jay Topkis and Martin London—beside me at the table, but I did not look at them. My attention was fixed on Judge Walter E. Hoffman. He was stage center, and he was about to begin the case of *United States of America* v. *Spiro T. Agnew.*

Judd Best, the Washington lawyer who had been with me from the beginning of the recent months of travail, entered the courtroom and sat down beside me. "Your letter of resignation has been delivered to the Secretary of State as you directed," he said quietly.

I nodded absently, keeping my attention on the judge, who through his questions to my senior counsel, Topkis, was now informing the observers that what they were about to witness was not an interlocutory proceeding concerning news leaks, but a criminal determination by the federal government against one Spiro T. Agnew—until a few moments before, the Vice-President of the United States. An audible murmur of surprise ran through the room, quickly followed by absolute silence. If anyone had accepted the judge's invitation to leave unless able to remain for the duration of the proceedings, I was not aware of it.

And I would have noticed anything that was unimportant at that moment. My mind was seeking diversion by concentrating on the immediate. I was numb—outside myself looking down on the scene as though it were a dream. Some buffer in my brain pushed away full realization of the enormity of the personal tragedy that was taking place. Grief and sorrow were held in a secret cage to be released later in a private place. I only knew I must not break in public. I could not give my enemies that satisfaction.

I stood to answer questions put directly to me by the court to be certain I understood the plea agreement. My fingers rested lightly on the table. There was no shaking; my voice was steady. Inside me another voice said, "It's only a play, only a play."

Earlier that day, I had said the same thing to Arthur J. Sohmer, my Chief of Staff, as I made my last journey as Vice-President of the United States—the relatively short drive on the expressway from the Executive Office Building in Washington to this courtroom in Baltimore's old Federal Building. We had gone several miles without a word from Art or the two Secret Service agents in the front seat. The gloom was as thick as a London fog. Finally, I broke the silence by remarking that life is unpredictable, and you have to play the cards you are dealt. We began to talk about Shakespeare's *As You Like It,* and the truth of the lines: "All the world's a stage, and all the men and women merely players . . ." I remember saying that I had a choice—either to live with the situation as it was or let it kill me. "Tomorrow," I said, "I will still have obligations to my family. My choice is to make the best I can of it."

The two agents, who were close to me and to our whole family, were visibly affected by the poignancy of the moment. Art Sohmer had been with me from the very beginning of my political career in the 1950's in Baltimore County. He had watched me go through good times and bad. It was his choice to accompany me through this final demeaning appearance. He said simply, "I was with you at the beginning and I'm going to be with you at the end."

Out of the corner of my eye, I could see that Art was wiping his eyes with his handkerchief. I felt a surge of emotion. I didn't dare look at him for fear of crying. So I focused on the idea that this was just a play and that I must perform my part creditably.

That self-deception was my device to keep myself in tight control, and it served me well then and later on, in the courtroom.

Now U.S. Attorney George Beall was presenting to the court "the Attorney General of the United States, the Honorable Elliot L. Richardson," as well as the Assistant Attorney General, Henry Petersen. Beall then handed the court a copy of the single-count criminal information alleging income tax evasion for the year 1967, which I had agreed not to contest. Topkis confirmed this, and Judge Hoffman began to address me again.

I quickly rose to my feet to answer a series of questions that confirmed my knowledge I was waiving my right to trial, and that the judge would find me guilty of the felony of tax evasion. Again, the inner voice saying, "Life's just a play—play out the role you have been given."

Then that was over, and I was listening to Elliot Richardson outline the accusations against me that would not be brought to trial. I knew this tainted testimony by heart, and my mind wandered.

What was I, Ted Agnew, doing in this courtroom, suddenly the defendant in a criminal trial? My whole experience with the law had been as a lawyer and teacher, not a felon. I loved the orderliness of the law, its rote and its unhurried logic. How many times had I stood in courtrooms like this as a respected officer of the court? How could a lifetime of work and accomplishment—that had led me to the second-highest office in a nation of two hundred and twenty million free people—be destroyed in an afternoon? The numbness in me spread. I felt vacant, drained, incapable of reacting to either pain or pleasure. I stared at the walnut paneling behind the bench, only half conscious of what was being said around me.

Now Judge Hoffman was calling on me again, this time to afford me the opportunity to comment prior to sentencing. As I got to my feet, a terrible fatigue came over me. I fought it back. Play the part, play the part, I told myself.

"Thank you, Your Honor," I said. Suddenly, new strength flowed through me. I was going to address the court, and that was something I knew how to do, had been trained to do. I picked up my prepared statement and was pleased to see that my hand was steady. I would play the part to the end.

"May I say, at the outset, I want to express my appreciation for the courtesy and cooperation extended to me through my counsel in their deliberations with the prosecutors and throughout the consultation on this matter," I began.

"My decision to resign and enter a plea of nolo contendere rests on my belief that the public interest requires a swift disposition of the problems which are facing me. I am advised that a full legal defense of the probable charges against me could consume several years. I am concerned that intense media interest in the case would distract public attention from important national problems, to the country's detriment.

"I am aware that witnesses are prepared to testify that I and my agents received payments from consulting engineers doing business with the State of Maryland during the period I was Governor.

"With the exception of the admission that follows, I categorically deny the assertions of illegal acts on my part made by government witnesses.

"I admit that I did receive payments during the year 1967 which were not expended for political purposes and that therefore these payments were income, taxable to me in that year, and that I so knew.

"I further acknowledge that contracts were awarded by state agencies in 1967 and other years to those who made such payments, and that I was aware of such awards. I am aware that government witnesses are prepared to testify that preferential treatment was accorded to the paying companies pursuant to an understanding with me when I was Governor. I stress, however, that no contracts were awarded to contractors who were not competent to perform the work and, in most instances, state contracts were awarded without any arrangement for the payment of money by the contractor.

"I deny that the payments in any way influenced my official actions. I am confident, moreover, that testimony presented in my behalf would make it clear that I at no time conducted my official duties as County Executive or Governor of Maryland in a manner harmful to the interests of the county or state, or my duties as Vice-President of the United States in a manner harmful to the nation; and I further assert that my acceptance of contributions was part of a long-established pattern of political fund-raising in the state. At no time have I enriched myself at the expense of my public trust.

"In all the circumstances, I have concluded that protracted proceedings before the grand jury, the Congress, and the courts, with the speculation and controversy inevitably surrounding them, would seriously prejudice the national interest.

"These, briefly stated, Your Honor, are the reasons that I am entering a plea of nolo contendere to the charge that I did receive payments in 1967 which I failed to report for the purposes of income taxation."

Judge Hoffman then summed up the proceedings and began the final disposition of the case. In the course of this he indicated that the statements of the parties—the forty-page exposition of evidence by the government and my one-page blanket denial of these assertions—were totally irrelevant, as far as the court was concerned. He allowed them in because they were "part of the understanding between the parties" and "because of the charges and countercharges which have received so much advance publicity." He went on to say that "the truth of these charges and countercharges can never be established by any judicial decision or action," and that "it would have been my preference to omit these statements and end the verbal warfare as to this tragic event in history."

The judge, after commenting about his usual disposition of income tax cases, asked me if I had anything further to say.

I said, "I have no further comments, Your Honor." My role was nearly over. Only remaining were the words that would change my life irreversibly and commit me to the disgrace of the label "convicted felon."

"It is the judgment of the court that imposition of any sentence be suspended for a period of three years, conditioned that you, Spiro T. Agnew, at all times will be of uniform good behavior, that you will not violate the laws of the United States or any state; that as a further condition of this probation, you are to pay a fine in the sum of ten thousand dollars within thirty days from this date, or otherwise stand committed for nonpayment of said fine; and that you shall not be required to be under the supervision of the probation officer of this court unless otherwise ordered by the court."

It was exactly 2:47 P.M. In just forty-three minutes my life had been drastically altered.

After Judge Hoffman left the courtroom, there was a mad scramble by the news media to get to the phones. I quickly shook hands with my lawyers and followed the Secret Service agents out through a side door. Later, I learned that the Attorney General and Assistant Attorney General, at the moment I left, had been making their way toward me to offer condolences. I am glad I was spared that ultimate hypocrisy.

The agents led me quickly through a narrow corridor and to a waiting elevator, which whisked me down to the side entrance of the courthouse where the cars were waiting. As I stepped out on the street, I was confronted by a few members of the press and television media. Most were at the main entrance on Calvert Street.

Recognizing a few faces from earlier political days, I stopped for a moment. Almost at once, a crowd gathered. Flashbulbs popped in the hazy gray afternoon light. Asked to comment on what had happened, I said that I had resigned "in the best interests of the nation" and "to spare my family from a brutalizing court fight that could have lasted two years."

Then Sohmer and I jumped in the back seat and we were off, with the follow-up car right behind us. As I looked out the rear window, I could see a horde of frustrated newsmen running toward the spot we had just left.

Although I felt some relief that the months of indecision and anxiety were finally over, my next destination was hardly one to improve my state of mind. Just the day before, my half-brother, Roy Pollard, had succumbed to a massive stroke. Now I would join his wife, Anne, at the funeral home. Judy and my elderly aunt—who had been as close as a mother to Roy and me—would meet me there.

At 3:15 P.M. we arrived at the Loring Beyer Funeral Home in Randallstown, Maryland. As we pulled to the rear parking lot, I saw a sizable press contingent waiting at the door. There was to be no privacy, not even in this moment of grief.

We got out of the car and I thanked Art. The Secret Service were having a shift change here, and Art would return to Washington with the relieved detail. When the new agents and I entered the funeral parlor, some of the press tried to accompany me. Someone from the funeral home stopped them at the door. I guess they expected to photograph me at the casket, but I wanted none of that. I believe even a public man is entitled to some privacy.

Once inside, I went immediately to Judy, Anne Pollard, and my aunt. One of our daughters, Susan, was also there. Friends were in the room. There was no emotional scene. Our family is not very demonstrative of inner feelings. Faces were drawn and eyes were a little glazed, but there were no tears. Judy looked hard at me to see how I was holding up. She is such a tower of strength in any crisis. I think she was relieved to see that I wasn't about to crack. My poor aunt, over eighty and not in the best of health, was bravely bearing up under the strain. I don't think she fully realized at that moment what had happened to me. It was a good thing. She had had about all she could handle in the death of one of her favorite nephews.

We stayed at the funeral home until about 7:00 P.M. It was difficult for me to receive my brother's and my friends knowing that the news of my resignation and conviction was being flashed all over the world. People tried to be considerate, but they couldn't avoid staring at me. Several times I wanted to say, "Stop staring at me. I'm not a freak on display. I'm a human being, just as you are, and I don't want my hurt to be examined so clinically."

By the time we had taken my aunt to her home near Towson, it was nearly eight o'clock. I had not eaten anything but a small breakfast, and I was quite hungry. We decided to stop at Sabatino's, a favorite restaurant in Baltimore's Little Italy, before returning to Kenwood. Judy and I and Susan had a quiet dinner. Later, an item written by a columnist made me seem insensitive and crass for "having the stomach" to celebrate at dinner after such a day. Well, the meal was not a wake, nor was it a morose discussion of our new low station in life. It was a family meal, one of the kind I hope we will continue to have, fair weather or foul.

Riding back home in the car, I put my head back against the cushion, closed my eyes, and the events of this difficult day replayed in my mind.

I remembered awakening at 7:00 A.M. after about two hours of sound sleep. There was a brief moment of unawareness, and then the realization of what the day was to be coursed through me in a nerve-wracking wave. While I was shaving I began to feel a little better, to think of a few good things—that I had arranged for my staff to be taken care of, and that at last everything would be out: there would be no more uncertainty.

When I arrived at my E.O.B. office at 9:20 A.M., Art Sohmer and my secretary, Mary Ellen Warner, were waiting for me with mail to be signed, and a deluge of last-minute details. David Keene, the staff member who had worked hard to arrange a now-canceled breakfast with some House members, was pressing to see me. Other staff members, also unaware that I was already well into my final hours as Vice-President, wanted to consult with me about ongoing projects. I simply had to put them off.

Mary Ellen told me that Judd Best was on his way over to discuss the final draft of the settlement papers. She had been my personal secretary for only a few years, but had worked in my office since I was governor. When she put my usual cup of coffee on the desk, I noticed that her hand was shaking. She was an excellent secretary, dedicated and totally loyal, as was Alice Fringer, who had begun with me in Baltimore County and had retired not long after I became Vice-President. When I look back on my days in public office, I am always impressed by the quality of the people whom I persuaded to work with me. Many of them are still close friends, and most keep in touch with Judy and me. The same thing is true of the Secret Service agents who were assigned to the vice-presidential detail during my time. I cannot say enough good things about these fine young professionals, who were thrown by circumstance into such close contact with the Agnew family.

Judd Best came in a little later and we went over the papers and scenario for the imminent drama. He was calm and unruffled, never losing his perspective or his sense of humor under the most difficult circumstances.

Shortly after 1:30 P.M., Jerry Parr, the Secret Service shift leader that morning, informed me that it was time to leave for Baltimore. I remember the distress on Mary Ellen's face as I was leaving. She hurried back into her office so that I wouldn't see the tears.

Then came the events I have already recounted here. I went over the whole day in my mind, and I could feel the depression returning. I reached over, took my wife's hand. She held on very tight. Somehow that made it better.

When I awakened the next morning from the deep sleep brought on by total emotional exhaustion, I wanted nothing more than to pull the covers over my head and withdraw from the human race. The terrible emptiness had returned and had brought an unwelcome companion, self-pity. "Why me?" I thought. "Why have I been singled out to be punished for things I did not do?"

But there was no time to withdraw from reality and brood. That very day I had responsibilities that must be performed—responsibilities that would force me to go to public places. The news media were already camped outside our home. I knew the reporters would be everywhere I went, recording my actions for the world to see.

We rolled out of the driveway past the clicking cameras and the shouts of the media people, and again headed for Baltimore. After stopping in Rogers Forge to pick up my sad and bewildered aunt, we returned to the funeral home. The news media, of course, were there in force. I did not stop to comment; the occasion was not appropriate. There were brief services for my deceased brother, Roy. Callously, questions were shouted at me by some reporters as the family moved to the cars. I ignored them, feeling some anger at this tasteless intrusion on a very private occasion.

At the cemetery, the media became even more aggressive, trampling nearby graves to get into position for close observation of the burial. As we left the graveside to move back to the vehicles, there was a similar press rush and a gravestone was knocked over. Then, while I was escorting my tearful aunt to the car, I noticed the final indignity—a microphone on a long pole was being held just over our heads to eavesdrop on our conversation. It was hardly the news media's finest hour.

CHAPTER TWO

SALT AND SOME PEPPER

The primary purpose of this book is to examine in detail the torrent of 1973 developments that culminated in the shocking events just told. But for the reader to understand fully how the second-ranking citizen of the United States could be so politically weak that he was destroyed by uncorroborated accusations, the background information that follows is necessary. Beyond this chapter, the book will focus on matters related to the Agnew investigation.

As the facts unfold in the subsequent chapters, the reader may well wonder why—equipped with such exact knowledge of the weakness of the case against me—I did not persevere and stand trial. Unfortunately, I did not then have access to the facts that you are going to read. It took five years of diligent digging, and the final resolution just two years ago of the cases of Hammerman, Wolff, Green, and Matz, for me to find out the entire story. Nor did I know in October 1973 that Richard Nixon had played me as a pawn in the desperate game for his survival. Had I known all these things, my decision to go quietly may well have been otherwise.

It was February 9, 1973, exactly three months after an elaborate celebration of my fifty-fourth birthday—insisted on, arranged, and financed by I. Harold (Bud) Hammerman, who was then my friend. *Air Force Two* cruised smoothly above the Pacific, bringing me home from an official mission to Southeast Asia. Through a few tufts of white clouds far below, the ocean reflected the clear blue sky. My mood was equally serene, and I felt confident that the future offered me bright promises of success.

Three weeks before, Richard M. Nixon had been inaugurated for his second term in the White House, and I had been sworn in again as Vice-President in a Capitol ceremony that marked the triumphant achievement of our new American majority. The President and I had earned a tremendous vote of confidence from the American people in our victory over George McGovern and Sargent Shriver, capturing forty-nine states and all the electoral votes except those of Massachusetts, the District of Columbia, and one vote in Virginia. We stood, virtually unchallenged, at a political peak. Furthermore, the Paris peace agreement on January 23—purporting to end the long and bloody war in Southeast Asia, with South Vietnam still an independent nation—appeared to have vindicated our long fight to achieve "peace with honor." At least that is what the President had said, and in those days I believed in the President.

During the administration's internecine struggles over Vietnam, it was generally accepted that I was the number-one hawk. I was convinced that the President was right in his tough decision to take strong action against the Communist forces, even at the risk of touching off violent protest demonstrations from the antiwar activists. I endorsed his refusal to accept a quick peace that would have amounted to surrender; his incursion into Cambodia; his decision to blockade Haiphong harbor and resume the bombing to check the enemy's Easter offensive in 1972, and his order for the precision bombing in December 1972 that ultimately forced Hanoi back to the bargaining table in Paris for the final settlement. We had been tough, but—it is now evident from the human rights abuses in Communist Indochina—not nearly tough enough.

Soon after the accord was announced, the President sent me as his personal emissary to the heads of eight Asian nations to assure them that the United States would continue to provide them with military and economic aid, and that we would remain a power in the Pacific. First, at Saigon, I conveyed Mr. Nixon's personal assurance to a skeptical President Nguyen Van Thieu that until the South Vietnamese people decided otherwise in a free election, our government would continue to recognize his as the only legitimate regime in South Vietnam; and that if the North Vietnamese violated the pact, we would react against them with force.

Coming events would more than justify Thieu's skepticism as the North Vietnamese forces later streamed south, hard on our heels, and destroyed the demoralized remnants of South Vietnam's army. In my judgment, the failure of the Nobel authorities to revoke the peace prize awarded to the duplicitous Le Duc Tho has cheapened this once coveted award.

I knew that Thieu had accepted the peace treaty most reluctantly, and only after Nixon had told him emphatically that we would sign it whether he did or not. Our separate action would have left him, without the essential help from the United States, to carry on a futile fight against his Russian-supported enemy. Gen. Alexander Haig, in Saigon as Nixon's representative, had told Thieu in plain army language that the South Vietnamese leader had to go along—or else. I did not know then how forceful the general could be in delivering such an ultimatum.

I left a somewhat reassured but still uneasy President Thieu and boarded *Air Force Two*, ostensibly for Thailand. Announcing Thailand as the destination was a necessary deception: we planned to stop in Cambodia if the tactical situation permitted. Once we were airborne and had completed final checks through secure communications, I decided to make the stop. I then informed the traveling press. Most of them, despite their understandable antipathy to being misdirected by politicians, realized why we had kept them in the dark so long.

There was a real reason to be careful. The Khmer Rouge were only five miles from Phnom Penh, and the airport was already under sporadic rocket attack. It was decided that we would make a steep approach, land and deplane quickly, and that *Air Force Two* would immediately take off again, circling out of range until we were ready to be picked up at the completion of our mission.

Helicopter gunships were ready to take me and principal staff members into the city. The rest went by armed motor convoy. As my chopper took off, we narrowly escaped tragedy. The assistant special agent in charge of my Secret Service detail, who had not yet had a chance to buckle in, was partly thrown out of the craft by a sudden sideways lurch of the aircraft. Fortunately, another agent grabbed him and hauled him back to safety. The injury he received in the struggle to climb back aboard required surgery later.

The capital of Cambodia was then a beautiful city, notwithstanding some war damage. We proceeded directly to the palace, which was heavily guarded by troops with automatic rifles ready, where I was met by General Lon Nol. I was shocked to see what a toll his recent stroke had taken physically. The robust man who had received me in Phnom Penh thirty months before bore little resemblance to the fragile, gray-faced officer who now required assistance to stand.

Mentally, he had lost no acuity. He was grateful for this demonstration of United States support. I told Gen. Lon Nol that we would continue sending him arms to assist his increasingly difficult effort to repel the Communist aggressors. I told him that I was pleased to see Sirik Matak—an influential former opponent—among those present, and suggested that he could answer some of his critics by expanding the political base of his government—by making more visible those former opponents who were now united with him out of common fear of the Communists. Soon, I knew, Congress would cut off the money for the United States bombing of the Communists inside Cambodia; then it would be impossible to save the poor people there from the brutality of the Khmer Rouge savages, who would eventually conquer the country and kill at least a million of its inhabitants before being succeeded by Le Duc Tho's equally brutal peace-prize pretties.

I brought Nixon's message of continued aid in my visits to Thailand, Laos, Indonesia, Singapore, Malaysia, and the Philippines. At Manila, I thanked President Marcos for his help in caring for our prisoners of war, who were freed by the peace pact, and hastening their return home. On the last day, *Air Force Two* took off from Malaysia's capital, Kuala Lumpur, touched down in Manila for my meeting with Marcos, and again in Honolulu, and landed finally at the Marine Air Base at El Toro, California —all in a single calendar day. Of course, the reason for the unusually long day was that we had flown eastward and crossed the International Date Line. I remember remarking, "This is the longest February ninth I ever saw—all the way from Kuala Lumpur to California."

The next day, after an overnight stay at Newport Beach, I gave a detailed report to the President, who was vacationing at the western "White House" at San Clemente. Later he told the press: "The Vice-President's trip served a very important purpose at this point in building the structure of peace, not only in Indochina but in the whole of Southeast Asia." Calling my mission a success, he said: "What happens in Indochina affects Thailand, Indonesia, Malaysia, and Singapore." Those words are equally true today and they point to a bleak future for our Asian friends.

I met with Mr. Nixon for an hour and a half, an unusually long session for us. His cordiality, plus his keen interest in my mission, gave me reason to hope that in our second term I could penetrate the wall he kept around him, and we could become more of a team than we had been in the first term. I had long desired to be his close partner, but he preferred to work with a controlled staff. I believe he had an inherent distrust of anyone who had an independent political identity. Even so, I supported his policies loyally —although I did not agree with them 100 percent.

While I praised him for refusing to withdraw unilaterally in Southeast Asia, I wanted him to go all out and win the war. I think he really wanted to knock out the North Vietnamese, but he was afraid he could not maintain public support: the Soviet Union would be encouraged to make other diversions, and marching mobs in the streets of America would cause Congress to cut off all funds for the war.

In criticizing President Kennedy for the indecision and bungling that led to the Bay of Pigs disaster in Cuba, Mr. Nixon once commented: "Whenever American prestige is thrown in the scale, we should not start things in the world unless we are prepared to finish them." That was precisely the problem in Vietnam. We should not have been in that fight unless we intended to win. We should have gone in with maximum non-nuclear power right away and achieved a lasting victory.

At the National Security Council (N.S.C.) meetings, we never discussed a knockout by heavy saturation bombing, such as was done to German cities in World War II, but we did talk about the possibility of destroying the dikes. That would have flooded large areas and finished North Vietnam. Taking out the dikes was rejected because it would have killed a lot of people through flooding and famine. The administration doves were eloquently concerned about the horrified editorials from the news media that such action would bring, but taking out the dikes would have won the war by striking at the heart of North's ability to sustain the aggression. It would have saved the lives of all those thousands of people whom the Communists later killed in South Vietnam, Laos, and Cambodia, and preserved the freedom of the additional millions who are suffering now under the yoke of the tyrranies that masquerade as "people's democracies."

Perhaps it is unfair to criticize the failure of recent Presidents to make authoritarian decisions that are cruel, ruthless, yet necessary to our nation's survival. Things have changed substantially since Harry Truman weighed the people of Hiroshima against the sons of America and faced up to his responsibility. Lyndon Johnson recognized this when he advised me privately just before I took office in 1969, "You may have an important office and a bully pulpit, but don't take on the big news organizations. They come out every day and you don't. Besides, they always have the last word."

Although the country cries out for leadership, the President's ability to lead effectively is being eroded by a popular obsession against even temporary governmental secrecy. The news media feel that it is their duty to discover by any means possible and immediately reveal every action the President may be contemplating. The harm in this comes not only from premature disclosure but from the use of inaccurate sources. Public officials are afraid to suggest that some limitations of the "public's right to know" may be in the national interest.

It was a sad thing for me to see Nixon at the National Security Council sessions, seated across the massive conference table with a dove at each elbow—Bill Rogers on the right hand and Mel Laird on the left. Rogers, the Secretary of State, and Laird, the Secretary of Defense, are both able and patriotic Americans, but they believed the war was already lost and they both had a fixed idea of getting out of Vietnam as fast as possible. I believe Bill Rogers is a genuine ideological dove—kind, compassionate and naïvely trustful of his fellowman. His longtime friends in the eastern liberal establishment knew him like a book and manipulated him shamelessly. Laird was a different kettle of fish. Pragmatic, evasive, with ice water in his veins, he was the ultimate professional politician. He feared that the aggressive action needed to win the war would enrage the Congress and split the country. He asked only, "What is politically expedient?"

Every time Nixon leaned toward a forceful action against Communist power, Rogers and Laird in effect would say, "Oh, you can't do that, Mr. President, the Russians would misunderstand it. We would be risking nuclear war." The shadow of the Russian bear inhibited a strong policy. Our military men knew how to win in Vietnam without nuclear involvement, but they weren't allowed to do it.

We also were plagued by leaks from the N.S.C. sessions, almost always from some dovish people on Kissinger's staff. The staff would prepare a series of options, from the most extreme on one side to the most extreme on the other, all the way across the spectrum from bombing to unilateral withdrawal. It was always the extreme option that was leaked to show undue belligerence or weakness. For instance, the news media might report that informed sources close to the N.S.C. said that we were considering unilateral withdrawal of all United States troops from Vietnam, or, on the other hand, that we were discussing the use of tactical nuclear weapons. Actually, the President went along with Laird's idea of "Vietnamization." By this was meant the gradual building up and training of South Vietnamese forces until they would be able to carry the combat responsibility without our troop involvement. That made a lot of sense, but it also required us to carry on a strong war effort until the South Vietnamese could take over. Vietnamization should have begun the moment President Kennedy put our first American soldier into Vietnam.

Mr. Nixon's cabinet was split over whether he should take a soft line in dealing with the "new mobilization" marchers who filled the streets of Washington and other cities in the fall of 1969 with their protests against the war. Henry Kissinger advocated a very hard line, saying that if we backed off, the Soviets would decide they could control our policies by influencing public opinion in the United States. I also backed the President on his November 3 speech which exhorted the "Silent Majority" of Americans to continue giving him their support so that he could govern despite the mobs. The White House switchboard lit up with telephone calls from people favoring his stand.

President Nixon said my Des Moines speech a few days later— in which I chastised the television networks for slanting their coverage against the administration—produced a wave of commendation, too. For Pat Buchanan and me, the crafting and polishing of that speech was a labor of love. I believe the reaction to my speech was even greater than the November 3 speech, not because I made it, but because the average American had been frustrated for so long about the proselytizing of some network commentators. The number of favorable responses was overwhelming.

I remember how enraged I was when I saw on television a gang of scruffy-looking characters proudly carrying a Viet Cong flag down Pennsylvania Avenue, while a national network commentator ran along beside them with his microphone deferentially extended for whatever seditious statements they might choose to make. Here was the same Viet Cong flag that was being carried into battle against Old Glory, and these traitors were being interviewed. It was an incredible thing to see the enemy flag carried down the streets of Washington and the networks treating the occasion as the display of a mere difference of opinion. It appeared that the networks' executives had fallen for that war-of-national-liberation line that the North Vietnamese Communists were peddling. Well, time has shown it was no civil war. "Big Minh," the Viet Cong hero in those days, told the *London Economist* in 1978 that instead of taking the role he had expected in the new government, he had been sent to a "reeducation center." Big Minh, he said, made big mistake.

Suppose this had been World War II and the demonstrators had been marching with a Nazi swastika banner. They would not have evoked sympathy for their compassion, but would have been justly condemned for being traitors to their country.

I was so proud of Nixon the day the troops went into the Cambodian sanctuaries in the spring of 1970 that I stopped him in the hall after he had announced it to the cabinet. "Mr. President," I said, "I admire you for having the courage to make that tough decision."

As Henry Kissinger said in his memoirs, it was the right decision. We would have been a lot better off—and so would the Cambodians today—if we had stuck to a more militant course of action to save them. It annoyed me to hear people complain about our "invasion" of Cambodia. The truth is that the North Vietnamese had invaded Cambodia with thousands of their soldiers months before we did anything about it. The Cambodians themselves have recently confirmed that to Western reporters. Prince Norodom Sihanouk had quietly let us know that he would like to have us come in there to suggest the North Vietnamese get the hell out of his country.

Although the North Vietnamese have steadfastly denied being

in Cambodia in 1970, that flimsy lie was ripped apart by the Pol
Pot government of Kampuchea, formerly the Khmer Rouge of
Cambodia. The Cambodian Khmer Rouge and the North Vietnamese fought together in 1970 against the Lon Nol government
and the Americans, but have since become bitter enemies. In a
recent interview with an American correspondent, a Pol Pot
spokesman admitted that the North Vietnamese and Viet Cong
were already present in great numbers in Cambodia—he says two
million—when the Americans went into the sanctuaries in 1970
at President Nixon's direction. The American incursion was to
prevent attacks by the Communists from protected Cambodian
bases, but the celebrity-led left-wingers in the United States
labeled it an "invasion" of a helpless country and another exhibi-
tion of "American imperialism."

As a result of North Vietnam's final victory in 1975, the Khmer
Rouge inherited Cambodia and by published estimates, killed up
to a million people. The North Vietnamese have since deposed
the Pol Pot regime, but both Vietnam and Cambodia are still
racked with strife. The Vietnamese are fleeing their oppressed
country by the thousands, risking their lives in flimsy boats to
escape for no known destination. They seem to feel that any place
is better. The whole of Indochina has turned to communism;
Thailand is under the Red threat and Malaysia and Singapore
have to be very nervous.

Mr. Nixon has said the televised pictures of the suffering in
Vietnam caused demoralization on our home front and raised the
question of whether America would ever again be able to fight
an enemy abroad with unity and strength of purpose at home.
Under current conditions, I don't think we could. Since President
Carter has pardoned the draft evaders and deserters, it is improb-
able that we could draft a civilian army successfully now unless
there were a direct attack on the North American continent—and
the Communists are too smart to do that. They have no need for
direct confrontation. They will continue to add satellites by financing and supporting "wars of national liberation" elsewhere.
If our government ever proposed to send United States forces into
such conflicts abroad, a high percentage of young people would
condemn the war as immoral and go away—figuring that the precedent had been set by Vietnam and they could easily come back
and be pardoned when it was all over. Also, I think the Soviet

aggression would have to be a clear-cut attack on us before we would respond with nuclear weapons. Would we fight for Western Europe again? I have grave doubts.

Europe's fate will largely hinge upon the maintenance of an obviously superior United States array of strategic nuclear weapons. That is why, at N.S.C. meetings, I questioned the concessions that ultimately were made in the Strategic Arms Limitation Treaty (SALT I), which Nixon signed with Leonid Brezhnev at Moscow in May 1972.

I found myself in unspoken alliance with Adm. Thomas H. Moorer, then chairman of the Joint Chiefs of Staff, and with most of the other military people. At one meeting I recall, Gerard Smith, our SALT I negotiator, was giving all the reasons why we should accede to the Russians' demand that there be no on-site inspections of weapons, because we had the capability to inspect by satellites. Then the discussion moved to missile throw-weights and how much more sophisticated our weapons were with MIRV's (Multiple Independently-Targeted Reentry Vehicles), and how, with a smaller throw-weight, one of our ICBM's, with its high accuracy and multiple warheads, would produce even better results than one of the much larger ICBM's of the Soviet Union.

I usually kept my mouth shut in those meetings because Bob Haldeman once told me, after I had participated perhaps too enthusiastically, "The President does not like you to take an opposite view at a cabinet meeting, or say anything that can be construed to be mildly not in accord with his thinking." In brief, I was told to keep quiet. But at this session, after waiting in vain for someone else to object, I said: "It doesn't make sense to me to negotiate an agreement which leaves the Russians with a great superiority in throw-weight. They are looking for an agreement to freeze these categories, which will allow them to stop worrying about numbers and put all their resources into developing their own technology. When they have improved their technology to the point that it is close to parity with ours, we are left with a crippling inferiority."

Tom Moorer's facial expressions showed me that he was in total agreement with me. I continued, "Furthermore, with regard to the inspections, maybe we can inspect now, but when we are frozen into the status quo and they devote all their energies to improving counter-surveillance, who is to say that ten years from now we'll be able to see what they are deploying?" Then I added, "Gentlemen, if two nations make an agreement to limit strategic nuclear weapons, and they intend to carry out that agreement, then neither should object to inspections to insure that the agreement is being performed. The only conclusion you can come to is that they're not going to play fair."

I was distressed about this. I could see that the military men were in agreement with me. The doves looked at me as if I were Attila the Hun. Gerry Smith said he didn't think we could get an agreement if we insisted on on-site inspections. The President just gave me a poker-player glance and someone raised another question.

Looking back, I now believe that Mr. Nixon's disaffection with me had its roots in my outspoken criticism at N.S.C. and cabinet meetings. I felt that a Vice-President should contribute, not just observe. Since I was given no chance to contribute in private, I had to do it in front of the family. The President did not have the inner confidence to take even implied criticism of his predetermined decisions.

Today, my SALT reservations still seem valid. Why are we always looking at the arms control issue from the Russians' standpoint? Why not look at it from ours? Instead, our press and the liberal community carp at the defense proponents unceasingly, saying we haven't been conciliatory, so gradually we soften our position while the Soviets stay right where they are and win concessions from us. It's a terrible thing. While the termites keep gnawing away at the foundations, we do nothing.

Gradually, I learned it was better to keep my objections to myself when I disagreed with Mr. Nixon's policies. When Bob Haldeman told me that the President would appreciate my not speaking up, I presumed that he was conveying a message from the top. But I would have appreciated it much more if the President himself had called me over and said, "Look, if you have something to say, let's talk about it privately. Don't say it at meetings because there are leaks, and I don't want the administration to look divided." But he never did that.

Nothing can illustrate better Mr. Nixon's dislike of personal confrontation and the lengths to which he would go to avoid it than this strange progression of events: The President of the

United States is always invited to the annual dinner of the Gridiron Club, a "fun" event run by prestigious news media people
for the purpose of roasting official Washington for the enjoyment
of everyone except the prime targets of their barbed humor. It
is generally conceded that the President of the United States,
being a prime target, does not particularly enjoy attending the
Gridiron dinner—unless his actions have pleased the media immediately prior thereto. Richard Nixon was no exception to the
rule, and to human memory, had never pleased the media either
before or after their annual bash. So he did what Presidents always do in such straits. He decided to send his Vice-President,
and he directed Mr. Haldeman to take care of the matter. Mr.
Haldeman had one of his assistants notify my scheduler to recommend the Gridiron dinner. He did so and I said no. You see,
the rule also applies to Vice-Presidents, and my activities had
not endeared me to the media. Moreover I was thoroughly ticked
off about the treatment I had been getting at the hands of the
big media.

A few days later, my scheduler was back with a renewal of
the request, this time identifying its source. "The President would
like you to attend," he said. Now, I had good reason to suspect
that every presidential request conveyed by staff did not originate with the man himself, so again I declined.

Weeks passed and I heard no more. It was about three weeks
before the event, and I was giving a speech in Hawaii—an assignment which I made no effort to avoid—in fact, accepted with
alacrity. Art Sohmer came in and said that Bob Haldeman had
called and told him to tell me that the President definitely wanted
me to attend the accursed Gridiron dinner.

At this particular time, I was more miffed than usual about
the lack of personal contact with Mr. Nixon, and I decided that
I would not go unless he asked me himself. I directed Sohmer to
so inform Bob Haldeman. Three hours later, Bryce Harlow, White
House counselor—whom I admired greatly for his wit and demeanor—was on the phone. Again I declined, exhibiting a streak
of Greek stubbornness that has often landed me in trouble.

I returned to the capital. Four days later, on a Sunday, I
received a phone call from the President—very unusual. We chatted for about ten minutes on a variety of subjects. He closed by
mentioning what a great job one of the cabinet had done on

Meet the Press that day. Then he paused a moment and continued about how important TV was. He paused again. I said it certainly was and that ended our conversation.

The following Monday afternoon, I was reviewing an economic policy memorandum in my office when I was given a handwritten letter from the President. With charming simplicity, he requested me to attend the Gridiron dinner, allowing that it would be a sacrifice but no more than Ike had demanded of him. He promised to go next year. Naturally, I went to the dinner. Unnaturally, I had a marvelous time.

I really would have enjoyed serving in the vice-presidency with Lyndon Johnson, because if anything had gone wrong, probably he himself would have picked up the phone and said, "Agnew, what the hell are you doing?" Or he would have said, "I've got a hell of a problem. Come over here. I want to talk to you about this."

Unfortunately, I could have no such man-to-man talk with President Nixon. Absolutely none. I was never allowed to come close enough to participate with him directly in any decision. Every time I went to see him and raised a subject for discussion, he would begin a rambling, time-consuming monologue. Then finally the phone would ring or Haldeman would come in, and there would be no time left for what I really had come to talk about. He successfully avoided any subject he didn't want to be pinned down on. He preferred keeping his decision-making within a very small group. I was not of the inner circle.

I disagreed completely—and still do—with President Nixon's initiative to "normalize" relations with the People's Republic of China. The American people—against the will of the majority, if the polls are correct—have been forced to go along with the Carter administration's decision to repudiate our mutual defense treaty with the free Chinese regime on Taiwan, and to give Peking the diplomatic and economic muscle to seriously impair the security and prosperity of the seventeen million people on the island. This is a strange way to reward a loyal ally whose hardworking and creative citizens have made their country a model success story for the capitalistic free-enterprise system.

I presume that my firm opposition to the policy of cozying up to Communist China was the main reason the White House froze me out of the Nixon decisions in that area. In mid-1971, while I was making a goodwill trip around the world, some of Mr. Nixon's aides put out the word that I was sent out of the country so as not to be in Henry Kissinger's way when he made his secret journey to China—the journey which paved the way for the President's visit there the following February. Then they compounded the felony by not notifying me until after the story broke in the press. I was in Kinshasa, then the capital of the Congo (now Zaire), when the story broke. Mr. Nixon certainly had no reason to believe that I would have leaked the story, because he well knew I never leaked anything—although I had access to much secret information through the National Security Council and daily C.I.A. briefings. But some of his assistants were aware of my sentiments about courting the Red Chinese, so they left me out.

I first began to feel isolated from the really important Nixon decisions after our 1968 election victory. The press had been bombarding me, portraying me as the neanderthal, gaffe-ridden vice-presidential candidate. Propagandized by the constant picking of my travelling press contingent, many of whom were still enraged that they hadn't predicted my selection as the candidate for Vice President, most of the senior Nixon staff believed I had really made a mess of the campaign. I was the dumb rookie who said the wrong things. I admit that I made mistakes, but so does every national candidate. If the media people like what you stand for they can be very forgiving, but if they are ideologically opposed, they harry you unmercifully. The staff should have realized that the real thrust of their effort was to get to Mr. Nixon (who was being very presidential and invulnerable) through the "new boy in school."

After the election, there appeared in the major press a spate of cartoons suggesting that the President was having really serious difficulty deciding what to do with me. In one, I was a slavering dog. Mr. Nixon was furtively handing me out the back door of the White House on a leash, saying, "Take him for a walk." It was really vicious, but I was not unfamiliar with the bestial barbs of the press, having once been likened by *The Washington Post* to Caligula's horse.

Unfortunately, however, that image of callous, animal stupidity permeated the beginning of our relationship. Some of the damage was repaired when I started building my own image and speaking out against the radicals who were undermining our country. Then the cartoonists magically transformed me from a stumbling, bumbling incompetent into an evil, dangerous man. First I was a clown, then a menace.

To the President's credit, he made an early effort to remedy the situation. Shortly after the inauguration in 1969, I was given an office in the White House—Sherman Adams's old office. I understand it became the office of Hamilton Jordan. It was one of the best locations in the West Wing, just down the hall from the Oval Office, but it proved impractical. The idea was that I would use presidential staff with my own staff and interchange them. This would require the staffs to work closely. Unfortunately, there were tremendous frictions between the White House staff and mine. I am told it has ever been thus.

As far as my cooperating with the White House staff to better serve the President was concerned, I soon learned that everything was run as a closed corporation. Haldeman and Ehrlichman didn't tell me what they were doing. There was a lot of secrecy and jealousy and vying for the President's attention among the senior people. I finally got disgusted and started spending more time with my own staff across the street in the Old Executive Office Building. Bob Haldeman came to me and said they needed more space in the West Wing; would I give up my office there, since I rarely used it anyway? I said I would. The press made a great deal out of the symbolism of my losing the White House office, but I had no objections. If the President had picked up the phone and asked me to come in and work with him, I would gladly have stayed. But he never did. Our only interchanges came at the staff level.

The antagonisms between my staff and the President's continued to build. His men did not like my top man, Art Sohmer; they thought he was incompetent. Although Art had weaknesses, he had strengths too; he knew how to handle people and he knew more about politics than anyone on the White House side of the road except perhaps Murray Chotiner and Bryce Harlow. His weaknesses were in staff organization, managing the unbelievable amount of paper the federal establishment generated, and in handling the bureaucracy itself. But he was more than adequately supported in those areas by Col. Mike Dunn, a brilliant career military officer with impeccable educational credentials. Mike became a Major General while in my service, and I can testify that he earned the promotions.

During the 1970 campaign I spoke for Republican candidates and defended the Nixon administration's policies all over the country. It was a bitter campaign, during which the raucous antiwar people were at the height of their frenetic activity. I found that I got the blame for what the media chose to construe as poor results. We did lose some House seats, but nowhere near the number usually expected in an off year and less than the Carter administration lost in 1978. We gained a few people in the Senate. The press said we had poor results because I was so divisive and had alienated the people. At that point, the President should have said: "That's ridiculous—we lost less than is usually lost by the President's party in an off-year election, and certainly less than we would have if the Vice-President had not been out there fighting." But there was absolute silence from the White House while all the criticism fell on my head.

I had been sent out on the point in 1970 and performed the mission assigned exactly, and the attitude of Mr. Nixon's staff was "Well, maybe he did commit excesses, but we won't criticize our own Vice-President." Any active public defense of me, however, was lacking. It was then that I realized how expendable the Vice-President was. Perhaps Mr. Nixon recalled having to do those tough jobs himself for Ike, and had gotten the same silent treatment, sometimes.

When we had a skull session at Key Biscayne, Florida, soon after the 1972 election, there was a lot of tough talk going around about cleaning house. In the upper echelons everybody's resignation was requested, and the word went forth that people who didn't do what the President wanted were going to have their resignations accepted.

I thought: "As a Vice-President who worked hard and contributed to our reelection by a huge majority, I will receive some praise this time. I will get a very big, important assignment."

But my actual assignment made me shudder.

At that same Key Biscayne session, the President sat silently as John Ehrlichman said: "We think you ought to spend most of your time working on the Bicentennial."

"The Bicentennial?" I could hardly believe my ears.

"Yes," they said. "It's the most important thing that has happened in a long time, and this should be your principal activity —to organize the most terrific Bicentennial that can be staged in 1976. Use your prestige and leadership to bring out the principles of Americanism."

"Gentlemen," I said, "I look upon the Bicentennial as a loser, because everybody has his own ideas about it and nobody can be the head of it without making a million enemies. A potential presidential candidate doesn't want to make any enemies." So I said, "No," and I made it stick.

Naturally, I was thinking ahead to 1976 because even my detractors agreed that I was the front-runner for the Republican presidential nomination. The early polls showed me way ahead of all other potential rivals.

However, I realized that I ultimately faced a spirited fight involving several other capable men. Ronald Reagan, John Connally, and Nelson Rockefeller were probably the top three potential contenders. Also, it had become obvious that Mr. Nixon, who had personally chosen me as his running mate in 1968, had cooled in his ardor and now directed his affections toward Connally.

Indeed, the President had toyed with the idea of dropping me in 1972 and substituting the former Governor of Texas, his new favorite, who had become the star of the cabinet as secretary of the treasury. Mr. Nixon made no secret of his admiration for Connally. I admire John too. I think he's a very capable, energetic man, a spellbinder as a speaker. He has great ability to project himself; he has charisma. That charisma is what the President admired most in him: Connally's outgoing, captivating nature was the antithesis of the indrawn Nixon personality. Mr. Nixon looked to him for the qualities he did not find within himself.

At first, I didn't believe the reports that the President was thinking of dumping me. He would often volunteer for my benefit in the presence of others, "That's just a lot of political talk. The biggest game in Washington is to create a fight between the President and the Vice-President."

However, I noticed that he became more remote towards me as his attachment to Connally grew. In a crisis, or simply when he wanted to expand on some subject to someone with whom he felt comfortable, Connally would be called to the Oval Office or to the President's hideaway in the Old Executive Office Building. The press noticed immediately that Connally was being brought into the inner circle while I was being kept out. I have no hostility towards John Connally. But naturally a rivalry grew up between us as the media tried to goad me into saying something against him. I remember that once, when I arrived late at a luncheon, I told this joke: "I'm sorry to be late. I did my best to hurry, but John Connally had me down at his ranch for a barbecue, and it took me an hour and a half to cut myself down from the spit."

As more and more rumors circulated about my being replaced on the ticket and the President did nothing to quash them, I started considering various possibilities for my future. I thought of writing a column or doing a television interview series. I knew, too, that the same left-wing Republicans who had fought my nomination at Miami Beach were now urging Nixon to let me go. But they did not want Connally; they despised him about as much as they did me. They preferred a liberal from the eastern establishment.

In the New Hampshire primary in March 1972, the youthful liberals of the Ripon Society staged a write-in campaign for Sen. Edward Brooke of Massachusetts as a replacement for me on the ticket. But my friends promoted a last-minute counter-drive for me, and I came in on top with 70 percent of the vote. That equalled the result for the President, who polled 69 percent in his race against the liberal California congressman, Paul McCloskey, and the conservative Ohio congressman, John Ashbrook.

As late as July, however, the "dump Agnew" efforts continued, with Sen. Jacob Javits of New York playing a leading role. Sen. Barry Goldwater of Arizona rebuked Javits and declared that it was an "absolute necessity" to keep me in the vice-presidency. "The Vice-President has built himself into a national figure with courage enough to say things that should be said," Goldwater asserted. "Any suggestions about dumping him at this time will alienate the Republican workers across this country. Agnew's popularity equals that of the President."

Senator Goldwater spoke out July 19 and Mr. Nixon got the message at once. Two days later, he called me into the Oval Office and told me he had decided that I would again be his running mate. I said: "Mr. President, I am delighted to have the chance to serve again with you, and I will do everything I can to see that we are reelected."

If he had not chosen me, I still would have campaigned for him. I have always considered public office a service. The pomp and flattery were never worth the sacrifice in personal privacy. I can honestly say that I never developed a big head in the vice-presidency. I made a strong bid to persuade Democrats and Independents to repudiate the Democrats' presidential nominee, Sen. George McGovern. "The Democratic party is controlled by an ideological elite," I said, and added that McGovern's policies were "repugnant" to the working people of the country. The sweeping victory of the Nixon-Agnew ticket proved that was true.

Then history began to repeat itself. Political power began to make a subtle shift, away from the President and towards me, because at the moment of his election to a second term, Mr. Nixon became a lame duck. He no longer had a political future. There would be no more exciting elections, no victories and no gratitude for presidential support. Of course he still retained a lot of power, but the politicians began instinctively turning away from the President, who could not run again, and towards his potential successor. As the front-runner, I got a lot of attention. The President slowly, almost imperceptibly, lost the attention of the party leaders as their attention focused on the selection of the nominee for 1976.

While I was in Southeast Asia in late January 1973, the newspapers carried stories saying that Mr. Nixon was already starting to build up Connally. I knew those tales came out of the White House, but I did not chew my fingernails and worry. I had my loyal constitutents in the Silent Majority, and I expected they would have the final word in the primaries and in the convention that would choose the Republicans' next presidential nominee. I also knew that I was completely in the clear on the Watergate scandal. Having been frozen out of the inner circle at the White House, I knew absolutely nothing about Watergate and nobody ever claimed I was tainted by it.

I never dreamed that both Connally and I would become the verbal targets of political assassins who were determined to ruin us both. I received the first hint of my own impending disaster while I was at Newport Beach, waiting to confer with the President after my trip to Southeast Asia.

On February 3, 1973, my attorney, George White, telephoned me from Maryland. He was extremely agitated. His voice was strained, and he sounded like a man under tremendous pressure. He said he had to speak to me immediately about a matter that was too dangerous to discuss over the telephone. I agreed that he should fly out at once and tell me the whole story.

CHAPTER THREE

THESE GUYS ARE DESPERATE

George White told me an incredible tale—of a federal investigation in Maryland that threatened to involve me.

He said that Lester Matz, a professional engineer from Baltimore County, who had built a lucrative practice from government work in Maryland, and Jerome B. Wolff, who had been one of my trusted advisers on technical matters since Baltimore County days, and whom I had named chairman of the State Roads Commission when I was Governor of Maryland, were making veiled threats against me that bordered on blackmail.

They both had been targeted in the initial Baltimore County phase of a widespread federal investigation. The probe had begun after anonymous tips to the Internal Revenue Service that certain engineering firms and contractors had paid kickbacks to political figures in Maryland, in return for contracts on highway projects and other construction work.

According to published reports, enough information was gathered through wiretaps to involve Matz's firm and others in payments to William E. Fornoff, who was then serving as County Executive Dale Anderson's principal assistant, and who had served me in the same capacity. On January 25, a county architect named Paul Gaudreau admitted to the federal prosecutors that he had been making payments to Fornoff. It is significant to note that Gaudreau also testified that he had made no such payments to Fornoff or to anyone else during the time that I was county executive.

Over and over again Gaudreau said he never gave me a dime. The probe widened, and other engineers implicated Jerry Wolff and Lester Matz. The prosecutors panicked Wolff and Matz, who by Wolff's own admission had been engaged in illegal activities together since the 1950's. As Russell T. Baker, Jr., one of the

42

prosecutors, bragged to reporters, he would call up a suspected engineer and ask if he had a criminal lawyer. Then he would advise the subject that he could be in trouble so he'd better get one and have him get in touch with the U.S. Attorney's office. It was also standard practice for a subpoena server to say: "Here's your subpoena. I want you to know you're in a hell of a lot of trouble."

When a witness came in for an interview with the prosecutors, they stimulated his natural uneasiness by a continuation of the same cold, hostile attitude. His answers were received with skepticism. There were frequent reminders that disgrace and jail were the penalties of perjury. The whole idea was to keep the witness frightened and fully aware of what it would be like to be a member of the prison population. All this was standard operating procedure for the Baltimore prosecutors, whom the media have called "bold young idealists."

White told me that Matz and Wolff had come in to see him while I was in Asia; that they were frantic with worry; and that they had made some very transparent threats against me, alleging they were in terrible trouble and they expected me to bail them out of it. They wanted me to use my influence as Vice-President to make the federal government stop investigating them. If I refused, they may have to say things that would be very embarrassing to me.

"In what way?" I asked.

"They will say they made kickback payments to you," White said.

"That's certainly not true," I retorted. "In the past, they have made campaign contributions, but those certainly weren't kickbacks; the money didn't go to me personally."

White interrogated me closely. "This is very serious," he said. "I want you to level with me about it."

"George, I am leveling with you about it," I said, becoming indignant. "There is just nothing to this. They are apparently in trouble, and they are trying to put the heat on me to extricate them, but I can't do anything for them."

Matz and Wolff were close friends who lived within a few blocks of each other in Baltimore County. I am sure that they had been conferring with each other and asking, "How do we get out of this bind?" They decided to carry their appeals and threats to George White. They frightened him and he was supposed to frighten me into rescuing them.

The prosecutor's records indicate Wolff told them that he and Matz had made "a spirited presentation" to White and warned him that I was "in imminent danger of being embarrassed, or worse" unless I interceded for them.

The federal agents served subpoenas on the consulting engineering firm of Matz, Childs and Associates, Inc., calling upon the company to produce its records. Matz and his partner, John Childs, were alarmed because they feared the inquiry would reveal a long-existing pattern of bonuses kicked back by employees to Matz, who then would use the cash in any way he pleased. Matz claimed a large part of it went to Maryland politicians to buy their influence.

Lester Matz did everything possible to create the impression that he was a close friend of mine. He apparently told the prosecutors that we celebrated milestone family vacations together. This is not true. He did make contributions to my campaign for governor, and he constantly sought favors by cultivating me.

However, we were never "friends," only acquaintances in a business-political sense. I have been inside his home once and that was an accidental thing. I had attended a tennis party at Jerome Wolff's house and, at Wolff's suggestion, I walked over to see Matz, who lived about two blocks away. That was all. Matz has never been in my home. I may have met with him seven or eight times. When someone is contributing to your campaigns, of course you have to meet him on a few occasions.

Matz sought to show our friendship by noting that we both owned condominiums on St. Croix in the Virgin Islands. But I had only a small equity in mine. I bought it because J. Walter Jones, a close friend and one of my campaign fund-raisers, had suggested it was a good investment. Unfortunately for me, a wave of terrorism made it the opposite, and I sold at a loss. St. Croix was a beautiful place, with a fine public golf course. I didn't learn until later that Matz had a condominium there, too.

White told me that Matz offered to hire him as his lawyer for a retainer of a thousand dollars a month when the federal investigation began in Baltimore County. White then went to U.S. Attorney Beall about this and said he was worried about a possible conflict of interest because of his close association with me. Beall replied that White would have no conflict of interest in representing Matz because the inquiry had nothing whatever to do with me.

White expressed concern that certain newspapers, because of their tremendous interest in "getting back" at me for my criticisms of the media, would try to discredit me through innuendo, linking me to the case. Beall said he and his assistants shared that apprehension about unfair publicity, and they were doing all that was humanly possible to protect the secrecy of their inquiry and to avoid any unfair comment about me.

Justice Department records show that on February 6, three days before White's telephone call to me, Beall met with Attorney General Richard Kleindienst and reported having "affirmative firsthand evidence that kickbacks were paid by architects and engineers to Baltimore County officials." But Beall specifically said he had no information that any such practices were in effect during my term as County Executive; therefore, rumors linking me to the case were all false.

Nevertheless, White reported to me that Matz and Wolff were threatening to implicate me. He expressed great fear that their threats could be extremely harmful to me; he knew that an honest man could be ruined by lies. I said I could not stop the investigation and I would not do so if I had the power. Furthermore, my conscience was clear. I knew that although some businessmen had made political contributions to my campaigns, I had taken no payoffs.

My friend, J. Walter Jones, a former Towson banker and real estate developer, has confirmed White's story about the blackmail threats against me. Jones said that while he was cruising on his yacht in Florida in late January 1973, he received an urgent message from my lawyer saying that Matz had warned White to have the Vice-President stop the Maryland investigation.

"Matz was completely convinced that the Vice-President could, in fact, stop it and would do so if enough pressure was put on him," Jones later said. "I must confess I took it rather lightly. I thought Matz wouldn't dare come out with blatant lies about the Vice-President of the United States. I didn't realize how terribly frightened Matz was, combined with how badly the

prosecutors wanted to 'get' Agnew. Matz told me they had wiretaps on his phone and that's how they got the information against
him. They had him cold."

Matz and Childs were in trouble because they paid fake bonuses to some of their employees. The employees were allowed
to keep only enough of the bonuses to pay the increases in their
personal income taxes that the bonuses caused. They had to kick
back all the rest to Matz and Childs. Since Matz and Childs had
not paid taxes on this company income, the I.R.S. had a solid
tax evasion case against them.

"I have long suspected that Matz extorted cash payments
from employees, developers and others with the story that he
was paying off various public officials in order to get favors,"
Jones said. "Matz actually created engineering problems and then
advised his clients that he could settle them by making cash
payoffs. It is my belief that Matz kept most of the cash, himself.
This would explain the large amount of cash he carried around
with him at all times. Matz invariably carried a wad of hundred
dollar bills. He spent large amounts on diamonds, furs and travel
with various girl friends. There was never a question in his mind
that Agnew could have stopped the investigation. He later displayed a great hatred for Agnew and for me because Agnew
refused to help him."

When Jones returned from his Florida vacation in early 1973,
Wolff also pleaded with him for help. Wolff said, "The prosecutors are not interested in me. They want the Vice-President."

By that time, Matz and Wolff were desperate. They were
rabbits, running for cover. They would do anything to escape
accountability for their acts.

I was amazed to learn that Jerry Wolff was threatening to implicate me in his financial mess. I felt as though I had been
stabbed in the back by a trusted friend. I was hurt, personally,
because I admired him as a very bright engineer, and I had
done everything I could to help him, all the way back to the
days when I was the Baltimore County Executive.

Wolff had worked for Baltimore County before my time there.
He is one of the most talented people I have ever met in government. Both an engineer and lawyer, extremely quick and able,
he could meet with a group of people and bring them to a con-
sensus to settle difficult questions. He also had the knack of

simplifying technical terms so that a busy executive could grasp the roots of an issue quickly and explain it to his constituency. When I was County Executive, we had a prominent citizens' committee, chaired by Samuel Hecht of the department store chain; this was an unpaid private group which advised me on budget and development priorities, as well as suggested new ways of doing things. I was particularly interested in guiding the county's rapid growth in the right way to keep its industrial base moving, but away from residential areas.

I admired Jerry Wolff's intellect, wit, and the way he was able to calm irate taxpayers. He was an absolutely charming man, but he always seemed in desperate trouble for money. He had had an unhappy marriage and his first wife had tried to extract the last pound of flesh from him in their divorce settlement. Nevertheless, Jerry lived like a millionaire. He had an expensive home with a swimming pool and a tennis court; he lived a Cadillac existence on a Volkswagen income. He spent money lavishly; in his statement to the prosecutors, he admitted having illegal money from several sources which he did not reveal—and which the prosecutors apparently never bothered to investigate. Obviously, they were not interested in prosecuting Wolff on these matters.

After I became Vice-President, I asked Jerry to leave the State Roads Commission and join my top staff as science and technical adviser. He accompanied me to Washington and proved very valuable, particularly in matters involving the National Aeronautics and Space Council, for which I had responsibility. In April 1970, Wolff told me that he could no longer manage on government pay. He said he was going to reenter engineering practice, but would very much appreciate being retained as a consultant to the Marine Council on a per diem basis, as he was in trouble financially. I agreed to retain him at a rate of one hundred dollars per day.

In nearly every assessment of the "evidence" against me that I have read, Jerome Wolff's notes and testimony are emphasized. The notes about engineering jobs awarded by Wolff as chairman of the State Roads Commission during my time as governor are always referred to as "documentary evidence" or "documentary corroboration." I am amazed that no investigative reporter has examined the Wolff statement objectively enough to see that it gives not a scintilla of persuasive evidence against me.

Wolff has never mentioned making any payments to me other than two legal campaign contributions. As an employee on a per diem, he would have been quite vulnerable to a kickback request, had I been as venal as the prosecutors tried to depict me. Just before the 1972 election, Wolff came into my office and said, "I'm not a rich man, but I want you to have this five hundred dollars because you've been very good to me." I took the money and turned it in to the campaign. I remember being very touched by his sincerity and loyalty.

Anyone reading Wolff's statement carefully will see he states unequivocally that I never asked him for either campaign contributions or payments of any type. At one point, he states he offered cash from his friends, but I had said I had enough cash. He further states that he has never made an illegal payment to me. In spite of this, I can point to hundreds of news stories that claim Wolff paid me off and passed a lie detector test that he had paid me off.* I now have the F.B.I. report of the polygraph test on Wolff. It states that he volunteered the fact that I had never asked him for any money and further, the polygraph report states Wolff said he has never personally given me any money.

Now, about Wolff's so-called "corroboration" of the others who testified against me: it consists only of his suspicions, or what Matz and others told him. You cannot corroborate the testimony of a witness—especially a witness whose statements are gaining him immunity—with someone's repetition of that witness's own self-serving statements. Wolff stated he knew I was being paid off because Matz told him so, or some one else told him so, or because he "inferred" or "had an awareness" that I was. Nowhere in Jerry Wolff's testimony or records is there any direct evidence to corroborate a payoff—no statements by me, no witnessing of money changing hands or even being acknowledged—nothing. Also, Matz said under polygraph examination that I never asked

* Typical of these stories is a *Time Magazine* report that was released early and picked up by hundreds of newspapers, including *The Washington Star*. Quoting *Time* as the source, the *Star* said, "Jerome Wolff, a key witness against Vice-President Agnew, in an investigation of an alleged kickback scandal, 'told the truth about delivering funds extorted from contractors to Agnew,' according to a lie detector test." *The Baltimore Evening Sun* also used the *Time* misinformation under the banner headline, "Lie Test Reportedly Passed by Former Aide of Agnew."

him for money. What is clear from the records of the case is that
Wolff, Matz and others engaged for a long time in illegal under-
takings that did not concern me, and that they were in fact co-
conspirators of long experience. Yet, the prosecutors were willing
to believe them as long as the Vice-President's hide was nailed to
the wall. They were well paid for their "evidence." In spite of
their admitted crimes, neither Wolff, nor Matz, nor Hammerman
has been convicted or will be convicted of any crime connected
with the Maryland kickback cases. This is not from lack of evidence, but from lack of prosecution. And the prosecutors still
maintain that no one was given immunity.

Wolff appealed to me to save him when the U.S. Attorney's
office first began tightening the screws on him. In a net-worth
investigation, they found he had money in safe-deposit boxes, and
they could document large expenditures of cash that he could
not explain. Thousands of dollars which he spent or secreted
apparently came from the mysterious illicit deals he mentioned
in his statement. He didn't dare report the illegal income, so
they had him in an impossible position.

Matz and Wolff are both very nervous and high-strung people.
As their troubles mounted, George White reported to me, they
were almost going out of their minds. They looked as though they
weren't sleeping; they stuttered; they wandered around aimlessly,
according to White, and their close friends reported they were
talking about committing suicide. Matz, who always told everyone his business anyway, was making dark hints about my involvement that began to circulate in Baltimore. Moreover, I was
told that Russell T. Baker, Jr., one of the "Gang of Four" prosecutors, was bragging at a Washington cocktail party that I was in
real trouble.*

I firmly resolved that despite their threats and pleas, I would
never allow Matz and Wolff to blackmail me. Upon returning
to Washington from my meeting with the President in California, I began my own inquiries into the Maryland case. On
February 13, I had breakfast with Attorney General Richard
Kleindienst, and expressed my concern that the investigation
could be used to smear me, although I was innocent. I warned

---

* The prosecutorial team in Baltimore consisted of George Beall, Barnet
Skolnik, Russell T. Baker, Jr., and Ronald Liebman.

him that politically active left-wing Democrats on the staff of U.S. Attorney Beall might have marked me as their ultimate target. I specifically mentioned Assistant U.S. Attorney Barnet Skolnik, who had served as an aide to Edmund Muskie during the Maine Senator's unsuccessful campaign for the 1972 Democratic presidential nomination.

There was no doubt that the young lawyers in the prosecutor's office were ideologically hostile to me, especially after my hardline campaigning against the anti-Vietnam crowd in 1970. Skolnik, who delighted in calling himself a radical, was publicly dismayed that he had been forced to prosecute the Catonsville Nine, a group of dissidents who had broken into a Baltimore County draft office and poured blood on the records. His heart really hadn't been in that case. Russell T. Baker, Jr., who had talked about me indiscreetly at a cocktail party, had been with the Peace Corps in Africa. Their personal animus against me made them go far beyond propriety in developing the case. In their eyes, I was a "bad man." They were out to get me.

Beall, a Republican, protested to me that his inquiry was nonpartisan and without political motivations. Justice Department records show that Kleindienst called Beall, questioned him about Skolnik's performance in Democratic partisan politics, and suggested that Skolnik assume a lower profile. Beall agreed to have his zealous young Democrat "stay in the background if that would eliminate some of the gossip circulating in Washington." In fact, however, I know of nothing Beall ever did to curb his eager assistant. Skolnik later went on to other prey— for a time being involved in prosecuting another prominent conservative, former F.B.I. chief L. Patrick Gray III. Skolnik left that job unfinished in March 1979 because, he said, "it didn't pay enough money."

I also spoke to the U. S. Attorney's brother, Sen. Glenn Beall, Jr., of Maryland, and told him, "Look; these people are out to destroy me, politically." He said he understood and indicated some worry about it. "But," he said, "George is very independent. He doesn't like me to talk to him about anything going on in the U. S. Attorney's office." One wonders if that prohibition continued during the time when Senator Beall was being scrutinized for accepting $185,000 in secret campaign funds from the notorious "Townhouse" operation. Herbert Kalmbach went to jail for his part in that operation, but the special prosecutor's office in Washington refused to do anything about the senators who received the money, claiming that the Justice Department should look into the matter. According to *The Wall Street Journal*, that meant that Glenn Beall's fate was largely up to George Beall, and, continued the *Journal*, "U. S. Attorney Beall doesn't intend to do anything about Senator Beall." The last observation on the subject in the *Wall Street Journal* article is as follows: "Moral: It can be more blessed to receive than to give, and it helps to have a brother who's a U. S. Attorney."

I also informed the President about the Maryland investigation, and I warned him that attempts were being made to implicate me in fund-raising abuses. "Some prosecutors in Baltimore are trying to hook me up to some serious violations," I said. "I think they are trying to embarrass the administration."

"They're always trying to do that," Mr. Nixon replied. "Don't worry about it. There's not going to be any problem." He brushed it off. I don't think he took it seriously.

Wolff has said that in late February or early March, he sent me a letter pleading for my help to "limit or terminate the investigation" of his financial affairs. I remember receiving such a letter, hand-delivered by I. H. (Bud) Hammerman II, the millionaire Baltimore real estate promoter who was active in my political inner circle and who had raised a considerable amount of campaign money for me.

The letter was a cry of anguish with an undertone of threats. In essence, Wolff said, "I'm in terrible trouble. I need help. I'm getting desperate, and I don't know what I'm going to do. If I go in and cooperate with the prosecutors, it may save me—but it will be very bad for a lot of people. Will you please help me?" That was the gist of it, but not the exact quotation.

I looked at the letter and told Hammerman, "Bud, I'm terribly disturbed by Jerry's problems, but I wish I hadn't even seen this letter." I didn't want to be connected with the troubles of Wolff and Matz in any way. The Watergate situation had made me very conscious of how easy it was for someone to accuse a public figure of obstructing justice. Certainly, I didn't want to get involved in covering up anybody's troubles with the law.

"Well, what do I tell him?" Hammerman demanded.

"You can't tell him anything," I replied.

"You've got to do something to stop this thing," Hammerman insisted.

"There's nothing I can do to stop it," I retorted. "I could easily be charged with obstructing justice."

"But Jerry's going crazy," continued Hammerman. "He's not well—not responsible for his actions, and he's going to involve a lot of people."

"Bud, I'd do anything possible to help Jerry, but what he's asking just cannot be done," I replied. We left the matter there with Hammerman being far from satisfied.

Based on a conversation with Hammerman Wolff later told the prosecutors: "Mr. Agnew was quite upset by the letter, but he did not give Hammerman any assurances that anything could be done." On that point, Wolff is correct.

Bud Hammerman was very much aware of his vulnerability in the Baltimore County investigation long before I ever heard of it. He was a close friend of Bill Fornoff and had been involved in politico-business with Lester Matz and Jerry Wolff since the middle 1950's. Moreover, Hammerman had worked closely with my lawyer and campaign manager, George White, from the early days of my gubernatorial run, so he was fully informed from several sources when the dominoes began to collapse.

Between late February and late August, when Hammerman finally abandoned his facade of friendship to me, he visited me quite a few times to report on the status of the investigation as revealed to him by the Baltimore County grapevine. He was terribly troubled about Wolff's mental condition, and I knew that his worries went beyond Wolff's health and well-being.

It would be dishonest for me to say that I was completely naïve about the political realities of fund-raising. Like most politicians, I knew we had to have the campaign money, and I knew that it came mainly from people who made money out of being politically "in." It was a wise policy for a candidate or officeholder to isolate himself as much as possible from the political collection process, but it wasn't always possible—particularly at the county level. The contributor always wanted to give the money to you personally so he was sure that you knew he was helping you. And he usually gave it in cash, for three reasons. First, he was giving to both parties, playing both sides of the street and hedging his bets, so he wanted no records made.

Second, he probably had not paid taxes on the cash; and third, he knew that in every campaign there was a great need for "walking around money," the legal tender for paid election-day workers and for other cash needs that did not look quite right on a detailed election expenditure report.

At the gubernatorial level, the collection of funds was entrusted to a few close political allies. Bud Hammerman was one of those who did this for me. I asked for no details because I wanted to be insulated from a process which always has gray overtones as to legality. Certainly, this attitude was wrong but it was, and still is, a way of life in politics. It is easy for a senator or a state legislator to be shocked at such impropriety. But the legislative branch does not have to finance the ticket. That responsibility has always rested with the top executive candidate—the governor, or mayor, or county executive—because the executive branch controls the patronage plums and the patronage plums are an incentive for contributions.

So when Hammerman began to sweat about Wolff, I had a good idea why. I was cognizant that Bud was in close contact with Jerry Wolff about engineering awards, and that he was keeping tabs on which friends were being rewarded for their loyalty. I was also generally aware that these friends would be the source of future campaign financing. But I didn't want to know the details.

There was something else. I suspected that Hammerman was giving Wolff money. While this was clearly wrong, I dismissed it from my mind by rationalizing that Hammerman was a millionaire and that he and Wolff had, past and present, many business ventures together. It wasn't, I convinced myself, any of my affair if Bud wanted to reward Jerry. Again, I know this was wrong, but it was the way I looked at it then. I never came to an active confrontation with my conscience because, as Wolff has testified, he and I never discussed the subject.

So during his visits, Hammerman would seek assurances from me that somehow the investigation could be halted. He would warn me that people in the prosecutor's office wanted my scalp, and were tempting Matz and Wolff to implicate me. He kept telling me, "These guys are desperate; I don't know what they will say." But in spite of the alarm bells that were being rung by Hammerman and George White, I never put any pressure on anyone to stop the investigation. I told Hammerman once, "Look, Bud, Watergate guarantees that even the slightest action on my part would be called a cover-up."

On April 12, six employees of Matz, Childs were called before the Baltimore grand jury and compelled to testify under "use immunity" imposed by a federal judge. Through this procedure, a witness can be forced to answer any question, with the assurance that anything he says cannot be used against him in a later criminal trial. In other words, he cannot incriminate himself, so his right to refuse to testify under the protection of the Fifth Amendment is abrogated. Though "use immunity" does not guarantee that he will not be prosecuted on the basis of evidence from other sources, it for all practical purposes assures "small fish" that they are off the hook. However, uncooperative "bigger fish" can have "use immunity" forced on them to catch still bigger fish, yet still be prosecuted by external evidence or for perjury if their stories do not jibe with the prosecutor's thesis. In practical effect, "use immunity" conferred as a reward by a prosecutor can be a tacit signal of total immunity; whereas "use immunity" forced on an unwilling witness is no protection against prosecution if the prosecutor can obtain evidence against him from another source.

The Matz, Childs officials admitted that they had received bonuses and had handed the money back after deducting whatever taxes they would have to pay on it. They were told that Matz would use it to pay off certain politicians, or for campaign contributions; but they had no actual knowledge of the eventual disposition of the money. Since the bonuses had been deducted as business expenses from the corporate income taxes, Matz and Childs were certain to face charges of income tax evasion.

Matz became even more frantic. He had to show where all that money had gone. I had been told by several people that he was a big spender who often went to ski resorts in Colorado and beaches in the Caribbean. The word was that he was frequently accompanied on these junkets by politicians and bureaucrats whom he entertained to promote his business. Also, Matz had the reputation of being very lavish with gifts, although he never made any gifts to me. Now he was facing the need to explain where he had spent thousands of dollars. The prosecutors were not interested in hearing about Anderson or Joseph Alton (at

that time County Executive of Anne Arundel County, Maryland),
because they thought they already had enough external evidence
to prosecute them. So the only thing for Matz to do to save his
skin was, in prosecutorial parlance, to "trade up" and say the
money had gone to me.

I had no idea how far he would go in his efforts to save himself
by ruining me. But I did not have long to wait before I found
out the full extent of his perfidy.

CHAPTER FOUR

WHO WOULD BELIEVE IT?

From the moment Lester Matz and Jerry Wolff received the ominous warning that they should retain criminal lawyers, the panic of each fed on that of the other. Ruthlessly and relentlessly, the prosecutors applied the pressure. Wolff and Matz would surely face prison unless they could answer a lot of troubling questions about untaxed money and net-worth bulges. In late April, I learned from J. Walter Jones just how frantically Matz was trying to manufacture a solution to his difficulties.

Jones related this account of events: Matz came to the Chesapeake National Bank in Towson, the county seat of Baltimore County, one day when Jones was presiding over an executive meeting as chairman of the board of directors. Matz insisted that Jones come out of the bank and meet him in his car because, he said, "I don't want to talk anywhere we might be bugged."

So the two men drove around in the car. Matz said he was in trouble because his own engineers had told the grand jury they had kicked back their bonuses to him. He claimed he had given the money as campaign contributions and could account for all of it except ten thousand dollars.

Jones said, "Lester, it's no problem at all. I've got a record of every penny you contributed to us, and I'll make you a list."

But that was not enough. Matz wanted the banker to say that Matz had given him the extra ten thousand dollars as a political gift, although he really had not. Jones refused.

Matz warned Jones emphatically that he must persuade me to have the investigation against him quashed—otherwise, I would be incriminated in it, too. Jones said he did his best to calm Matz, recognizing that Matz was not in control of himself and was capable of doing something foolish.

A few days later, Matz returned to the Towson bank. He appeared extremely nervous. His face was flushed and he said he could not sleep at night for worrying—even sedatives did not help.

Matz told Jones he was being heavily pressured by his lawyer, Joseph H. H. Kaplan, to go to the prosecutors and tell them, "I made illegal contributions to Agnew."

Jones had been shocked. "That can't be true," he said. "Who would believe it?"

"It's not a question of who will believe it," Matz retorted. "If I make the statement, that will destroy Agnew."

"You need people to back you up on things like that," Jones said.

"I've got people who will back me up," Matz replied. Then he stressed his warning: "If Agnew does not stop this investigation, he will find himself in deep trouble."

At this point, Jones recalled, "Matz literally fell apart, angrily shouting like a madman."

Jones became indignant and declared: "I've had enough of this abuse from you. From this point on, if you have anything to say to me, I'll talk to your lawyer. I'm going to give him a list of the contributions you gave me, but I won't make up any."

So Jones went to one of Matz's lawyers, Arnold Weiner, gave him the list and said: "Lester wants me to say there is ten thousand dollars additional he contributed but it didn't get written down. That just didn't happen."

Weiner replied, "All you can say is the truth."

When I learned of Matz's hysterical threats to implicate me in his mess, I decided to seek help from the White House. I gave Bob Haldeman a complete summary of the Maryland problem, assured him of my own innocence, but expressed concern that I could, nevertheless, be seriously harmed by false charges. I suggested that given the way the big media were going after the Watergate matter, we could expect no restraint or objectivity on their part. They would have a field day reporting every wild rumor that surfaced and would apply all their old prejudices against the administration—particularly against me, because of my speeches in Des Moines and the South against media excesses. I warned Haldeman the President would be attacked on another front.

I asked if someone from the White House would alert Sen. Glenn Beall, the U. S. Attorney's brother, that political opponents would try to embarrass the administration by doing everything possible to involve me in the case. At that time, I did not know the depth of George Beall's personal hostility towards me. I knew we had disagreed politically on key issues, but after all, I had cleared his appointment as U. S. Attorney—an appointment I could have blocked easily.

Briefed by Haldeman, Mr. Nixon later commented on this in his *Memoirs*: "I was very concerned at the prospect of Agnew's being dragged through the mud unfairly, but in view of all the other problems and our strained relations with Capitol Hill, I did not see how we could do anything to help him. In fact, the climate was such that anything we did to try to help might boomerang and be made to appear that we were trying to cover up for him."

At Haldeman's suggestion, I asked former White House counsel, Charles Colson, to recommend a capable criminal lawyer who was familiar with the workings of the U. S. Attorney's office. He suggested his partner, Judd Best. So Best became my liaison with the prosecutors in Baltimore.

The President and his top people were totally absorbed in their own problems arising from the Watergate scandal, which—although I was blissfully unaware of it—was about to blow up in their faces. As I stated earlier, having never been accepted in the White House inner circle, I took no part in the frantic maneuvering that was going on in mid-April.

On April 19, White House Counsel John Dean declared that he would not become "a scapegoat in the Watergate case." On that same day, Judd Best had his first meeting with George Beall in Baltimore. The United States Attorney later filed a memorandum of their conversation:

April 19, 1973, 10:30 A.M.—Mr. Best in the office. He advised me that he represented Agnew; that his client had heard "cocktail-party conversation" to the effect that we had an investigation in this office involving him, and that there was deep concern about possible newspaper publicity on the investigation, which his client would be seriously hurt by, and which could not possibly be answered appropriately.

I told Best that the investigation did not involve his client and that we were very sensitive to the problems of prejudicial publicity.

Best reported to me Beall's assurances in essentially the same words. They sounded sincere, but I was still concerned, knowing of Russell T. Baker, Jr.'s cocktail conversation of Matz's and Wolff's early veiled threats to George White, and having learned just a few days before of Matz's aggressive challenge issued through Walter Jones.

It was around this time that the person I depended upon most for clearheaded counsel began to come apart at the seams. George White, my close friend, political counselor, and personal attorney, began to visit me frequently with all kinds of "horror stories" about how Matz and Wolff were gradually being forced to implicate me in the continuing investigation. Long known as one of the best trial lawyers in Baltimore, White was a person I had come to rely on for cool, orderly advice on a variety of subjects. I was shocked to see him becoming very nervous and confused about the progress of the investigation. Instead of calm, reasoned advice, I was getting only a lot of glum hand-wringing and ominous predictions of disaster. All this was terribly out of character for George. I think that Arnold Weiner, the very experienced criminal lawyer Matz and Wolff had retained, was feeding White the gloomiest possible picture of what was happening in the U. S. Attorney's office, because his clients were clinging to the hope that a sufficiently worried Agnew would, in some magical way, stop the investigation. To add to that, White was going through some critical financial problems of his own. I guess his world seemed to be collapsing. Whatever the reason, it put a lot of extra pressure on me at a time when I already had a full plate of problems.

On April 30, after weeks of agonizing, President Nixon finally announced the resignations of Haldeman, Ehrlichman, Dean, and Kleindienst. Elliot Richardson, the secretary of defense, was switched over to become Attorney General. That turned out to be bad news for me.

Nixon would soon grow to detest Richardson. As Watergate diminished the President's power, Richardson changed from a transparent toady to a sanctimonious lecturer on morals. I don't know why Mr. Nixon put him in charge of the Justice Department, except that he may have considered this a gesture towards his enemies of the eastern establishment. Nixon had a compulsion for giving important positions to people who were doctrinally opposed to him. After the didactic Richardson had chosen Archibald Cox as the special Watergate prosecutor and delivered Mr. Nixon into the clutches of his worst enemies, the President realized his mistake. But his realization came too late.

On August 22, when he was under heavy pressure from the Watergate prosecutors, the President held a press conference at San Clemente. The day before, I had held my own press conference, attributing directly to the Justice Department the leaks that the media were publishing about the investigation. Richardson had responded immediately, denying that his department was responsible. Of course, the President got questions on this subject. He condemned the leaks very strongly, saying he would demand the immediate dismissal of any Justice Department employee found to be responsible for leaks. I phoned the President to thank him for his support and to congratulate him on his handling of the press questions. He was very bitter about Richardson, referring to him during our conversation as "that little Ivy League pipsqueak s.o.b."

Elliot Richardson was one of those who tried to block my nomination for Vice-President at the Miami Beach convention. After Nixon had chosen me, the left-wingers drummed up a little band of delegates on the floor who showed their dissatisfaction by registering a protest vote for George Romney. My trouble with the eastern liberal Republican establishment dates back to the time when I led a national committee to draft Nelson Rockefeller for the presidency.

I admired Rockefeller greatly. He was very successful as Governor of New York; he favored a strong foreign policy to confront the threat of communism in the world; he had good ideas about how to make state government work for the benefit of the people, and about how to use the federal bureaucracy most effectively. I had been active in the National Association of Counties and in the various governors' associations, and I realized that local governments were getting a raw deal: they had an insufficient tax base to provide enough revenues to execute their responsibilities. Rockefeller agreed, and we both favored a greater sharing of tax revenues for state and local governments. Revenue sharing, bastardized by the incompetence of the Nixon Domestic Council staff, later became a poor substitute for what was needed.

I was also very friendly with Ronald Reagan and ideologically compatible with him in many ways, but thought his two years as Governor of California could not match Rockefeller's long years of practical experience. A lot of people considered Rockefeller very liberal and dovish on foreign policy, but he was not. He was harder than Nixon, and a lot more hawkish about the mission of America in the world. Later, when he was a member of the Foreign Intelligence Advisory Board, I had an opportunity to exchange views with him on several occasions. I can assure you that Nelson Rockefeller would not have presided over the destruction of C.I.A. effectiveness that we have been witnessing in recent years.

Many admirers expected Rockefeller to announce his candidacy for the presidency when he called a New York press conference on March 21, 1968. I was even more confident that he would announce because he had personally assured me that he had made up his mind to run. We had talked when I introduced him at the *Ahepa* (a Greek lodge) convention in Washington only a few days before.

It was pure happenstance that March 21 was the day for my regularly scheduled Thursday press conference in Annapolis. My staff suggested that we set up a television set so that I could share in the moment of glory as the great Rockefeller rocket blasted off. After all, said my advisers, I had been the first governor to press for the Rockefeller candidacy, and I should take the credit. Unfortunately, the rocket fizzled on the launching pad. Rockefeller said: "I have decided today to reiterate unequivocally that I am not a candidate campaigning directly or indirectly for the presidency of the United States."

His announcement left me furious and humiliated. He had not even shown me the courtesy of informing me of his intentions in advance. He finally telephoned me hours afterwards, but only when the word had gone out on the wires that I was mad as a hornet. Some time later, when Rockefeller switched once more and belatedly tried to seize the nomination at Miami Beach, he still held the allegiance of some members of my Maryland delegation—those who were aligned with liberal Republican Sen. Charles Mathias. I had long before declared my support would go to Richard Nixon. As leader of the delegation, I tried to deliver the entire bloc of Maryland votes to him. My efforts were not successful. George Beall, who would later oppose me in a much more serious way, was one of those I could not move. He stayed with Rockefeller to the end.

We had a bitter argument among our delegates. Because John Mitchell had sworn me to secrecy, I could not tell them that Mitchell had visited me three days before the voting and told me that it was 90 percent certain that I was going to be the vice-presidential nominee. But I did everything else I could do to swing Maryland votes to Mr. Nixon. The people in Sen. Mathias's orbit did not come around, so the Maryland delegation remained split, eighteen to eight in favor of Nixon.

When Beall's recommended appointment as federal prosecutor for Maryland came to my attention—every Maryland appointment went across my desk and was subject to my approval when I was Vice-President—I remember holding it a couple of days and thinking, "George Beall was stubborn as a mule at the convention and he is not on our team, so why should we make him the U. S. Attorney?"

Old Maryland friends interceded for Beall, so I finally talked to others who were opposed and concluded that since we were trying to reunify the party, I should let bygones be bygones. So I put my approval on the Beall nomination. It has often crossed my mind that this was a crucial decision. If a different U. S. Attorney had looked at the case being so eagerly and ruthlessly developed by his left-wing Democratic assistants, he might have been more objective about the self-serving testimony of the witnesses who dragged me into their troubles to save their own skins. Or perhaps he would not have retained people of incompatible political beliefs at all.

While recalling the 1968 political campaign, I might mention an incident which shows that contrary to all the published lies about my "graft" and "greed," I turned down a quarter of a

million dollars in cash that was offered me as a campaign contribution.

This story has been related to me several times by friends in
the Baltimore Greek community. This is what they say happened: The Greek-Americans all over the United States were so
excited about the selection of the first vice-presidential candidate
of Greek blood that they enthusiastically began pouring money
into the Nixon-Agnew coffers. A group of Greek-American businessmen in Chicago called Gus Constantine, who was very active
in fund-raising for us in Baltimore, and announced they had collected $250,000. Constantine referred them to Walter Jones, who
was area chairman for the Nixon-Agnew ticket.

Jones asked, "How do we go about getting the money?"

"Someone is flying it down today," came the reply. "But be
clear on one thing. This is for our brother, Spiro, not for Nixon.
Most of us are Democrats, and we don't want to contribute to
Nixon."

Jones didn't think it would be very smart to point out that all
the money went into the same pot for the same purpose, so he
simply asked for the list of the contributors' names, which had
to be reported in compliance with the election laws.

"There are no names," the Chicagoan replied. "The money is
in a suitcase. It's for Agnew personally."

Evidently the Chicago businessmen of Greek ancestry had
simply canvassed the Greek community and collected a quarter
of a million dollars for "Spiro, the Greek." They wanted to give
it to Spiro Agnew, not to the Nixon Committee or to the Republican party, and they wanted to hand it to me personally.

My plane, by coincidence, was due to land in Chicago on the
afternoon Jones received the telephone call about the money. He
became alarmed over the possibility that some eager donor would
rush up to me at the airport and present me with a suitcase full
of money.

I assume some of the givers did not know about the techni-
calities of reporting campaign contributions; others probably
knew but did not want to be identified as contributors to a
Republican candidate, even if of Greek extraction, and perhaps
some of the money had not been reported to the I.R.S. For one
reason or another they did not want their names listed, but Jones
told them: "We have to have the names." He telephoned my

plane and got campaign adviser George White on the line. "George," he said, "don't let anyone hand the Governor anything you can't identify while he is in Chicago."

The point of the story is that there are many opportunities for a major political candidate to get his hands on cash if he is of a venal nature. I have never considered political money *my* money. That is why the I.R.S. never found the supposed hundreds of thousands in kickbacks. They just didn't exist. Whatever contributions were made were spent in the campaigns.

The allegations of the confessed bribers and extortioners that they were acting to satisfy my "gargantuan appetite for cash" are patently ridiculous. There was the time when Lester Matz said he wanted to give five thousand dollars to me for Rockefeller's campaign. "How do you want it?" he asked, and I said, "By check." If I were as venal as my accusers say, it would have been easy for me to answer, "Cash, Lester," and put the five thousand in my pocket.

The opportunities I had to make money on my decisions as governor were limitless. But I was a reform governor, and I refused to play the old game of machine politics. In most previous Maryland administrations, a lot of political influence went into the selection of state judges. Ambitious politicians would have their friends offer up to fifty thousand dollars in return for an appointment to a judgeship. When I became governor, I made sure that that practice did not penetrate my administration. I laid the law down clearly: "There will be no tying of any judicial appointments to any financial contributions to the party."

We never accepted a contribution tied to a judgeship, and we never solicited judges for contributions. That was well known to everyone in Maryland politics, and it was quite a variation from past Maryland practice.

During the gubernatorial campaign of 1966, I realized it would be impossible to see all the people who wanted to express support in the hope their support would not be forgotten if we were successful. We had a committee that carried out the responsibility for raising party funds; Walter Jones, Bud Hammerman, and George White were among its members. I believe they will remember well that I made it clear to them that they must not promise anything to anyone in return for a contribution.

My two years as governor were noteworthy for a major tax

reform program and a strong effort to provide Maryland with a new and less cumbersome constitution. Other accomplishments and activities are fully set forth in the official record of the Agnew administration, which has now been published by the state of Maryland. Many will remember my time as governor because of a confrontation I had with Baltimore's black leaders during the disorders that followed the tragic murder of Martin Luther King, Jr. Intimidated by the militants' accusations that any black who spoke against a black was an "Uncle Tom," the moderate leaders seemed unable to find the resolve to condemn the rioting and arson.

I took a strong stand against the Cambridge riot, engineered by H. Rap Brown, and against the campus upheavals at Bowie State College. My actions were anathema to the liberal establishment, which claimed I had suddenly switched from liberal to conservative on the issue of race relations. This was not true. I have never been liberal when it comes to condoning violence and the intentional destruction of property.

It is my firm conviction that the hostility generated by my actions during the riots was directly responsible for the antagonism of the liberal media during the 1968 presidential campaign. Mr. Nixon and I might have begun our years in a different climate had not each of us been branded as being "without compassion" because of our refusal to sanction civil disobedience that abrogated the rights of others.

Although no one, not even my enemies, has attempted to implicate me in the Watergate scandal, I must say here that I think the break-in incident was overblown and the shock expressed largely phony. I don't condone it, but the major parties have been penetrating and spying on each other for many years. What was most reprehensible about Watergate was the cover-up and lying that followed the break-in. The President should have dismissed everybody directly involved, burned the tapes, and taken responsibility for the actions of his subordinates. The liberal intellectuals and the left-wingers would have screamed for awhile, but there would have been no impeachment and that would have been the end of it.

So in spite of my being free of the taint of Watergate, I was destined to learn in a very painful way that political enmity of unscrupulous prosecutors, coupled with a weakened President, can destroy a Vice-President. The collection of unverified testimony, improperly referred to as "corroborated"; the leaking of it to the news media; the fabrication and leaking of damaging accusations and wholly unsubstantiated rumors convicted me before I ever had a chance to defend myself. Worst of all, these things convicted me in the minds of the President and those members of Congress who might otherwise have made sure that I was given a congressional investigation and supported me as I faced my accusers in a nationally televised impeachment hearing.

Some have speculated that Congress was disinterested in my plight because the case against me was so strong. It is certainly true that the Justice Department did everything possible to create that impression—both to the Congress and the White House. However, my real problem was in some ways similar to the legislative problem President Carter faces in dealing with the Congress every day. He is not—nor was I—a member of the club.

When one comes to the executive branch of the federal government from state or local government, rather than from the House or Senate, he comes as a stranger—without the many close friendships that members of Congress develop through years of working together. While I had a few close friends in the Congress, I did not have the broad base of acquaintances needed to support my effort to obtain a hearing.

There were other reasons, more coldly political, for turning me away. The White House itself was not supporting me. On the contrary, it was quietly cutting my legs from under me. The Democratic majority in the Congress knew Mr. Nixon was in trouble and that he faced possible impeachment or resignation. They did not want to rehabilitate a strong successor who could unite the Republican party. All these factors taken together made it easy for the Congress to ignore my problem.

CHAPTER FIVE

HOW CAN WE PROVE IT?

On May 18, 1973, Joseph H. H. Kaplan, a lawyer representing Lester Matz and John Childs, telephoned Assistant U. S. Attorney Russell T. Baker, Jr., at Baltimore, proposing a deal. He requested total immunity for his clients as a reward for testimony that would lead the prosecutors to a major break in their investigation of Maryland politicians and professional contractors.

Baker replied that Kaplan's clients were sure to be indicted on charges of making payments in return for contracts to William Fornoff, the chief assistant to Dale Anderson, my successor as County Executive of Baltimore County. Kaplan said they knew that, but hinted he had some information that was really sensational—however, there was some question whether the government would even be interested in the information they could supply.

As Kaplan had intended, this incongruous teaser thoroughly whetted Baker's interest. The prosecutor reminded the lawyer that Matz and Childs ". . . might be able to earn immunity if they were to cooperate fully and truthfully." Kaplan then said his clients had no evidence against Anderson and he thought the government already had enough to convict Fornoff, so he doubted they would offer his clients immunity for any more information on him. Then Kaplan played his ace. Matz, he said, could provide some testimony against the Vice-President of the United States but, he quickly continued, he assumed the prosecutors would not wish to investigate the Vice-President.

"What do you mean by that?" Baker retorted, according to one of his own memoranda of the conversation, an intriguing document which I have obtained from the Justice Department's files and about which I will comment further, later.

Baker virtuously declared (so he says in his memo), "This

office is interested in doing its job, which is investigating and prosecuting federal crimes. Since Agnew left Baltimore County public office in 1966, all federal statutes of limitations had [*sic*] run and Agnew has not been a subject of this investigation."

But Kaplan pressed on. He stated, according to another of Baker's memos, that "there had been dealings between the Vice-President and his clients while Agnew was County Executive and Governor of Maryland and that they continued to have dealings with him *up to the present time.*"

Kaplan said Matz and Childs would talk, if given immunity, but were reluctant to say anything that would destroy the business they had built up over many years. Baker promised to "minimize harm to the business." But he added they had better hurry, because *The Washington Post* had three reporters snooping around; if they did not come in soon, he "would proceed towards indictment of Matz and Childs."

The really interesting things about Baker's memoranda of May 18 are that he wrote two memos about the same conversation, and that he states he discussed *four* subjects with Kaplan. One of these was possible immunity for Matz and Childs, but the other three listed in the memo have been painted out with black ink. The second memo is characterized by Baker as a *"discussion of informal deals"* (italics mine). What the deals were is a puzzle. However, it is clear that Joseph Kaplan had more than one stack of pancakes on the griddle, and it is equally clear that the bargaining session involved more than the fate of Matz and Childs.

I have reliable and confidential information that Matz first told his "payments to Agnew" tale to Kaplan in hopes he could pressure George White into convincing me to intercede in the investigation. The Matz allegations provided Joe Kaplan with a wonderful negotiating tool, because the prosecutors were also looking into reports that a large and illegal campaign contribution from corporate funds had been made—in cash—to the committee that raised money for Sen. Joseph Tydings, the Maryland Democrat, in his 1970 reelection campaign—which he lost to Glenn Beall, Jr. Kaplan, as Tydings' campaign treasurer, was directly accountable for any campaign-money irregularities.

Matz told several people that Kaplan relayed the "payments to Agnew" story to Baker without even consulting his client in advance. When Matz asked Kaplan the reason for this irregular procedure, Kaplan is said to have replied that the prosecutors told him: "Get Matz in here to talk about Agnew or we will proceed against you in the Tydings case."

Kaplan was reported to be lying awake and worrying at night over his problems. I suspect he was in deep trouble; otherwise, why would he run in ahead of his clients and say he could deliver the Vice-President?

Beall and his youthful assistants have been depicted in print as shouting for joy after Kaplan's telephone call on May 18; they eagerly seized the chance to win national fame by prosecuting a Vice-President of the United States. Skolnik, according to one account, told Beall: "Keep up the pressure, George. Keep hammering at Matz and soon enough he will serve up Agnew."

On the same day, Archibald Cox was named the special Watergate prosecutor and promised to follow the trail of that scandal all the way into "the Oval Office." That was a clear signal that Richard Nixon would be a target of any Cox-managed investigation of the Watergate cover-up. And if Mr. Nixon lost the presidency, who would then become President of the United States? I would, of course. Unless I could be pushed out of the way beforehand—perhaps by smearing me with this scheme which the Baltimore "Gang of Four" so zealously embraced.

For the next two weeks, Kaplan stalled. He said Matz and Childs were worried about the danger that my ruination, after the shock of Watergate, might cause too great a trauma for the nation to bear. Baker fired back that if they would not talk, the government would grant them use immunity to compel their testimony against me before the grand jury. If the prosecutors were forced to take this course, Baker continued, Matz and Childs would still be prosecuted and there would be no deals available to them. Both Baker and Kaplan were well aware that the evidence of the Matz, Childs employees and of Fornoff's testimony, coupled with a net-worth investigation, would be more than enough to sink Matz.

It would be appropriate here for me to comment on a very sharp prosecutorial tool called immunity. Like a scalpel or a chain saw, it can accomplish an enormous amount of work quickly. But its use requires skill and restraint. Restraint is not a dominant quality among the politically ambitious, and it was

certainly lacking in the Justice Department when they agreed
that the Baltimore prosecutors had a strong case against me on
the bases of Matz's accusations and Wolff's assumptions.

It is ironic that immunity came into favor during the early
days of the Nixon administration, and that I strongly supported
the concept. I saw it as a way of getting to the narcotics big
shots by compelling the pusher on the street to implicate the
higher-ups. This looked like an attractive way to break organized
crime. However, danger lies in the fact that the hardened criminal, even at the lowest level, seldom breaks. The prospect of
jail is neither new nor intimidating to him. But the white-collar
criminal, never before in trouble, not only breaks but collapses
and often bends the truth to save himself from incarceration.
His currency for salvation is the ambitious prosecutor's desire
to "trade up"—to make headlines by bagging big quarry. Immunity then becomes bribery and extortion sanctioned by the law.
Upon convictions obtained by such uses of immunity, careers are
born. James Thompson, the loudmouthed Governor of Illinois,
is a case in point.

Immunity leaves the fairness of prosecution bilaterally in the
hands of the prosecutors and their bosses in the Attorney General's office in Washington. When both have lost their impartiality, there is no rein—unless it is the President of the United States
—and we know that the President, at the time of my case, had
the bit in his own mouth.

Where the bait is a political and philosophical enemy of some
importance, the prosecutor is sorely tempted to believe lies and
to encourage further lies. In the investigation of Spiro Agnew,
the temptation proved irresistible.

On June 4, in the Baltimore Federal courthouse, William Fornoff pleaded guilty to having "received substantial quantities of
money" from businessmen having contracts with Baltimore
County, and having delivered the cash to "another public official"
whom the media identified as County Executive Dale Anderson.
In return for his testimony, the government recommended that
Fornoff be spared from a jail term. In a sealed document presented to the court, Fornoff also named the businessmen accused
of having bribed him. Lester Matz and Jerome Wolff were on
that list.

After Fornoff's plea, Matz instantly realized that he was implicated in the Dale Anderson case. He could no longer remain silent; he had to do something to stay out of jail. Kaplan had been urging Matz all along to throw me to the wolves. So, on the very next day, Kaplan again telephoned the U. S. Attorney's office. His clients had decided "in the national interest," he said, that they would consider a deal. Kaplan demanded total immunity from prosecution on all charges in return for their information, which he claimed "was sufficient to convict a high federal official of serious offenses." Baker and Skolnik refused to promise the payoff without detailed information about the "high federal official."

Kaplan said the case would amount to more than "a mere swearing match" between his clients and me. My alleged offense was, he claimed, "a substantial federal crime and not just a campaign contribution violation." Skolnik warned that if Kaplan's clients told lies or held back anything, all deals they got from the government for easy treatment would be "null and void."

On June 7, in identical letters of negotiation sent to Matz, Childs, and Wolff, Beall specified his terms: first, he must hear all the information before making any deal. Second, he did not want any more evidence on someone he already had—for instance, on Fornoff. Beall went on to say the investigation had produced evidence of several serious offenses on Matz's part in addition to those about which Matz might be prepared to talk.

On June 11, apparently in fear that the Beall letter might frighten Matz into changing his mind about accusing me, Baker advised Kaplan that the letter "did not necessarily mean that the government would inevitably charge and prosecute Matz and Childs for bribery, whether or not they refused to cooperate." The haggling continued as Baker and Beall used the carrot-and-stick technique. It is difficult to tell exactly what happened at the time because the memos are so heavily censored. (Minor examples of such censoring appear in Appendix.)

Wolff swung back and forth, unable to decide whether to cooperate. He was torn between two emotions—a frantic desire to save himself from jail, and a terrible feeling of guilt about his mistreatment of me. He was well aware of my regard for him and knew how much I had done for him throughout his career, and he hesitated to reward me by sticking a knife in my back.

His lawyer, Arnold Weiner, told the prosecutors that Wolff was on the brink of suicide.

Weiner and my former attorney, George White, are good friends in a professional way. They are both very good trial men, and White made no secret of his respect for Weiner as a criminal lawyer. Weiner was fully experienced, having spent quite some time as an Assistant U. S. Attorney in that same Baltimore office. At this point in the investigation, White was in almost daily contact with Weiner, and Weiner gave him a blow-by-blow account of Wolff's torment—along with broad hints that Wolff would be a devastating witness against me because of his little notebook in which he had recorded, chapter and verse, an alleged conspiracy between Hammerman, himself, and me. Actually, the notebook contained nothing that incriminated me. It contained a record of engineering awards and notes based on Wolff's conjectures and conclusions and, of course, what Hammerman told him.

Nonetheless, White became increasingly morose and on more than one occasion told me that for all intents and purposes my life was over, my career finished, and I would probably end up in jail.

An insight into the eagerness of the prosecutors to implicate me may be gained by knowledge that the Baltimore "Gang of Four" went to Richardson on June 12, the day after Baker took pains to advise Kaplan that Matz and Childs might escape prosecution in spite of Beall's tough letter. They told Richardson they were on the verge of receiving information from attorneys who represented the subjects of an investigation—one which could damage the Vice-President personally. At that point, the only information they had was a secondhand story from a worried Kaplan.

On June 13, Weiner asked total immunity for Wolff. This is George Beall's own memorandum of his meeting with Weiner:

> I fenced with him for awhile as to the difficulty for us to predict what our posture would be without knowing in greater detail what Wolff would be able to contribute to the investigation. He insisted Wolff was a "victim" of the Baltimore County system and that we should not be particularly interested in pursuing him criminally. I dis-

agreed with his characterization of Wolff and suggested that, from our standpoint, the corruptors were just slightly less culpable than the public officials who were the object of their affections. . . . He pressed and wanted to know if we would consider immunity for Wolff. I said that we would consider all of the alternative possibilities with respect to his client, depending upon the information he gives, his candor and reliability and adherence to the agreement which we suggested in our letter.

A George Beall memo in the prosecutorial files indicates that on June 15, during the time that Baker was encouraging Kaplan's efforts to bring Matz in to testify, Arnold Weiner stopped by to see Beall with a "bizarre story with respect to leaks from this office which came to him at the Maryland Bar Association meeting yesterday." Weiner added that "the story was potentially harmful to the members of the U. S. Attorney's office." I have an idea what that story was, although like many others, it is not revealed in the prosecutors' files. A highly respected lawyer in a premier firm called me about that time, saying Skolnik had mentioned during a conversation about another case that he had to have a postponement because he was so tied up in the Agnew investigation. The lawyer had been shocked at this indiscretion on the part of an officer of the government, who was supposed to know how to keep his mouth shut. No wonder so many damaging leaks became the prosecutorial trademark of the Baltimore "Gang of Four."

Meanwhile, Matz and Childs had decided, finally, to use me as their escape hatch. They signed letters of negotiation spelling out the terms for the plea bargaining and their testimony. On June 21, Kaplan and Weiner met with Beall, Skolnik, and Baker. Baker's memorandum of this conference—a document heavily censored before the Justice Department would release it—quotes Weiner as saying that Matz could testify about payments to me.

According to this document, Matz claimed he had given me up to forty-four thousand dollars, including one twenty-thousand-dollar payment while I was governor and the remainder in a series of visits to me when I was Vice-President. "One payment was apparently delivered to Agnew in the basement of the White House itself," the memo said.

I don't remember whether Matz visited me in my White House office (incidentally, it was not in the basement), but I can assure you that he delivered no kickbacks to me there or anywhere else. Just about every politically oriented person I knew wanted to stop by at the West Wing of the White House to say hello. As my scheduler John Damgard often said, Matz would have been in to see me every other day, if I had allowed it.

The same memo contains the following outrageous fabrication, told to Weiner by Matz and dutifully relayed to the prosecutors. According to Baker's memo, someone close to Matz wanted a federal job in Maryland that was within the control of the Vice-President's office. Walter Jones told Matz the job would cost twenty-five hundred dollars, and it was arranged between Matz and Jones that the payment was to be delivered in the Vice-President's office. On the appointed day, Matz met his friend across the street from the Vice-President's office. The man only had a thousand dollars, and Matz agreed to lend him the additional fifteen hundred that he needed. Matz took the money in cash into the Vice-President's office and "placed it on the corner of Agnew's desk," the memo reads. "Jones and Agnew," it says, "were in the room when Matz placed the money on the desk, but neither of them picked it up before Matz left." And Matz's friend, according to this memorandum, later got the job.

During my years in executive political offices, I guess I got thousands of jobs of one type or another for friends and friends-of-friends. But I did not sell any of them—neither the most prestigious nor the most lowly. Any of those I appointed or recommended for appointment can verify that; not even my adversaries bothered to accuse me of this at any time during my career.

That piece of fiction was seized upon by the prosecutors as the centerpiece of their charge I had accepted cash from Matz while I was Vice-President. They believed they could make Jones testify that he had been in my office at the time and had witnessed the transfer of the money. Then their case would not depend solely on the testimony of a few trapped men desperately trying to save themselves by offering me as a sacrifice; it could be corroborated by J. Walter Jones, the respected banker who had been identified with my political career for a long time.

But they ran into a sticky problem. Jones said yes, he certainly was in my office that day with Matz, but no cash transfer had taken place. The truth, said Jones, is that Matz sent a twenty-five hundred dollar *check* to the Nixon-Agnew reelection campaign fund, and Jones then supplied Matz's covering letter confirming the check. So the prosecutors—confronted by the check, Matz's letter, and Jones's testimony—then did a lot of clandestine modification. They stuck to the story of the twenty-five hundred dollars, but became very fuzzy about Jones being in my office at that time. The reason is clear: Jones's testimony destroyed their case for the so-called payment by Matz in the Vice-President's office. This was a typical performance by the federal attorneys in Baltimore.

From the word *go*—from the first day Weiner quoted Matz as saying "I paid off the Vice-President"—the prosecutors never showed the slightest incredulity about the charge. On the contrary, their actions revealed their keen desire to make a case. They never expressed any doubt; they said in effect, "How can we nail it down? How can we prove it?"

Unquestionably, George Beall was a very weak U. S. Attorney. He was never really in command of his office. Skolnik, the old hand, led George around by the nose. A skimming of the Cohen-Witcover book, *A Heartbeat Away*, reveals starkly the romanticized self-portrait painted by the Baltimore "Gang of Four." They were, in their own eyes, the tough TV law-enforcement types. Witnesses who resented their high-handed tactics and became unwilling to grovel were called "bad men."

The prosecutors reveled in intimidation and repeated to their chroniclers self-aggrandizing happenings, such as Wolff's statement that his blood froze when Skolnik said, "I got Congressman Johnson, and I'll get you." Their technique was to terrorize witnesses. In *Heartbeat*, it is said that Skolnik chased uncooperative witnesses with special delight. "He would hammer at the witness unceasingly, threatening imprisonment and the disgrace that went with it" . . . "[Once the witness] decide[d] to cooperate . . . he became malleable, often zealous, willing to report fact and *hearsay*" (italics mine).* And, I might also add, willing to compose fiction.

The rude tactics they used in their initial contact with poten-

---

* *A Heartbeat Away*, Cohen, Richard M., and Witcover, Jules, p. 72.

tial witnesses are another example of their abuse of their authority. When they phoned my old friend, Harry A. Dundore, Sr., a retired businessman who had no connection with government awards whatever, the first thing they said to him was their old line, "Do you have a criminal lawyer?" When he replied that he did not, they told him perhaps he'd better get one. That alone is enough to scare a law-abiding citizen to death. Then they told him they didn't want to discuss the case on the phone, but that it was serious and his lawyer should contact them.

In their effort to show that I had illegally received money, they immunized scores of witnesses who had done business with the county or state, or who had contributed to my campaigns. But they could get no one to say I had ever extorted money from them, or that I had ever indicated I would withhold work unless they made a payment to me. Some businessmen came to me with campaign contributions. I didn't chase after them. They also went to other politicians, past and present, of both parties.

Where the money was used is the determining factor. If it went for personal use and had been solicited in direct exchange for political payoff, it was graft. If it went to a political campaign and had been voluntarily given, it was a campaign contribution. I received no bribes. I engaged in no extortion. Both Wolff and Matz stated in their polygraph tests that I had never asked them for money. That is part of the prosecutors' own records.

Yet the prosecutors set out to make somebody testify that I had extorted money and received bribes. The witnesses knew what the prosecutors wanted. They wanted to implicate me criminally. The minute a witness would say, "I don't know of any misconduct by Agnew," the prosecutors would say, "We'll immunize you and take you before the grand jury. If you lie, you'll go to jail for perjury. If you refuse to testify, you'll go to jail for contempt of court. So you might as well tell us. We know more about what you've been doing than you think we do."

The frightened witnesses indeed became "malleable." Especially when they were reminded of the horrors of jail. The prosecutors told one witness: "You're a very nice-looking man. Certainly, you don't want to be thrown into jail with a lot of thugs who will treat you like their girl friend."

It isn't hard to see why such insinuations would make a man's blood run cold. The prosecutors used these and other rough tactics in their determination to get me. These men, in violation of my constitutional rights, assumed that I was guilty unless proved innocent, and they persuaded frightened men to testify against me in return for easier treatment.

Federal Judge Hoffman, during a conference with my attorneys and the prosecutors, said he was not unfamiliar with prosecutorial indiscretions—previously he had reviewed a grand jury transcript from another jurisdiction in which the prosecutors had browbeaten one witness and accused another of lying. Judge Hoffman called it a disgraceful performance by the government.

CHAPTER SIX

STRIKE WHILE THE IRON IS HOT

The files of the Justice Department on the Agnew case are fascinating. They would be even more so if they were not so well decorated with the black ink-blots of the prosecutor-censors. Even so, they have revealed to me long after the event the machinations of the U. S. Attorney's office in Baltimore, as the "Gang of Four" constructed their fragile case against me and the Department of Justice used it to force my resignation from the vice-presidency. Attorney General Elliot Richardson proposed to confront me with the allegations of the witnesses, who had made their deals with the prosecutors, and to demand that I resign. By a not-so-strange coincidence, this rush for my resignation occurred just as Richardson was beginning to believe that the President himself was cracking under the strain of the Watergate scandal and must soon leave the presidency.

The records show that U. S. Attorney George Beall received a phone call from Attorney General Richardson's assistant on July 3. The Attorney General was terribly busy and would have to cancel the appointment Mr. Beall had previously made with him for that day.

Beall accepted the postponement and was berated by Skolnik for his timidity. In *A Heartbeat Away*, Skolnik is reported to have said, "God damn it. Call the secretary up and tell her that we must see the Attorney General today." Beall obediently called back, insisted that the matter was very urgent, and eventually prevailed. So the Baltimore Four went to Washington for the second time, armed only with the narratives of attorneys Kaplan and Weiner, to tell Richardson that two men in deep trouble themselves would implicate the Vice-President of the United States—if it would help them escape their own difficulties.

The three-hour meeting in the Attorney General's office was

interrupted repeatedly because Richardson had to take a series of urgent telephone calls from the White House. It later came out that Mr. Nixon had been burning up the wires with angry protests about an unsubstantiated story in the press, which said that Watergate Special Prosecutor Cox was probing government expenditures of about $1.5 million on the President's San Clemente home.

The President demanded that Richardson get Cox to deny unequivocally that any inquiry was being made into the Casa Pacifica financing, and to do it immediately. Nixon's ranting and raving so upset the Attorney General, according to Richardson's staff, that the proper Bostonian considered resigning then and there. One reason he did not quit was that he believed the President was losing control, emotionally and mentally, and might soon have to hand the presidency over to me. That was a horrible prospect to the Attorney General, who seems to have been determined I should never reside in the White House.

Richardson has been quoted as saying that the Baltimore prosecutors so impressed him with their tale about me that he soon became convinced it was true. Having prosecuted similar charges as a U.S. Attorney in Massachusetts, he thought the Marylanders had "more complete and convincing testimony than I had ever been able to assemble in my own investigations." The startling assessment was based solely on the unverified, unquestioned narratives by lawyers Kaplan and Weiner as relayed to Richardson by the Baltimore Four.

By past accounts, Richardson did not need much to convince him about charges against public officials. In 1966, when he was running for Attorney General of Massachusetts, he accused his opponent, Francis Bellotti, of lacking the moral sensitivity to fill the office because he accepted an improper retainer-fee. Richardson won the election. Press reports say that he was upbraided by Judge Webster Thayer, who presided over the notorious Sacco-Vanzetti trial, for using tactics against an Italian-American that he would never have considered using against a member of his own class. According to columnist Kevin Phillips:

Hostility toward ethnic politicians appears to run in Richardson's family. His maternal uncle, Henry Lee Shattuck, hated Boston's Irish wardheelers so much that he

paid $35,000 out of his own money for the private investi-
gation that led to Mayor James Curley's imprisonment
for fraud in 1947. Such moralizing against corruption is
easy for the rich Lees, Shattucks, and Richardsons. Even
when Elliot Richardson was a young man, his unearned
income from inheritances was $100,000 a year. New En-
gland fortunes like this were not built on seamy courthouse graft; they were built on the higher morality of
three generations of ethnic millworkers paid $11 a week
and dead in their graves at 43.

But what was the sum total of this "most complete and convincing testimony" that the Baltimore prosecutor now offered a
credulous Richardson? It consisted of nothing except the payoff
story of Lester Matz and the speculations and hearsay of Jerome
Wolff, which their lawyers had outlined along with Matz's demands that the government must pay a high price for it by granting him total immunity from prosecution. Matz himself had not
yet come in and testified under oath. Wolff at this point had
not even signed a letter of negotiation.

Baker's memorandum of the July 3 meeting states: "The
Attorney General indicated that he was greatly concerned for
the nation if these allegations proved accurate, particularly in
view of the Watergate matter. He directed that the investigation
should be a thorough one. He also indicated that it would probably be advisable at some later point to confront the Vice-President with the allegations in order to give him an opportunity to
clear himself, if possible."

Before the Matz fabrications had turned the investigation in
my direction, my lawyer, Judd Best, had discussed with George
Beall the possibility that my testimony might be needed. We
believed it was constitutionally inappropriate for the Vice-President to appear before any grand jury, and had so advised Beall.
Beall now relayed this information to Richardson, who indicated
I might be questioned by deposition. Richardson seemed to be
preoccupied with speculation about the judicial vulnerability of
the President and the Vice-President. On June 25, he received
a very long memo from Assistant Attorney General Dixon about
whether or not a President is subject to judicial subpoena.

Beall said Matz was "unwilling to cooperate except in exchange for total immunity." Baker's memorandum goes on to add: "The Attorney General did not in any way indicate that total immunity was an impossibility. Instead, he suggested that total immunity should probably depend upon the extent of the corroboration which could be mustered in support of Mr. Matz's allegations." Baker says that Richardson "did understand, however, that negotiations could not proceed with Mr. Matz and his attorneys unless we could indicate that immunity was a possibility." The Attorney General's attitude is summed up in *Heartbeat* as follows: "Richardson grasped the dimensions of what the Baltimoreans were telling him, but he never challenged the authenticity of it. From the very first the resignation of Vice-President Agnew was seen by the Attorney General as the most direct, desirable way to serve the public interest."

When Richardson suggested that he should tell President Nixon about the charges against me, the prosecutors emphatically objected. They were afraid the word would get back to me and I would break the news of my being a target. They had not yet nailed down either Matz or Wolff, and they were afraid a public statement from me would change their minds—scare them off. Their plan was to sneak up behind me without warning. They were also cool to Richardson's idea of confronting me with the evidence and giving me a chance to assert my innocence. They knew their evidence would be tainted—bought from a dubious character in exchange for total immunity—and they knew I would fight.

Kaplan and Weiner repeated their demand for total immunity at a meeting with the prosecutors the same day. Beall told them "immunity was a possibility," and that it depended upon the corroboration. A few days later, Matz came in and detailed the story previously told by his lawyers. On July 9, my attorney, Judd Best, made another of his periodic telephone calls to Beall to find out the latest developments. Beall said he could not discuss the matter over the phone, that Best should call back for a meeting. The next day Best called again, but Beall said he had decided it was not appropriate for them to talk any more. In effect, Beall said, "Don't call me; I'll call you."

"I understand," Best replied. He knew then that, despite their denials, the investigators were really aiming at me—that they must have some new testimony linking me to the case. They did.

Much later, I learned that Jerry Wolff came in on July 10 and made a detailed statement to the prosecutors. I am convinced that Wolff—who is, as I have said, one of the brightest men I have ever known in or out of the government—did so only because he was frightened half to death. He was terribly nervous, and threatening suicide. The prosecutors drove him to the point where he felt compelled to give them something, yet he could not do the totally dishonest thing—turning against me altogether and saying he *knew* I had received payments for my personal use.

A careful reading of his statement shows that he repeated only what Bud Hammerman had told him: in essence, that Hammerman was collecting money from contractors and engineers and dividing it three ways: giving 25 percent to Wolff, 50 percent to me, and keeping 25 percent for himself. I suspected that Hammerman had for years been giving money to Wolff, who was, as I mentioned earlier, always in a financial squeeze because of his first wife's claims for support and his own high style of living.

Hammerman's story about paying 50 percent of the money he collected to me is an outright lie. I have denied it many times and will continue to deny it to my dying day. I knew that Hammerman was raising funds; he was constantly telling me that financing campaigns was a year-in, year-out job, that you could not wait until election years to get the amount of money needed. But I didn't ask for details. Of course, I was aware that the really substantial givers were people who did business with the state and that consulting engineers were a traditional source of political money. But I insisted that all jobs go to qualified people. However, we gave jobs to our friends more often than to those who had opposed us. Not all of our friends were contributors to our campaigns, but most were. Some contributed to both sides.

Wolff never got the story of Hammerman's alleged payoffs to me from any source except Hammerman, or from some other Hammerman crony who heard it from Hammerman. In his statement to the prosecutors, Wolff used all kinds of vague expressions, such as he "felt" or "sensed" or "believed" or "assumed" what Hammerman and I were doing, but he did not say outright that he had any definite direct knowledge Hammerman was "kicking back" to me.* There was an excellent reason: he had

* For Wolff's statement to the prosecutors in its entirety, see Appendix.

no such information, so he did not provide any real corroboration. Wolff's notes supposedly put the nails in my coffin, but except for hearsay and speculation, they did not actually involve me.

The saddest thing about this case is that as soon as Wolff went to the prosecutors, the people I was depending on to help me immediately assumed I was guilty. The prosecutors, the United States Attorney, the Nixon administration people, assumed the witnesses were telling the truth when actually they were "trading up," telling the prosecutors what they wanted to hear and negotiating their own salvation by implicating the "big man."

The reader may wonder, as I do now, why some intrepid investigative reporter has not questioned the weight of the testimony against me that was set forth in the highly publicized forty-page compendium of "evidence." Wolff's statement was there for all to assess. The only person in a position to corroborate Matz was Jones, who pronounced him a liar. There is absolutely no corroboration of Green's or Hammerman's stories, except their own self-serving declarations made to each other or to associates. Moreover, Matz and Green had double motives for deception—to get themselves off the hook, and to get extra cash for themselves, blaming the heavy withdrawals from their firms on greedy politicians. Hammerman had substantial cash needs for his wooing of the big financiers in New York so that he could move his Baltimore development projects forward.

The records which I have obtained from the Justice Department's files show that the Baltimore Four met with the Attorney General for nearly three hours on July 11 to speed up consolidation of the case before I became aware of the charges to be made against me.

Richardson called for proof that the payments Lester Matz claimed he made to me were connected with business he received from the state of Maryland. Beall and Baker said Matz alleged such a link. The Attorney General then observed, "There are at least two lines of defense available to Mr. Agnew: one, that the payments were only political contributions and two, that Matz's story was a total fabrication—that in fact, Matz had been cheating his partner and using the money generated by the company for his own purposes."

Richardson said that only an elaborate net-worth investigation of my finances might determine whether or not "Mr. Agnew had

in fact received the money and converted it to his personal use."
There was no proof of that in the mere allegations of Matz and
Wolff.

Richardson expressed grave concern about "the consequences
for the ability to govern," especially in view of President Nixon's
difficulties arising from Watergate. The Attorney General wondered how to handle this case in a way that would "minimize
harm to the nation"; he suggested confronting me and giving me
the opportunity to refute the charges or to resign. At that time,
I was being kept in the dark about the allegations against me.

Skolnik, the demon investigator, has been quoted as saying he
considered Richardson's proposals "amusing but insane." The
young Assistant U.S. Attorney then proceeded to tell the Attorney General how the case should be handled. He told Richardson
that he must never reveal to me anything but the bare outlines
of the case, lest I should have an opportunity "to manufacture
and tailor evidence and documents." Skolnik's own technique
was to encourage the suspect to "hang himself." He proposed
contacting other potential witnesses and making them talk by
whatever methods proved most effective, and to defer any confrontation with me.

Richardson said the President had a right to be fully informed
about the charges against the Vice-President, but not immediately; "the Vice-President might establish that he was innocent
and that the allegations against him were totally false." So why
bother the President with another problem on top of his Watergate troubles? The transparency of their excuse to avoid informing the President need not be explained, other than to say Mr.
Richardson's subsequent conduct proved beyond any doubt that
giving the President problems was not of major concern to him.

The Baltimore prosecutors feared that information given to the
President might be "leaked" to me. It would never do for me to
be forewarned about the knife that was poised to stab me in the
back: Richardson promised to "exercise discretion" and not tell
Nixon too much.

He ordered the team to "strike while the iron is hot" and wrap
up the case. But he insisted that he must make the final decision
on any grants of immunity to witnesses in payment for their testimony used in building "the case against the Vice-President."
He feared it would not look good to have all the key witnesses

bought with promises of complete immunity; if the government had only witnesses of that sort, the case would look suspicious to the grand jury and to the public. I totally agree: The chief witnesses were all men in deep trouble with the law, who testified against me to save their own skins. And up to the very end, the Attorney General and the Baltimore "Gang of Four" insisted that no immunity had been granted. The fact that Wolff, Matz, and Hammerman, in spite of their confessions, have no criminal records today proves otherwise.

Ronald S. Liebman has detailed the prosecutors' techniques in a devastating way in his private memorandum of July 17, relating a meeting which he and Baker had that day with Brendan Sullivan, a lawyer from the well-known firm of Edward Bennett Williams. Sullivan was the attorney for Allen Green, another engineer accused of making payments to Maryland politicians in return for contracts.

"Baker advised Sullivan to inform Green that we are not just fishing with respect to information of corrupt activities performed by his client," Liebman wrote. "We are interested in Green's personal tax difficulties."

Then Baker told Sullivan, "The government does not and will not buy half a witness." The prosecutors would make concessions only after "we knew what we were buying," and that would consist of all his information about payments to Maryland politicians.

There could not be a better illustration of the lack of decency in the Baltimore U.S. Attorney's office than this casual reference to "buying" a witness. The gross appeal to a frightened wrongdoer that he can sell testimony incriminating someone else in order to protect himself, is bad enough. But to add that the "government does not and will not buy half a witness" is a clear signal that the potential witness will be expected to provide all the testimony the prosecutor wants to obtain from him. Otherwise, how would the prosecutor be aware when the witness had told only half of what he knew?

With self-serving professions of nobility, Richardson and the prosecutors claimed they did not "buy" any testimony, but the candid admissions by Liebman in his private memorandum show, as the young attorney said, that they "bought" an entire witness in every instance; they refused to "buy" only half of one.

CHAPTER SEVEN

THE POINT OF NO RETURN

According to Mr. Nixon's memoirs, he awakened very early on July 12 with severe chest pains. Despite a temperature of 102 degrees, he completed a full schedule that day. At Dr. Walter Tkach's insistence, he was driven to Bethesda Naval Hospital in the evening. He was found to be suffering from viral pneumonia and was admitted to the hospital.

I did not learn that the President was ill until he was on his way to the hospital. My recollection is that I received a call from a White House staff member, who advised it was nothing serious and that it should be played down as far as media questions were concerned. There was a fear that adversaries in the Congress and Watergate-preoccupied press would imply that the illness was the onset of emotional problems, or worse.

The next morning General Haig informed me the President was doing fine and wanted me to carry on my regular schedule which, of course, included whatever cabinet, leadership, or National Security Council meetings had been previously set up. Any meetings scheduled were not to be cancelled. I was to take over the chair and follow the regular agenda. I made it a point to conduct these meetings—which were held in the Cabinet Room next to the Oval Office—from my own chair and not from the President's. And even though I was convinced that Mr. Nixon's illness was not serious, the empty presidential chair—its back slightly higher than the rest—made me more aware than I had ever been of the awesome responsibilities that were always only a step away. I was conscious that others in the room were also aware of that fact.

On Monday, July 16, while in the hospital, Nixon received the shocking news from General Haig that Bob Haldeman's former assistant, Alex Butterfield, had revealed to the Watergate committee the existence of the White House taping system.

Several days passed before I was allowed to see the President at Bethesda or even talk to him on the phone, although he saw and talked to Haig, Press Secretary Ziegler, Kissinger, and George Shultz during that time. As I said before, I was not a member of the "in" group—any more than Harry Truman was during the Roosevelt years. When I finally did see Mr. Nixon, he was sitting in a chair and looked quite well. We talked for about half an hour, mainly about Butterfield's revelation of the tapes and the Watergate situation generally. There was no mention of my impending problem, and I didn't feel that it was the proper time to discuss it. I doubt the President was even thinking about it because, at this point, nothing had come out in the press. The prosecutors and Richardson had not yet confided their intentions to General Haig.

Abruptly, Mr. Nixon asked me what I thought he should do about the tapes. He said he knew there would be demands to let the tapes tell the truth about what had transpired in the secrecy of the Oval Office since the break-in. He was terribly concerned about matters on the tapes that might affect the national security; also, he was uncomfortable about discussions he had had with individuals that they thought were entirely private. He added that much of the time he wasn't even conscious the machine was there, and really didn't know what was on the tapes.

I advised him to destroy the tapes. I thought then, and believe today, that the tapes should have been burned. For a man not to protect himself against the hostile interpretation and dissemination of what amounts to his own private, unguarded remarks just doesn't make good sense. The way the tapes were used was manifestly unfair to Nixon and a violation of his civil rights, in my opinion.

When he returned to the White House on July 20, the President told his staff that because of his illness and the mounting attacks over Watergate, they would be hearing comments suggesting he should consider either slowing down his work or resigning. He rejected those ideas with one word: "poppycock."

The day after Butterfield's revelation to the world that the

President maintained a secret taping system—July 17—Assistant
U. S. Attorneys Baker and Liebman met Brendan Sullivan.
Sullivan came in to negotiate a deal for Allen and Max Green,
principals in the Green Associates, Inc. Both brothers were in
serious income tax trouble with the federal government. Here
again, I was a convenient piece of bait.

Myriad witnesses previously interrogated by the Baltimore
Four had led the prosecutors to the Green consulting-engineer
firm, which was quite prominent, not only in Maryland but on
the entire East Coast. The Green outfit had received substantial
awards from the state of Maryland and other governmental enti-
ties before I became governor.

To my knowledge, I have never met Max Green, who was active mostly in Pennsylvania. The firm maintained a major office
there as well as in Maryland. However, I had known Allen Green
since my county executive days. How we met is interesting.

In 1962, not long after I took office in Baltimore County, I received a call from Sen. Glenn Beall, Sr., the father of Glenn, Jr.,
and George Beall. I had known Beall, Sr., ever since I first became involved in county politics in 1957. The senator said he had
a good friend, a consulting engineer named Allen Green, who
had been active in fund-raising for his campaigns. Green, he said,
wanted to meet me. He had not been doing any work to speak of
in Baltimore County, and the senator thought he could be of
service. Green headed a very large and experienced firm. Beall
closed by remarking that Green could be really helpful to me in
raising campaign money, and that he highly recommended my
seeing him.

Being a neophyte in such matters, I was grateful for the suggestion; and, of course, I wanted to please Senator Beall, who
was one of the most powerful and senior members of the party
in Maryland. In due course, Green arranged an appointment,
and a few days later we talked.

Allen Green is a soft-spoken, suave man. He played his sales
job very low key. I was impressed with the credentials of his organization and consulted Albert Kaltenbach, head of the county
engineering department, about his getting some work from the
county. Kaltenbach told me that there was no question about the
qualifications of the Green firm. We gave them work and the

county engineers were well satisfied with the results.

Over the years, I had come to know and like Allen Green. He contributed generously to our campaigns, and his work increased as the big jobs expanded. I should digress here a moment to explain that the very large construction projects required sizable firms with high performance capability. So the big consulting-engineering groups did not have heavy competition with regard to the more complicated and extensive projects. They all did well. Moreover, the big jobs always seemed to become bigger while in progress, as the government usually added to the job while it was underway. This resulted from the rapid growth of the county and the need to constantly extend services.

Allen Green told the prosecutors that he was kicking back engineering fees to me. He was caught in the same cash-generating problems that beset Matz and Childs and was undoubtedly advised to "trade up" with the rest of those similarly implicated.

Green did make contributions to me for political purposes. He insisted on making most of them in cash and handing them to me personally. He told me that was the way he operated with Senator Beall, Sr., and other politicians of both parties. The money that Green gave me was used for political campaigns. Some was reported under other names, some was given in cash to other candidates I wanted to help, some went for "walking-around money," and some, I freely admit, went for entertaining and wooing influential civic leaders—particularly those of large organized groups, whose endorsements were important to the major candidates.

Allen Green told the prosecutors he introduced me to Senator Beall, Sr. It is ridiculous for him to assert that. How could two of the best-known and important Republicans in the state of Maryland—where you could count Republican officeholders on your fingers—not know each other? This fabrication is no more true than his claim that his contributions were kickbacks delivered at my insistence.

How close the Green family's connections were to the Beall family, I did not realize—until I learned much later that Richard Beall, the younger brother of Glenn, Jr., and George, was employed as a consulting engineer by the Green firm in Pennsylvania. When Allen Green visited me in Washington, he would often remark that he was going to drop in at Sen. Glenn Beall, Jr.'s, office before he returned to Baltimore.

Allen Green, like many others whose business thrived on being close to well known political figures, lost no opportunity to ingratiate himself. John Damgard, formerly my appointments chief, used to get irritated at the constant pressure Green applied to get close to me. Green pressed me to appear at the parties he gave, usually large formal affairs at his country club; he arranged with my scheduler once a year to come to our apartment in the Sheraton Park hotel "to present a small holiday remembrance." Although the initiative for these meetings was always his, my wife and I, out of a sense of awkwardness, would ask the Greens to come for dinner. The gifts were expensive but we didn't know how to turn them off without offending the Greens. We did give them gifts in return, but could not afford such lavish ones as those we received. They usually gave us watches or pieces of jewelry. I later was told that Green had an arrangement with a jeweler friend and bought these items in quantity for substantial discounts. I doubt that the Agnews were the only recipients of gifts from Green.

The gifts Allen Green presented raise a question in themselves. If Green was already kicking back thousands of dollars to me for my personal use, why the need to give me expensive presents?

John Damgard, Gen. Mike Dunn, and Art Sohmer hated to see Green come into the office. He always had a problem he wanted help with—a relative who wanted to get into medical school, a recommendation for a friend to one of the service academies, help with a politician in Central America to get a construction job there, a contact with a Greek bureaucrat for the same purpose—there seemed to be no end to his requests for the Vice-President's office to assist him. I have a file of his requests that I copied before I left office. Because he was one of my firmest supporters and helped me politically, I never stonewalled his attempts to "use" the Vice-President's office. But I told Dunn and Sohmer not to do anything improper or even questionable on his behalf, and they didn't. Allen Green did not get one successful result that I know of out of his multiple entreaties.

Justice Department internal records show that the Baltimore prosecutors met with the Attorney General again on July 27 and told him that press publicity of the Agnew investigation was imminent. He sought assurances that a federal criminal case could be brought against me, and he was told that the charges could be based on statutes concerning income tax evasion, extortion, conspiracy, bribery, and conflict of interest. Clearly, they were preparing to throw the book at me.

Richardson expressed concern that the government's case would be gravely weakened in the eyes of a jury and the American people if all the main witnesses won immunity in exchange for testifying against me. This must have been tongue in cheek in view of Richardson's knowing that all of them were on their knees begging for a deal, and that the prosecutors were telling them Beall's letter didn't mean they "positively" couldn't "earn" total immunity. It all depended, said the prosecutors, on the "quality of the evidence." The witnesses would have had to have been stupid not to know that the more they implicated me, the higher the "quality of the evidence."

Well, of the four witnesses relied on by the prosecutors, only one—Hammerman—was prosecuted in connection with the Agnew case, and his case was thrown out on appeal because he had been made improper promises in exchange for his testimony.

The prosecutors told Richardson they were thinking in terms of total immunity for Wolff, Matz, and Childs—and that it was a substantial possibility for Allen Green, but not for Hammerman or J. Walter Jones. My friend Jones was steadfastly refusing to take the bait and help himself by lying about me. He insisted we were both innocent, that he had no information whatever to aid this attempt to railroad me out of the vice-presidency.

At last, Richardson said, he had made up his mind to tell the President about the case. He had refrained from doing so, he said, as long as there was a considerable "possibility of exoneration." The Baltimore Four said they could not see any tenable defense for me, based upon the evidence. They strongly opposed advising me in any detail about the allegations. They were determined to present me with a formal letter outlining the charges, as if I were some common criminal—not the Vice-President of the United States.

They would also use the letter as a device to force me to deliver all of my personal financial papers and campaign records.

This is how the authors of *Heartbeat* described the young law-yers' clever tactics: "Enough was requested—personal bank records and tax returns—to *suck him in*; when he complied, the prosecutors hoped, they could hit him with a second request for more incriminating material" (italics mine). Actually, there was no material I would have refused them, because nothing in my possession incriminated me in any way.

The prosecutors realized that the great, gaping hole in their case against me was their lack of proof that I had ever converted to my personal use any of the thousands of dollars which were supposedly illegally given to me. At their request, Internal Rev-enue agents began swarming everywhere, collecting the tiniest bits of information about everyone the Agnew family had ever had contact with since I was county executive. My attorneys estimated there were as many as two hundred agents all across the country working on my case at one time or another. They were trying to build a net-worth case to show that like Matz and Wolff, I had been spending money lavishly, making big invest-ments, and otherwise showing expenditures far above my re-ported income. Unfortunately for the zealous investigators, they could not find any such evidence, nor any secret cache of cash because I had none: no such thing existed. And if there was no corroboration of the tainted testimony that I had received these bribes, the case against me would collapse.

Nevertheless, the charges against me would serve their pur-pose: they would smear my reputation, ruin my public image, and prove devastating to my hopes of becoming President.

It is clear to me now in retrospect that the White House was tipped off in advance: they knew Richardson would authorize release of the letter from George Beall to me stating I was under investigation. Richardson told General Haig some time in late July the Justice Department was moving against me. The At-torney General knew that, when he told General Haig, he was in effect telling the President. Until much later I did not know Haig knew about the letter before I did. They were playing a double game.

At three o'clock in the afternoon of August 1, 1973, Judd Best arrived at George Beall's office in Baltimore and received the letter that made me the first Vice-President in United States history to be officially placed under criminal investigation.

United States Department of Justice

UNITED STATES ATTORNEY

DISTRICT OF MARYLAND
405 UNITED STATES COURT HOUSE
FAYETTE AND CALVERT STREETS
BALTIMORE, MARYLAND 21202

August 1, 1973

Judah Best, Esquire
1735 New York Avenue, N. W.
Washington, D. C. 20006

RE: **Spiro T. Agnew**

Dear Mr. Best:

This office is now conducting an investigation of allegations concerning possible violations by your client and others of federal criminal statutes, including but not limited to Section 371 (conspiracy), Section 1951 (extortion), and Section 1952 (extortion and bribery) of Title 18, United States Code, and certain criminal provisions of the tax laws of the United States (Title 26, United States Code).

It is possible that your client may choose to cooperate with this investigation. It is, therefore, the purpose of this letter to invite your client, or his authorized representative, to produce and deliver to this office on either Tuesday, August 7, 1973, or Thursday, August 9, 1973, at 10:00 in the morning or 2:00 in the afternoon, whichever is more convenient for your client, the following materials, to the extent that such materials are now in or under his actual or constructive possession, dominion, or control:

(a) All bank statements, cancelled checks, check vouchers, check stubs, check books, deposit tickets, and savings account books (a copy of any active savings account book will be sufficient), for any and all checking and savings bank accounts in the United States and elsewhere in which your client has or had any beneficial interest or over which he has or had any control for the period January 1, 1967, to the present;

(b) Any and all retained copies of federal and state income tax returns for the period January 1, 1967, to the present.

I would appreciate your notifying me personally, on or before Monday, August 6, 1973, as to whether or not your client chooses to accept the invitation tendered by this letter.

In view of the serious nature of the allegations now under investigation by this office, any production of materials by your client, or his authorized representative, pursuant to this invitation must be completely voluntary on his part. Your client should understand that under the Fifth Amendment to the United States Constitution, he has a right not to produce the requested materials if he believes that the materials might tend to incriminate him. He should also understand that, should he choose to produce materials, they could be used against him in a criminal case, should any charges be returned naming him as a defendant.

I await your reply.

Very truly yours,

(signed)
George Beall
United States Attorney

I felt frustrated and helpless.

There was a terrible cumulative weight in the chain of circumstances against my interest that were piling up in all quarters: the President's mounting problems with Watergate, a hostile Attorney General, hostile prosecutors, a mostly unfriendly news media. I was beset by an ideologically attuned group of people who were all against me on the basis of my beliefs and the way I was conducting my public responsibilities, and most of them would profit by my destruction. They wanted to wreck my life.

It was a frightening situation. All of a sudden my enemies found in their hands a weapon to get rid of me. Subsequent events proved they did not hesitate to use it.

CHAPTER EIGHT

WE THINK YOU SHOULD RESIGN

In early August 1973, I found myself in a strange and dangerous situation that had never before confronted a Vice-President of the United States.

I was locked in battle with high officials at the Department of Justice and the White House—officials of the same administration I served. These brothers were determined to force me out of office without even bothering to question the quality of the evidence against me developed by a hostile prosecuting team in Baltimore.

Gen. Alexander Haig, who had virtually become the de facto President for all other matters while Richard Nixon struggled desperately to escape the entangling web of Watergate, apparently arrogated unto himself certain judgments that made the administration's commitment to my departure from the vice-presidency irreversible.

By late July, Elliot Richardson had been ready to seek the President's approval to proceed formally against me. He wanted permission to authorize the prosecutors to notify me by letter that I was under investigation for serious crimes, and he asked Haig for an appointment with Mr. Nixon for that purpose.* Once such a letter was sent, it was certain to be discovered by the press—and the President's control over the case would vanish.

Haig stalled him on the appointment, even though he knew its purpose, for several days. Richardson decided to go ahead without the President's permission, and did. The letter was delivered to my attorney and five days later, leaked to the press. I am convinced that Haig did not want Nixon to be confronted with the need to make a clear decision on that letter. The Presi-

* The letter was subsequently delivered to Judd Best on August 1, as detailed in the preceding chapter.

95

dent wanted to maintain the fiction that he was supporting me, and I presume Richardson was passed a quiet signal to do the dirty work on his own. In this way, Mr. Nixon could avoid alienating my supporters.

Moreover, after the letter was leaked, Richardson was finally allowed to brief the President before I was given a chance to say a word in my defense. As the reader will see from what follows, Haig had no intention of allowing me to be heard at all.

Under the general's orders, Richardson first called presidential attorneys J. Fred Buzhardt and Leonard Garment to his home on Sunday, August 5, and informed them of the testimony against me. This was the first time the White House lawyers had learned any details of the case; the Justice Department had deliberately kept the President and his men in the dark until the point of no return had been passed, for fear they might help me prepare my defense or even direct Richardson to drop the case.

A Heartbeat Away frankly states that by writing the formal letter informing me I was under "criminal investigation," the prosecutors had succeeded in their intention of cutting off any possibility that the President "might try to quash the whole enterprise." Therefore, the authors say, the issue for Nixon became not "how the investigation could be derailed, but how Agnew could be compelled to resign."

The control that an incumbent administration retains over a potential prosecution until the very last moment is designed to safeguard the rights of an accused person. It is not accidental, but fundamental to our system of justice. However, it can be destroyed by the enormous impact of adverse and prejudicial publicity. That is why criminal investigations are required to be conducted in secrecy, and it is also why Richardson and the "Gang of Four" made no serious effort to control the misinformation and leaks in my case until the damage had been done.

An excellent example of control properly exercised took place in the investigation of the federal Rayburn Office Building scandal by U. S. Attorney Steve Sachs, George Beall's immediate predecessor. The federal grand jury in Baltimore actually recommended indictments in that case against Victor Frenkil, the contractor. Implicated in the mess were Sen. Russell Long and the late Congressman Hale Boggs of Louisiana. Attorney General John Mitchell refused to authorize the signing of the indictment and the case was abandoned. I am sure Mitchell concluded that Long and Boggs would be wrongfully ruined by tainted testimony, so he refused to allow the case to proceed.

After being briefed by the Justice men, Buzhardt and Garment recommended to Nixon that I be forced to quit. He had their briefing paper on his desk on Monday when Richardson came in and laid out the case against me.

Richardson later commented:

> The President appeared to be ready to believe it. His reaction was remarkably objective and deliberate . . . He was disturbed and concerned with the correctness of any action or anything he did or did not do. At first he thought he ought to have an independent assessment of the evidence from Henry Petersen and me, on the basis of which he could then decide whether or not the situation called for Agnew's resignation. He later concluded that he ought not to try to be fully informed about the state of the evidence, and that his position ought to be more insulated . . . It was ordered that Petersen would assess it.

Nixon says in his *Memoirs*, "I knew that we were dealing with political dynamite and that I had to be scrupulously careful . . ." The President had already received word from John Mitchell that I believed Richardson was out to get me, and that I was convinced the Attorney General saw himself as my potential rival for the presidency.

"Objectively I recognized the weight of Richardson's evidence, but emotionally I was still on Agnew's side," Nixon writes. "I wanted to believe him. I told Richardson that I expected him to assume full responsibility for seeing to it that Agnew was not railroaded by biased U. S. Attorneys and a predatory press corps."

As soon as the Attorney General returned to his office, he received a telephone call from General Haig. Haig ordered him to see me immediately and show me the full scope of the case that had been built against me. Then Haig telephoned me to tell me that the President had directed the Attorney General to call on me that afternoon to outline the evidence. I later learned through a Justice Department memo that the White House hoped that this presentation would frighten me into resigning at once. That would have rescued Nixon from a political predicament.

At 3:15 that Monday afternoon, the Attorney General strode into my suite in the Old Executive Office Building. He seemed even more stiff and starchy than I had remembered him from previous encounters. The proper Bostonian was definitely hostile.

"I am here because the President asked me to come," he began. "I would not have been here otherwise."

We went through the cold formalities. I introduced my lawyer, Judd Best, and my new team of additional attorneys, Jay H. Topkis and Martin London, of the Manhattan law firm of Paul, Weiss, Rifkind, Wharton & Garrison. Both liberal Democrats, Topkis and London did not share my political views. But they proved to be tigers in defending me against the attempt to railroad me into prison. They had a long-standing and fundamental distrust of Richard Nixon that served me better than I realized at the time.

From the very outset, Richardson treated me, not as the Vice-President of the United States, but as a criminal. He would not show me any of his "evidence" nor let me read anything. He simply sketched the bare bones of the case against me and emphasized how serious he thought it was.

Richardson said Lester Matz and Allen Green could testify that they had paid money "directly to the Vice-President"; that Matz would say he made one payment after I had become Vice-President in regard to some work for the federal government; that Green alleged periodic payments while I was governor and later, the most recent one "at a family Christmas gathering in 1972." Six or eight other engineers had made payments, he said, "which they believed were intended for the Vice-President" when I had been governor, through J. Walter Jones or Bud Hammerman. He insisted that these cash donations were regarded by the donors not simply as gifts or political contributions, but as necessary to obtain county or state business. Richardson said Jerome B. Wolff could testify that he regularly submitted a list of architects and engineers eligible for state contracts from which I, as governor, would select primarily those who had made such contributions.

I listened to this farrago of lies with rising indignation. It was all I could do to restrain my temper and maintain my composure in the face of these outrageous accusations. "The whole thing is a fabrication," I said, "and Matz is crazy."

It was a normal thing, I explained, for the Governor of Maryland to select architects and engineers for state jobs; that had been done by every governor in every administration for many years. I also said these businessmen had always made contributions for political purposes, in most cases to the Democrats who usually controlled the state government. When in 1966 I became one of Maryland's few Republican governors, the same engineers transferred their attentions to me because I was then in a position to hand out the jobs they wanted. Of course, I would give the jobs to my friends whenever they were fully qualified to do the work; why on earth should I give them to my enemies?

I did not run after these men; they ran after me. I recalled that Green had been introduced to me by the late U. S. Sen. J. Glenn Beall, Sr., the prosecutor's father. Every time Green had seen me, it was at his own insistence. He was constantly seeking my help; I had a thick file of his requests, which I had turned down because they were unreasonable or improper. We had no conversations about kickbacks—ever.

As for Lester Matz and his professed friendship, I said, I had seen him about four times in my five years as Vice-President. "He has constantly been thundering to get in," I said, "and crying that he has not been able to get any help."

Without mincing words, I told Richardson that I had no confidence whatever in Beall. He was weak and inexperienced and had lost control of his office to his zealous assistants. He had let these arrogant youngsters run wild. I therefore asked that the case be transferred to an experienced, professional, independent prosecutor who would view the charges objectively, without prejudice. Richardson refused. He expressed total confidence in his Baltimore team.

Judd Best also complained that the prosecutors were using high-handed tactics and threats to make reluctant witnesses talk. One of their favorite tricks was to tell them, "You'd better get on the boat or it will be leaving without you." Another was to say, "Talk, or you'll be indicted." Faced with such frightening threats and the prospect of prison, a witness would say anything.

Best also protested that Assistant U. S. Attorney Baker had said at a cocktail party, "We're breathing down Agnew's neck." Best said the prosecutors treated me with contempt, calling me "Agnew" rather than "Mr. Agnew" or "the Vice-President." This may seem like a trivial thing, but it was not; it clearly reflected their arrogance and bias.

I demanded to know why the prosecutors believed I had collected all the thousands of dollars in payments alleged by the lying witnesses when my complete financial data, which I had willingly turned over to them, would clearly show that I had no great wealth. Most of my modest assets were invested in the house I had recently bought in the Maryland suburbs of Washington—the government did not provide me with a free residence, as it has done for subsequent Vice-Presidents, so I had to furnish my own. The General Services Administration paid only for minor changes in the house to provide separate facilities for the Secret Service and for protective alterations required by them. Incredibly, the government is still trying to charge me for those expenses, too, in spite of the fact the Secret Service occupied at least 25 percent of the house and has never paid a penny of the rent they had agreed to.

I said the letter delivered to me on August 1, demanding outrageously detailed personal data within six days, came to me totally without warning. To put together the information would take weeks. It seemed clear that the prosecutors were trying to throw together a case—and Richardson had admitted they did not have sufficient corroborative evidence—so that they could rush it to a grand jury. I told Richardson he must realize that an indictment would mean my destruction, the end of a career I had built up through fifteen years of struggle. His cold, totally unsympathetic attitude while relating this screed let me know immediately that I was dealing with a closed mind, a mind operating within the rule that the end justified the means.

Topkis observed that if there were ever a need for a special prosecutor removed from any political role in the same state as the accused official, it was this one. But Richardson replied, "It is not at all clear to me that this is so." He would not agree to that, but he would request Henry Petersen, the Assistant Attorney General, "to make an independent assessment of the evidence."

London asked for a more specific summary of the charges, or

much more than the vague outline given to us so far. Richardson demurred. He admitted that "various potentially corroborative steps had not been taken—for example, to check on whether a meeting had taken place at the time and place on which a witness said it occurred." My lawyers and I were amazed to hear the Attorney General thus admit that he had accepted the witnesses' charges without bothering to begin even the preliminary steps of corroboration. Richardson explained that he was trying to "avoid leaks" and preserve the secrecy of the inquiry. In light of the cascade of leaks that later came pouring out of the Justice Department, I view that weak excuse with grim amusement.

As Richardson left my office, he said he would have Petersen review the entire case and then call my lawyers about the next move.

The Attorney General had failed in his mission. He had not panicked me into resigning on the spot. Proof of the real purpose of his visit can be found in a Justice Department memorandum written by Russell T. Baker, Jr., the next day, concerning a telephone talk with George Beall.

Beall said Richardson's meeting with me had arisen from "*pressure* from the White House that was *designed* to force a confrontation which would result in the Vice-President's *resignation*" (italics mine). "When the meeting did not produce the desired result," the memorandum went on, "the White House suggested that more detailed disclosures be made to the Vice-President in the hopes that he would become convinced that the case against him was so strong that he should resign."

Even today, when I review the irrefutable sequence of events, I find it difficult to comprehend the callous self-interest which dominated the actions of the White House at this point. Bear in mind that the President had not granted my request to see him. Without even an opportunity to be heard in my own defense, I was to be jettisoned, a political weight too heavy to allow the presidential plane—now laboring on its last engine—to remain airborne. Yet at that point I never would have believed that Richard Nixon, the man who thought loyalty the cardinal virtue, would not stand strong and presidential behind his Vice-President. In retrospect, what had happened to Bob Haldeman should have taught me better. How much influence General Haig had on Mr. Nixon's decisions at this time I cannot say for sure, but the man at the top must remain accountable. And Nixon's inherent reluctance to face unpleasant confrontations makes my attempted execution without a hearing not out of character.

Immediately after Richardson left my office, I renewed my demands for an appointment to meet with the President and tell him my side of the story. I was shocked and incensed because Nixon didn't even call me. I was held off by his staff until word came in the afternoon that the President had flown to Camp David. Art Sohmer, my Chief of Staff, and I stayed in my office waiting for a telephone call, expecting me to be asked to join the President at his Maryland mountain retreat. We waited until nearly nine o'clock that night, when finally Sohmer came in from his office and said: "We have just learned that *The Wall Street Journal* will break the story for tomorrow's edition. They have Beall's letter. Jerry Landauer just read it to Marsh Thomson over the phone."

"It had to come from Beall's office or someone at Justice," I said. "We've got to see the President—right now."

"There's something else," said Sohmer. "We are not going to Camp David. The President is sending Bryce Harlow here to see you—tonight."

Harlow was one of the few men in the White House whom I felt I knew well. He had been a close friend of President Eisenhower, a speech writer and counselor to both Eisenhower and Nixon, and was regarded as one of the wisest men in the Republican party. He was also in a small inner group of people who had privately aligned themselves with me for the future. We had been keeping the existence of this committee a closely held secret. When the right time came for me to announce as a candidate for President, Bryce would have been on my team. So I felt I could trust him.

At 9:15 P.M., Harlow came into my office. He was accompanied by General Haig. I sat behind my desk, facing Haig on my left, Harlow on my right. They did not appear to be hostile. They were troubled and serious and glum, and extremely ill at ease.

"Well," I asked, "when am I going to see the President?" They said the President had been "floored by the news" of the charges against me and had flown to Camp David to consider this latest blow against the very survival of his administration. The President, they said, had sent them to talk to me about my case.

Richardson had briefed them on the prosecutors' version and told them my indictment was "inevitable."

They went through a long recital about how hard it was for the President, beset by enemies from every quarter, to govern; what terrible complications I was causing for him; that my problem was another straw on an overloaded camel's back. I do not recall that either Haig or Harlow ever asked me, "Are you guilty of these charges?" They just beat around the bush, talking about how bad the situation was.

Haig did most of the talking. He uttered a lot of words that said very little, evidence that he had mastered the language of the Washington bureaucracy. He spoke of "sustainable allegations," "uncontrollable circumstances," "points of no return," "foreclosed options" and "the ability to carry out the responsibilities of the Constitutional office." I watched him intently, fascinated by this virtuoso performance yet impatient for him to get to the point. After Haig wound down, I looked at Bryce. He just sat there and stared at me in total anguish. "This is a national crisis," Harlow said. "Congress will undoubtedly act. You will be impeached."

Finally, I asked. "What are you here to tell me? What do you want?"

Haig said, "We think you should resign."

"Resign?" I fired back. "Without even having a chance to talk to the President?"

"Yes, resign immediately," Haig said. "This case is so serious there is no other way it can be resolved."

"Did the President send you down here to say that?" I asked.

"We are not here on our own," the General said. "We have been with the President all evening at Camp David, thoroughly discussing the matter. We came here to tell you that you should resign—tonight."

"You mean the President wants me to resign right now?"

"Yes."

I became incensed. I stood up and began pacing the floor. "This is ridiculous, to receive such a message second hand," I said. "I'm not going to resign. I'm not going to do anything until I see the President. I want to see him just as soon as I can."

Art Sohmer lost his temper, too, and some harsh words were exchanged between him and the President's emissaries, who in effect had brought the traditional suicide pistol into my office and laid it on my desk.

Shortly thereafter, I ushered Haig and Harlow out of my office. I was seething with rage, frustration, and despair. I could not imagine that they could think I would resign without even talking to the President and having at least a chance to defend myself. Harlow knew better than that. I was disappointed in him, because I had a very great affection for him—and I still do. When I was in Washington in 1978 and found out he was critically ill in a hospital, I sent him a handwritten note, saying "the past is the past," and I wished him a speedy recovery.

It was even more disappointing to think that Mr. Nixon would send two trusted associates to me with orders to shove me out of the vice-presidency. Here was renewed evidence that he strongly resisted dealing with any personal crisis on a man-to-man basis. Apparently he could not bring himself to discuss this personally with me, but hoped that his emissaries could quickly get rid of this new problem that was adding to his Watergate woes.

Looking back, I can see now that the White House strategists must have told each other, in so many words, Agnew has got to go, but we have to be careful not to anger his constituency in Middle America. Send Richardson in to paint the blackest possible picture. Afterward, let Agnew stew all day. Then send Harlow and Haig to see him. He likes Harlow and trusts him. See if we can't get the resignation now.

Haig and Harlow left me with the bitter conclusion that I was definitely not part of the team. They were not concerned about me. They were only worried about the President. I was just a pawn on the chess board to be played in whatever way would help Nixon to survive. The White House had ruled, "The Vice-President is expendable."

On Tuesday, August 7, the newspapers broke the story about "the criminal investigation of the Vice-President" and the flood of media publicity began to engulf me. On the same day, I won my appointment with the President. I went down to see him in the hope that all was not lost—that in this hour of crisis, I could convince him of my innocence and we could fight as a team against our common enemies.

CHAPTER NINE

NOTHING TO HIDE

Although Haig and Harlow claimed to speak for Richard Nixon in demanding that I resign at once, I clung to the belief that the President himself would help me when he heard my side of the story in reply to the version peddled to him so persuasively by Elliot Richardson. Furthermore, I felt that Mr. Nixon at least owed me an objective view of the evidence out of loyalty, since I had never run out on him. I had been totally faithful to him through five stormy years of our adversaries' attacks on issues ranging from the Vietnam War to domestic violence, so he should be equally loyal to me.

I had staunchly defended him on Watergate, despite all the testimony that poured forth against him day after day in the Senate committee hearings of that awful summer of 1973. I thought Mr. Nixon had been unjustly maligned, that he had been victimized by some ambitious people in the Committee to Re-Elect the President; and that it was out of fidelity to his aides that he was not forthcoming about everything. I really did not think he had any knowledge about the Watergate cover-up, but in view of the revelations on his own tapes, I now realize that he did. He admits it in his *Memoirs*.

It was the cover-up more than the inept, amateurish breaking in at the Democratic headquarters that destroyed Richard Nixon's presidency. I do not believe that the President was called on to authorize or that he even knew in advance about the burglary. The details of what the Committee to Re-Elect the President was doing had been carefully separated from the official duties of the President, because opponents were ever alert to the impropriety of mixing politics with official duties. Where the President mishandled the matter was in not acting decisively to investigate at once and expose any White House involvement.

105

He then could have acted selectively to discharge, reprimand, or defend those accused, according to the degree of their involvement. The public—far more objective than most of us believe— would have placed the proper weight on the crime, and the Nixon haters would have had no opportunity to construct day by day the image of a dishonest, sneaky individual, running until cornered. I never did think the break-in at a party headquarters by unsupervised subordinates was a big enough crime to drive a President out of office. Certainly, such wrongs should be punished, but it is common knowledge that party offices have been wiretapped and broken into in the past by political opponents looking for some last-minute edge to assure or turn an election. Never, in such cases, were the candidates themselves held accountable for the breaking and entering.

It is known now that Lyndon Johnson put me under surveillance in October 1968, when he thought I had been in contact with President Thieu through Anna Chennault. He feared Nixon was trying to keep South Vietnam from going along with his efforts to end the Vietnam War before the election on terms which President Thieu considered unsatisfactory. I did not learn about it until the truth came out several years later, but I did not resent it. If I had been President and had had the same suspicions as Lyndon Johnson, I might have done the same thing, as a national security measure. Naturally I disliked the intrusion on my privacy, and if Johnson had checked on me for political or personal reasons, it would have been absolutely wrong. But the national security purpose, when it is legitimate and clearly defined, supersedes everything else—and surveillance for that reason is justified. After all, if we don't save our country from its enemies, we won't have any rights at all.

The real reason for the Watergate break-in is still a mystery to me. It was a stupid blunder and ten times compounded by the administration's foolish attempts to cover it up. Nixon himself did not expect it to turn out to be such a serious issue. He did not realize until too late how badly his opponents wanted to find anything at all to drive him out of office. Having been beaten at the polls in the crushing defeat of the McGovern-Shriver ticket, the left-wingers determined to reverse the election results by forcing Nixon out of the presidency by a process which amounted to a coup d'état. However, they would have gained nothing by kicking out Nixon only to have me come into power as his successor. They knew that I was more of a conservative than he was on major domestic and foreign policy issues. They had reason to think I would have slowed down the drift toward accommodation-at-any-cost with the Soviet Union and the People's Republic of China. To quote an old colloquial expression, replacing Nixon with me would have been "swapping the devil for the witch." So to make their revolution a success, they had to get rid of me first.

I believed that once Nixon realized the ultimate purpose of the attack on me, he would see we were in this fight together; and that if our enemies killed off one of us politically, they would then concentrate on destroying the other. The President, being Commander in Chief and head of the executive establishment, still had great power and he could help me, if he would.

So I still harbored much hope when the President received me on August 7 in his hideaway, the suite of rooms just below mine in the Old Executive Office Building. Here, Mr. Nixon liked to slump down in an easy chair, prop his feet up on a hassock, read, and meditate. It was one of his private havens away from the furors of the West Wing.

He greeted me warmly at the door and led me to an easy chair, talking all the while about inconsequentials so as not to allow the gaps in conversation he found so uncomfortable. When we were seated, the monologue continued, mainly about his meeting with Richardson and the briefing that Richardson had given him about my problems. He seemed sympathetic and solicitous—indignant about the investigation in Baltimore. He said he understood the pressures on a governor to raise money for the ticket, and he understood where and how that money had to be raised. During all this, I had no opportunity to do other than briefly interject a word of agreement or a nod of understanding.

When he finally subsided, it no longer seemed appropriate to talk about the abrupt resignation request conveyed by Haig and Harlow the night before.

I expressed my concern about testimony obtained by promises of immunity, especially in cases heavily affected by politics.

The President said he would caution the Justice Department about that.

I complained about the obvious delight of the Baltimore Four that they were successfully entangling me in their investigation.

He said, "It's terrible. It's horrible."

"Can you function effectively as Vice-President?" he asked. I assured him I could.

I laid out the fundamental problem that we just did not seem able to get across to Richardson and to the White House lawyers —who considered this an "open-and-shut case"—that the evidence was not "irrefutable" and that there was no independent corroboration.

"All they've got," I said, "is the testimony of a few men who have done business together for years. They were caught in a tax evasion problem and they saw a hell of a good way to extricate themselves from it by dragging me in."

I told the President that the Matz, Childs engineers had testified about paying back their bonuses to Matz; and the net-worth checkup had shown that Matz and Jerome Wolff had spent thousands of dollars for which they could not account except by saying they gave the money to politicians. I noted that Matz and Wolff had been implicated by Baltimore County Administrative Officer Fornoff, who was caught by a wiretap receiving payments for county contracts. Fornoff was employed in the same capacity when I was county executive, but had testified he received no kickbacks during my time. Also that Paul Gaudreau, one of the most important contractors involved in the Fornoff case, had said in his statement to the prosecutors that he was never asked for money in all the time he had done business with the county while I was the executive. Fornoff had said the same thing; both cleared me completely.

Now, the prosecutors did have a real "open-and-shut case" against these witnesses, who had, in their expensive life-styles, spent a lot of money unreported as income and were caught cold on tax evasion charges. After Fornoff pleaded guilty and accused them of payoffs, they had to admit being involved. It was then that Matz claimed he gave money to me I told Mr. Nixon. Jerry Wolff never said he personally knew of any payoffs to me; he simply reported a scheme that Bud Hammerman, whom he later implicated, had told him about.

Assuming for the sake of discussion that payments were made, I told the President, there was still no proof the money went into my pocket. It was just my word against Hammerman's in one case; my word against Green's in another; and my word against Matz's in another; there was nothing to refute in Wolff's statement because he said he had no direct knowledge about any money given to me. Moreover, all these people knew each other well; lived in the same neighborhood; had done business together; and had undoubtedly been in close contact with each other since this investigation began.

After Fornoff's plea, the accused men were facing jail, I continued. When Kaplan had brought my name into the matter, they were urged by the prosecutors to say that some of the unaccounted-for money had gone to me. I was convinced, I told him, that the prosecutors made it clear to them, "If you will just deliver Agnew to us, things will be a lot easier for you"; and I was convinced that their lawyers had told them, "You're caught but you have a powerful bargaining tool—the Vice-President of the United States." Richardson, I said, had backed up the government lawyers in Baltimore from the first day they brought Weiner's story to him. He trusted them, but not me.

"I don't think I'm getting a fair shake out of Richardson," I told the President. "I want an independent review of the case."

"Maybe these people are trying to railroad you, as you say," the President said. "I know you don't have any confidence in Richardson." He laughed morosely. "I've had my troubles with him, too. Look, I'll tell you what; I'm going to appoint Henry Petersen to take this thing over and do an independent review of everything that has been done and report back to me. He's a very fair man, a real professional, and I have confidence in his integrity."

Because Richardson had mentioned Petersen at the meeting in my office the day before, I was a little surprised that Nixon acted as if the thought had just struck him. However, I desperately wanted to believe the President had been persuaded I was not being treated fairly and that he wanted to rectify that. If Mr. Nixon, with all his Watergate troubles, believed Petersen was unprejudiced and objective, then I wanted to believe that, also.

"Well," I said, "if you think he's a fair man—fine."

Just before I left, I informed the President I was going to hold a press conference the following day, to defend myself before the American people against the outrageous leaks that were appearing with increasing frequency in the news media. He was less than enthusiastic about that, probably because he was being excoriated for dodging the press, but he contented himself with cautioning me against making any statements that might hurt me later.

During the whole time I was in the hideaway not once was there the slightest suggestion that I should consider resignation. In spite of the Haig-Harlow visit the night before, I felt there was no need for me to bring up the subject.

After an hour and a half with the President, I went out of his office feeling a surge of hope. I remember telephoning Bud Hammerman and Walter Jones, who were then being pressured beyond belief to testify against me: "Petersen is going to be taking a new look at this case. I think you can look forward to fairer treatment now, because he has the reputation of being thoroughly professional."

On that same August 7, Petersen testified before the Senate committee about his role in the Watergate break-in case. He had been criticized heavily for not having pursued the investigation thoroughly; he was smarting over the charge that he had bungled it.

The Justice Department files show that at 8:45 P.M., Petersen answered a telephone call at his home. The President was calling to congratulate him on his performance before Sen. Sam Ervin's committee. "You did a good job; you did exactly right in telling it straight out," Nixon said.

Then the President began discussing "the Agnew matter" and said he was certain Petersen would do a very careful job. All he wanted, he said, was the truth; but he was very much concerned that persons who had been receiving or making payments "would be immunized in order to make a case against the Vice-President."

Nixon told Petersen to be especially careful about the type of persons to be immunized. "When you are dealing with the Vice-President," he said, "you are not dealing with a Boston politician."

Nixon's remarks, as quoted in the memorandum which Petersen sent to Richardson, indicate that the President had been impressed by my warnings to him against immunizing witnesses who would tell lies about me in hopes of staying out of jail. Although surrounded by men who were pressuring him to hustle me out of the vice-presidency, Mr. Nixon apparently was trying to give me a chance to be saved.

Unfortunately, Petersen had a motive—that I didn't then recognize—for being less than objective in reviewing my case. Having been ridiculed for flubbing the Watergate investigation, he sought to restore his reputation as a fearless, competent prosecutor by being tough on me. Nixon was counting on Petersen to be his friend inside the Justice Department and to protect him against Richardson and his Harvard mafia. Too late, I found out that I was tapped to be the source of Petersen's rehabilitation and of Nixon's, too.

I have since learned from a review of the Justice Department's own files that on August 7, Petersen suggested to Richardson that a letter be written to me giving some details of the charges, including "the companies involved and the manner of payment." This letter, he said, would "put the ball in the Vice-President's court and place him in such a position that he could never claim that he was not given an opportunity to respond to the charges."

Petersen also said the President might want a full memorandum on the case and was entitled to have one in order to decide his future actions. When George Beall left the meeting with his Justice Department superiors and relayed their views to his three zealous young assistants in Baltimore, they reacted with a negative blast. Russell T. Baker, Jr., protested that to provide more information to either the President or me would be "a great mistake"; it would "weaken the case"; that "Agnew would not resign."

Baker said further that in my confrontation with Richardson I had already had my opportunity "to take the honorable course but had, like most other politicians, claimed that the whole thing was a frame-up." Baker's statement, which I obtained from the Justice Department's own records, is evidence of his obvious bias against me.

Petersen joined in the telephone call to Baltimore and told Baker "the extent of the White House pressure" for a letter which would save the Attorney General from being forced to talk to me again in person. Petersen also said the President, as the senior political officer of the government, had a right to know all the facts developed in the investigation so that he could properly determine his future course—for example, "whether or not to force the Vice-President to resign or to take a hands-off attitude about the whole thing."

Baker repeated the Baltimore prosecutors' strong objections to sending anything in writing to the White House. Why should the President know as much about this case as the Assistant U.S. Attorneys in Baltimore? Who was he to have such information?

Beall came back on the telephone line. Baker told him, "We are not raising the red flag of rebellion here in Baltimore, but we are members of the team and we feel the team is making a very serious error."

The next day, August 8, the Baltimore prosecutors met with Petersen and Deputy Attorney General William D. Ruckelshaus and repeated their protests against any more disclosures of evidence to me or to the President. They wanted to continue treating me as if I were a common criminal. They had told the world, through their carefully-leaked letter of August 1, that the Vice-President of the United States was under "criminal investigation." They knew full well that the letter alone was enough to besmirch my reputation. That is why they wrote it and leaked it to the press. Now they fought fiercely to keep me from learning anything more about their case, and they resisted informing even the President. They must have been afraid to show Nixon that— as I repeatedly charged—they had no corroboration but simply the tainted evidence from the accusing witnesses. If they had been forced to detail their evidence and to admit they had obtained it by promises of immunity or freedom, the President would have seen that I was right: that the case on its merits would not stand up in court. It therefore became imperative, from the prosecutors' standpoint, to keep Nixon in the dark.

On the afternoon of August 8, I presented my own defense to the American people, with the strongest possible assertions of innocence, at a press conference in an auditorium on the fourth floor of the Old Executive Office Building:

"Because of defamatory statements that are being leaked to the news media by sources that the news reports refer to as close to the investigation," I began, "I cannot adhere to my original intention to remain silent following my initial statement a few days ago, which asserted my innocence and which indicated I would have nothing further to say until the investigation was completed.

"Under normal circumstances, the traditional safeguard of secrecy under such proceedings would protect the subject. But apparently this protection is not to be extended to the Vice-President of the United States.

"Well, I have no intention to be skewered in this fashion. And since I have no intention to be so skewered, I called this press conference, to label as false and scurrilous and malicious these rumors, these assertions and accusations that are being circulated and to answer your questions regarding them, and any other questions that I might be able to answer concerning the general situation."

Almost the first crack out of the box, some reporter brought up the story that I had received a thousand dollars a week in kickbacks.* "Do you deny the charges?" he asked.

"I am denying them outright and I am labeling them—and I think a person in my position at a time like this might be permitted this departure from normal language—as damned lies," I retorted.

"Mr. Vice-President," someone else asked, "have you ever received money for your personal use from any person, contractor, doing business with the state of Maryland or the federal government?"

My answer: "Absolutely not. I've been aware, through rumor, of this investigation since February," I said. "Friends of mine have indicated to me that there have been rumors in the cocktail circuit that various allegations coming out of the investigation have mentioned my name." So, I recalled hiring Judd Best as my counsel in April, and that he told the prosecutor I would "in no way attempt to impede the investigation." I also remembered that U.S. Attorney George Beall specifically told Best I was by no means a target of the inquiry. Yet on August 2, my

* On August 7, Knight Newspapers under the by-line of Saul Friedman, a friend of Barnet Skolnik, broke a sensational story that was picked up in headlines by such prominent newspapers as *The Chicago Tribune*. The story alleged that a close friend and former aide of mine was helping the prosecutors track down allegations that a thousand dollars per week was being funneled to me from contractors when I was Baltimore County executive and that the payments may have continued after I became Vice-President. These ridiculous assertions were later dropped by the prosecutors, but the damage had already been done. I believe Friedman got this information from Skolnik.

attorney handed me the prosecutors' letter that I was under investigation.

A few hours before the press conference, White House Deputy Press Secretary Gerald Warren had told newsmen there was "no reason for the President to change his confidence in the Vice-President." Asked if I considered that an ample vote of confidence, I replied, "Although I welcome the President's support, I think the office of the Vice-President is an important enough one that the man has to stand on his own feet. So I'm not spending my time looking around to see who's supporting me. I'm defending myself."

Some of the reporters could not understand why the Maryland U.S. Attorney, a Republican, would be going after the Vice-President in a Republican administration. I could not explain why the Justice Department was leaking so many stories against me, either. "I have no knowledge of who is leaking this information," I said. "As you ladies and gentlemen know, one of the things the press does best is protect its sources. I could not comment in response to the motives of the individuals because I don't know who they are. I would say this: the accusations that are being made, if they do come from people who are also under investigation, must be looked at as accusations coming from those who have found themselves in very deep trouble, who are looking to extricate themselves from this trouble and are flirting with the idea that they can obtain immunity or reduced charges, perhaps, by doing so."

When asked, "Have you ever had a political slush fund financed by a Baltimore County contractor?" I answered, No.

When asked if the campaign records would include gifts from Maryland contractors, I replied, "I would suspect that they do because anyone who's been around the political scene in the United States, who would expect that campaign contributions don't come from contractors doing state and federal business, is quite naïve.

"I had some people who were in the engineering business who were longtime friends and political supporters," I said. "I did not ever have any financial transactions with these people. I did consult with them. I did listen to their complaints. I did allow them access, as most political figures do, to persons who are supportive of their political campaigns."

I recalled that several years previously, I had been offered a bribe but delayed reporting it because "I was very inexperienced and quite uninformed about such matters at the time." I thought it had occurred while I was the Baltimore County Executive, and was running for governor in the summer of 1966.

Frank H. Newell, the former county attorney, later confirmed that I had told him I was offered two hundred thousand dollars in campaign contributions if as governor I would help to keep slot machines legal in four Maryland counties, where they were supposed to be eliminated by 1968 under an act of the legislature.

Newell ridiculed my report because I refused to give him the names of the people who had relayed the message to me. I explained that the offer was relayed to me by people not involved in the slot machine business who themselves were innocent, and I didn't want them to be hurt. Newell claimed my report was "a hoax, political tomfoolery." But I knew better. The truth is that all sorts of special interests persuade individuals who are politically close to Maryland governors to suggest the signing or vetoing of bills that would affect their interests. It is also true that generous gifts are often proposed. But, I repeat, I never accepted such offers, and I never made a decision against the welfare of the people of Maryland or the people of the United States.

I said at my press conference that I had "no expectation of being indicted" and no intention of stepping down, even temporarily, until these charges were cleared up. "I have nothing to hide," I said.

Someone asked if the accusations against me would hurt my prospects for winning the presidency in 1976. "I am not really thinking about that right now," I replied. "I am thinking about having my innocence affirmed."

Moments after I ended my half-hour news conference, telegrams and telephone calls began pouring into my offices. They ran overwhelmingly in my favor, as Americans across the land congratulated me upon my strong defense of my own integrity. One Western Union employee said it was "a mountain of telegrams," and my press secretary called it "a hurricane of paper." The messages reassured me that, in spite of all my enemies, my friends still believed in me. Their encouragement gave me new heart to carry on my fight which had to be waged against foes inside my own party's administration.

CHAPTER TEN

FIRST ONE IN GETS THE BEST DEAL

My defiant refusal to be pressured into an instant resignation rocked Elliot Richardson back on his heels. He realized that despite all his claims of an airtight case against me, he could not be sure of winning it in court. He probably could have persuaded a grand jury to indict me; the prosecutors usually control the grand jury and bring in only witnesses they have carefully coached—often in return for promises of leniency hinting at immunity—and the accused person cannot have a lawyer present to cross-examine them.

Since Attorney General Richardson had only tainted evidence against me, he met on the evening of August 9 with Henry Petersen and the Baltimore prosecutors, and told them—according to his own Justice Department's records—to make sure they were building an airtight case. He prodded them to move towards the goal of an indictment in mid-September. I could be first indicted on charges of bribery, extortion, and conspiracy, and later—if he found any evidence—there could be a second indictment on charges of tax evasion. Always in Richardson's mind was the gnawing fear that Richard Nixon would soon have to leave the presidency, so I must be knocked out of the line of succession before it was too late.

My lawyers, Jay Topkis and Martin London, had met with Henry Petersen and his deputy, Philip T. White, and said I would cooperate by granting an interview, making a deposition, or possibly even appearing before the grand jury. I agreed to turn over my personal financial statements after a reasonable period of time to assemble them. If I had been engaged in all the terrible schemes alleged by my accusers, those documents would have been devastating. They would have shown a net-worth bulge

116

impossible to cover up. But I had no inexplicable net-worth increase; and I had no money obtained illegally.

On August 10, Richardson suffered another setback. Henry Petersen called in Plato Cacheris, the lawyer for J. Walter Jones, in an effort to persuade Cacheris's client, my staunch friend, to testify against me. Jones had received a letter from the U. S. Attorney's office saying he was under investigation in connection with his political fund-raising activities. The letter from Beall to Cacheris offered "limited immunity," saying Jones's testimony and documents would not be used against him "directly or indirectly, in any criminal case, even should such disclosure constitute evidence of crimes committed by him."

The prosecutors were eager to enlist Jones; they had to get a respected businessman not associated with the tight little cabal of accused engineers to lend respectability to their case. They needed a friend of mine who had no tax problems and was less likely to be charged with sacrificing me to save himself. But the prosecutors had nothing against Jones except the statements of some witnesses in the Dale Anderson case who called the banker a "bag man" for me in Baltimore County. Jones, from the days of my campaign for County Executive, had been one of my principal fund-raisers. He was a member of my finance committee, along with George White and Bud Hammerman, when I ran for Governor of Maryland in 1966. During the presidential campaign he was a regional finance chairman for the Nixon-Agnew ticket under Maury Stans.

There is no doubt that whatever job Walter Jones undertakes he does it thoroughly and does it well. He was an enthusiastic, aggressive seeker of campaign contributions. Knowing the Maryland politico-business community as he did, he was impatient when offered excuses instead of contributions by people who were giving lip service to my campaign and who, he knew, had given heavily in past (and in some cases the same) campaigns.

Whether his efforts are for politics or for charity, an aggressive fund-raiser does not endear himself to the people he is "putting the arm on." Walter was no exception.

So it was hardly surprising that when the Baltimore prosecutors began to interrogate potential witnesses in the contractor-professional community, using the disgraceful heavy-handed techniques so dear to Skolnik and Baker, a few of the hard-pressed and intimidated selected Walter Jones as a convenient escape valve.

The prosecutors made no secret to these potential witnesses that I was the target of the investigation. The witnesses knew Jones was their only link to me—their release from the trouble that the "Gang of Four" assured them they would most certainly be in if they didn't cooperate. They probably rationalized that because Jones had pressured them, how did they know the money he collected did not go for kickbacks to me?

When Jones's lawyer, Plato Cacheris, was presented with the allegations that his client was a "bag man" for me and had the choice of testifying against me or going to jail, he related the options to his client. Jones knew they had no corroboration of these lies and no income tax case against him. He flatly refused to sell me out. He asserted his own innocence and his confidence in mine. Through Cacheris, he categorically denied Matz's wild tale of a payoff to me in my vice-presidential office. Jones had been present on the day of that alleged payment and knew it had never happened. He would not provide evidence against me, his lawyer said, because "it would not be true."

Cacheris also warned the Justice Department that the witnesses against me, notably Green, Matz and Wolff, were "people of not the best reputation," and recalled how Matz and Wolff had demanded I stop the investigation of their financial problems or else they would involve me in the mess. But the Assistant Attorney General, my only hope for an unbiased review, had his mind made up. Petersen told Cacheris to tell Jones that between him and Hammerman, "First one in gets the best deal."

Of primary importance to the prosecutors was the need to establish at least one of Matz's numerous fairy tales mentioned in the Kaplan memo of June 22, 1973 (see Chapter Five). They concluded, therefore, that on April 20, 1971, Matz paid twenty-five hundred dollars cash to me in my vice-presidential office. Matz had called Jones and complained that his requests to see me had been ignored; that I had been treating him shabbily; that I had not helped him to get any business from the federal government; that I had forgotten old friends. The complaints came about because Jones had solicited him for a contribution for the Nixon reelection campaign. So to placate a political supporter, Jones suggested I invite Matz to my office.

He brought along one of his secretaries who wanted to meet me. It enabled Matz to show off a little bit. I gave her a charm bracelet—a usual vice-presidential giveaway—because I thought it would make him happy. After she left the room, Matz and Jones and I sat down. Matz said, "I want to give you a campaign contribution, but I need your help in getting some work." I said, "I will recommend you and do what I can to help you, but I have no control over awarding work." He seemed satisfied and arrangements were made for him to send a check to Jones, which he did, along with a letter.

Jones is convinced that the prosecutors told Matz his earlier testimony was not enough to buy his immunity; that they told him in so many words, "You've got to say you gave money to Agnew while he was Vice-President. You need somebody to back up your story." Then, and only then, did he concoct the lie about the so-called payoff in my office. This is Jones's own account of the incident:

"I called Matz and asked him to help raise funds for the 1972 campaign. He was angry because Agnew was not getting any federal contracts for him, and said, 'I'm not going to work for him.' He complained that Agnew, as Vice-President, was ignoring his old friends. He asked me, 'When are you going to see him again?' I said, 'Tomorrow.' His whole manner changed. He said, 'I am going to be in Washington tomorrow with my secretary and, God, you know, if I could introduce her to the Vice-President, that would be great.'

"I said, 'I'll see what I can do.' So I called Ted and said, 'Matz wants to see you with his girl friend. It will take about five minutes.' So he said, 'O.K.' When I got to Agnew's office, Matz was there with the girl and you would have thought he owned the office, he was swaggering around so much. Ted gave her a little charm bracelet with the Vice-President's seal on it, and Matz said he was going to work for Ted. The girl left, but I stayed in there with Matz the whole time he was in the office.

"Matz did not hand over any money to Agnew. That was unthinkable. Here was the Vice-President of the United States in his office, with the American flag behind him. Furthermore, Matz brought his girl friend over. Would he have invited a secretary by saying, 'Hey, come with me, I'm going to bribe the Vice-President?'

"The frightening thing is that it appears to me that the prosecutors suppressed evidence. They knew that Matz had testified in the Dale Anderson case that he had been angry with Agnew and had given twenty-five hundred dollars, his only contribution to the 1972 campaign. He mailed the check to me with a letter saying he was enclosing it. They knew that I had listed the check as a legal campaign contribution. So the prosecutors had to give up trying to make me say that I saw the twenty-five hundred in cash paid by Matz to Agnew. It never happened. They knew it never happened. They must have said, 'How do we handle this?' So they changed their evidence to fit their theory. They said there was some doubt that I had been there."

In talking about it later, Jones told a reporter: "The heart of the whole case was Matz's claim that he had paid cash to Agnew when Ted was Vice-President. If Matz had not told his lies, there would have been no 'Agnew case' and Agnew would have become President."

Having failed to force Jones to testify against me, the prosecutors turned their screws on Bud Hammerman. Justice Department records show that they were applying the heat to Hammerman as early as July 18. While his lawyers were angling for a deal, Hammerman was assuring me he would remain my faithful friend until death. A memorandum by Ronald S. Liebman said he and George Beall and Russell Baker, Jr., met that day with Hammerman's lawyers, Sidney Sachs and Hal Witt. Beall told them, "We have developed hard information indicating that Hammerman . . . was at the center of a corrupt conspiracy involving the State Roads Commission and high state officials for the years 1967, 1968, and 1969. . . . Hammerman participated as a bag man for engineers who paid him large amounts of cash."

"We are not fishing," the prosecutors said. They warned that Hammerman had better talk fast, that he "does not have the luxury of taking several weeks to agonize over a decision." Most significant of all is this sentence in Liebman's memorandum: "The attorneys were advised that when we enter into a relationship, we always buy the whole witness."

The Baltimore Four had already "bought" Matz, Wolff, and Green. But while those three were telling lies against me, Hammerman was assuring me: "You don't have to worry about me turning tail like those guys. I'm your friend, and our family doesn't do that."

He was referring to the role of his father, Sam Hammerman, who made all those millions back in the "frontier" days of Baltimore County. Old Sam was a "wheeler-dealer." (I mean this as no disrespect to his memory, because I would apply the same term to the late Jay Gould, John D. Rockefeller, or Joseph Kennedy.) Actually, Sam Hammerman engendered a lot of respect among the tough old pols of the all-powerful Democratic organization in Baltimore County during the 1930's, 1940's, and 1950's. He was known as a stand-up guy. On more than one occasion he refused to testify against politicians who were accused of wrongdoing.

The government had a case against Bud Hammerman on income tax evasion charges because he had spent large amounts of money that did not show in his tax returns, and he had had no way to explain where he got all that cash. Also, Jerry Wolff's record of payments received from Hammerman corroborated the testimony of the engineers, who said Hammerman called them and demanded the payments. This was real corroboration, not the fake corroboration that the prosecutors had said Wolff provided for Hammerman's testimony against me.

Unknown to me, Bud Hammerman caved in to the threats to send him to jail and signed a statement August 17. I will answer that statement now, point by point.

I will say, at the outset, that Bud Hammerman is a charming man, and for several years he completely fooled me into believing he was my friend. He was helpful with political groups, he always wrote congratulatory letters when our friends experienced a success, always sent little commemorative gifts to me and Judy and to members of my staff. It may have been calculated, I realize now, but that's true of most business people. I don't hate him for that; it's human nature. He was very useful as a fund-raiser for the Republicans in Maryland after having given large amounts to the Democrats. He was a little too aggressive sometimes, but he was generally thoughtful and considerate of everyone. Frankly, I liked him.

It is not true, as he claims, that he has known me "ever since we attended junior high school together in Baltimore," or that we "distributed circulars together" after school. I bought a lot

from him when I built my house at Lutherville, when I came out
of the army in 1946. That was our first meeting that I remember.
When I was elected Baltimore County Executive in 1962, he gave
money to my opponent. But he began cultivating me immediately
after my victory, showering me with entertainment, travel, and
gifts. Later as an important member of my finance committee,
he also raised a considerable sum in my successful campaign for
governor in 1966. Evidently he saw a great opportunity to become a member of the inner circle around the Governor—to use
his friendship with me as a golden key to open the doors to many
lucrative business deals, and even to dream about being at my
side if I were elected to national office.

Only much later did I realize I had been naïve; that Hammerman had been using me—when I was Governor and then Vice-
President—for his own profit. He was the kind of man who
employed his money to be close to political power. It built up
his own image tremendously. When he wanted to borrow money
from a New York bank, it was helpful to be known as a personal
friend of the Vice-President's. He made sure he introduced me
to all those bankers so they would know we were close. I was an
asset. He used me to generate capital and to enhance his own
reputation.

If this were not such a tragedy, I would laugh at Hammerman's claim, that, shortly after I became Governor, I "advised"
him Maryland had a long-standing system whereby engineers
made substantial cash contributions for political purposes and
shared in contracts awarded by the chairman of the State Roads
Commission. His statement is ridiculous. He did not need me to
"advise" him of that. The system had, indeed, been going on for
many years under the Democrats. As Sam Hammerman and his
son, Bud, had built up their multi-million-dollar real estate and
mortgage banking business, they had regularly made political
contributions—nearly always to the Democrats, who are the ruling party in Maryland, controlling the legislature as well as the
city governments of Baltimore and Baltimore County.

Hammerman did raise campaign funds from engineers as well
as from other businessmen. But I purposely stayed out of that
field. I wanted to know as little about the gray areas of fund-
raising as possible. I would tell him, "Don't give me any details."

Therefore, I have no way of knowing how much money Hammerman may have collected from any donor.

As I have said earlier, I totally deny Hammerman's tale that he divided the money on the basis of one fourth to himself, one fourth to Jerry Wolff, and one half to me. This is a total fabrication, probably to justify his giving Wolff a smaller portion under their arrangement. I never knew of any such understanding.

Hammerman also told another string of lies in claiming he kept money for me in a safe-deposit box—that I would ask him how many "papers" he had to deliver to me, each "paper" supposedly equalling a thousand dollars.

I know now that Hammerman was collecting money from businessmen and telling them it was for payoffs to politicians. But he has no proof the money went to me. In fact, it did not. He has verified that he had some safe-deposit boxes, but that does not prove the money inside was mine; he could just as easily have said he gave it to George Beall or to Barnet Skolnik.

How can a safe-deposit record corroborate that the money was mine? The record merely shows that Hammerman had the box. It was his box. It didn't have my name on it.

During the period of the investigation, I had two safe-deposit boxes—one in Towson at Chesapeake National Bank and one in Washington at the First National Bank across from the Executive Office Building. Naturally, the I.R.S. checked into these immediately. The bank records in each case will verify that there was very little traffic to either box during the time Hammerman was allegedly passing these large amounts of cash to me. The only things in the boxes were my insurance policies, my will, and my personal family records. No cash. Now, one doesn't carry large amounts of cash on his person and the Secret Service men who were with me day and night would have been curious if I had tried to bury it in a shoe box, as the prosecutors suggested I had done when my net-worth investigation came up dry of all those tens of thousands I was said to have taken.

Hammerman is also supposed to have "corroborated" Wolff's story about the division of the payments. But all Hammerman did was to say directly the same thing Wolff had reported as secondhand information from Hammerman himself. Hammerman cannot corroborate himself. The prosecutors simply got the same story twice. But there is no documentation to support the tale at all.

For that matter Hammerman could have been keeping all the money he collected, except for the amounts he gave to Wolff, and using it in his widespread enterprises for which he always needed loads of cash. He had multiple business interests in Maryland and elsewhere; he was generating large amounts of money to finance them, and entertaining heavily. He certainly got money from somewhere, and he couldn't prove where it came from.

It is true that during the eight years or so I knew him, Hammerman gave me personal gifts amounting to perhaps nine or ten thousand dollars. I do not know the exact amount. I did not keep an account of these gifts. He knew that I had accumulated very little savings from my modest earnings, and had no outside income. I could not possibly make ends meet on my twenty-five-thousand-dollar salary as Governor or sixty-five-thousand-dollar salary as Vice-President and fulfill all the financial and social obligations of those offices. Rich men can do so from their reserves, but I had no reserves. So Bud would sometimes come to me and say: "Look, Ted, I'm wealthy and I know you have all sorts of financial pressures. So take this thousand dollars; it's a gift from me."

I didn't think it was wrong to take a gift from a wealthy friend, who apparently wanted nothing in return except close proximity to me. I want to emphasize that Hammerman was not a contractor and *did no business with the state of Maryland while I was Governor, nor with the federal government while I was Vice-President*. Therefore, his gifts to me cannot by any stretch of the imagination be considered kickbacks.

Occasionally when we were in New York City, Hammerman would go into Sulka's and buy me some ties. At various times he gave me a robe, a jacket, some opal cuff links, and as a birthday gift, a dozen shirts. But it is untrue that he outfitted me at Brooks Brothers with suits. During the 1968 campaign, a Baltimore reporter manufactured the story that I wore expensive silk suits. Apparently, he couldn't tell silk from polyester. The story has been repeated a hundred times. I have never had a silk suit in my life. I bought my suits from a Baltimore wholesale tailoring outfit known as English-American and paid for them myself. I still buy them there. The I.R.S. found that out when they conducted their net-worth examination. They didn't come from Hammerman and they didn't cost a lot, anyway—about $125 apiece at that time.

At various times we exchanged gifts. For instance, I gave him cuff links and an inscribed silver box. After all, he was my friend.

His steady line to me was, "Look, Ted, I'm not hurting for money. It's my pleasure to do things for you."

I knew that I was being used by this man, but used, I thought, within the bounds of propriety. Of course I was stupid to take his money, even as a gift. If my head had been screwed on right, I wouldn't have done it. Although he would say "Accept this as a friend," I was unconsciously being obligated. I realize that now, when it's too late.

I have read a ridiculous claim that Hammerman even paid for installing a new kitchen in my apartment in the Sheraton Park Hotel. That is untrue. The truth is that when Judy and I first looked at the apartment in early 1969, the kitchen was in horrible shape—so broken-down and antiquated that we refused to use it. I said, "Before I rent this place, I want a new kitchen," and the man from the hotel office replied, "OK, you'll get a new kitchen."

The hotel managers were eager to please me. They wanted to have the Vice-President as a resident in their hotel, just as they had wanted Vice-President Lyndon Johnson, who had occupied the same apartment there a few years before. They offered me a celebrity discount, not because of any Hammerman influence, but the same discount given to Lyndon Johnson and to Earl Warren when he was Chief Justice and to John Connally as Secretary of the Treasury, and many others.

The I.R.S. later made a claim against me for taxes on the value of the kitchen, saying it was a gift from Hammerman, who was friendly with the Sheraton people and who had accompanied Judy and me when we looked at the apartment. But that silly claim was later abandoned when I proved that the management put in the kitchen. I paid rent for it and the kitchen is still there. I didn't package it and take it home with me.

The prosecutors related the wildest tales by Hammerman as if they were the gospel truth—despite denials by responsible individuals. For instance, they said he told them a certain large financial institution received a state bonding contract while I was Governor of Maryland only after I had insisted that it make a substantial cash "contribution."

Hammerman quoted me as telling him that the principals of that firm were "a cheap bunch" who "don't give you any money" and as saying they would not get the contract until they paid.

"Hammerman carried that message to the appropriate person; a substantial cash contribution was made; the institution got the bond business," the prosecutors said in their forty-page statement issued after my resignation.

I may have called them a cheap bunch. They had had the state bonding business for many years under Democratic administrations, but they were not lavish with their contributions to Republicans. As I recall, Hammerman told me they were going to do more for Republicans.

But Alex Brown and Sons, the Baltimore investment banking house which received a $220 million state bond-issue contract in 1968, flatly denied any such payment. George W. Seger, administrative partner of the firm—which freely cooperated with the investigators in the case—said in a story reported by Lee Baylin in *The Baltimore Evening Sun* on October 12, 1973, "Alex Brown and Sons states categorically that it never made any cash contribution or payment directly or indirectly in order to get this particular state bond business or any other business of the state of Maryland. Moreover, no partner or anyone else associated with the firm made any cash payment."

In retrospect, I realize I should have suspected that Hammerman, by lavishing attention and gifts on me, was using my name as a reference to open doors for himself in the New York financial world. He got away with an incredible deception one day in the spring of 1971, when he arranged for me to brief several investment executives at a private breakfast at a New York hotel. I spoke chiefly about foreign affairs and President Nixon's dealings with the Soviet Union and China. I never mentioned anything about Hammerman's project.

Lo and behold! I found out much later that Hammerman had remained to meet privately with these same executives immediately after my departure and had put the arm on them for a contribution to one of his own enterprises. He was trying to raise money to build a forty-million-dollar hotel, office, and apartment complex on the Baltimore waterfront. He had used me as bait.

Roger G. Kennedy, a senior vice-president of the Ford Foundation, was among the New York breakfast guests. I did not know it then, but the Ford Foundation had backed out of a tentative commitment to help finance the Baltimore development. Kennedy later said he wondered if I would solicit money for Hammerman, even indirectly. Of course I did not, because I had no idea of Hammerman's secret purpose in bringing me there.

Kennedy concluded that Hammerman had simply decided to "trot out a big politician and demonstrate how many big shots he knew . . . to impress a bunch of very senior investment types that Hammerman was a man of stature." About three weeks later, at my request, Kennedy met with me in my office. He later said he thought that finally he was going to get the pitch for Hammerman. He was wrong. I spent forty-five minutes telling him that the Ford Foundation should stop financing a lot of ultra-liberal activities. That was at a time when many students were rampaging against the Vietnam War; in that same spring, the May Day marchers brought havoc to the beautiful city of Washington.

Hammerman remained loyal through the 1972 election campaign, raising a considerable amount of money for the Nixon-Agnew ticket. Immediately after the election, he began promoting me for the presidency. On my fifty-fourth birthday, November 9, he staged an expensive party for me in a Washington hotel ballroom, where he displayed a huge banner: "SPIRO OF '76." He brought about five hundred people in to show what good friends we were, and how he was going to be close by when I rode into the White House.

A gigantic birthday cake was served. The baker had planned to copy the vice-presidential seal in the icing, but that proved too difficult.* So the official seal itself, which is placed on the lectern wherever the Vice-President speaks, was installed as if it were part of the cake. A day or two after the party, Hammerman's

---

* This was the seal that was good enough for every Vice-President from John Adams to Gerald Ford, but somehow did not satisfy Nelson Rockefeller. He declared it a "tired old bird with its wings down" and had it replaced by a more aggressive eagle—perhaps one better equipped to engage its presidential counterpart in battle.

office called and asked, "What happened to the seal on the cake?"

Bud wanted it, but the members of my Secret Service detail had other ideas. They were far too professional to question my choice of associates, but I could tell Hammerman was not one of their favorite people. Too frequently, he persuaded me to put him in the immediate vice-presidential party, compounding their logistical problems. They were aware that he was exploiting his relationship with me, and they did nothing that would further his objectives. So they reclaimed the decorative seal. I think they feared it would wind up as a conversation piece in the Hammerman home or office.

Hammerman continued to promote me for the presidency through the spring of 1973, although my staff and I did all we could to discourage him. I even wrote him a letter asking him to desist from the public statements he was making. In politics, timing is everything and it was far too early for me, positioned as advantageously as I was, to show any overt interest in the 1976 presidential election. There was no chance that a Vice-President would be overlooked as a candidate and, in my case, my popularity in the party was recognized by all. Those hard campaigns had laid a perfect base as far as the party loyalists were concerned. Moreover, my campaigning for congressmen and governors had put a lot of political I.O.U.'s in my pocket. My friends believed that my total noninvolvement in Watergate made me shine by contrast, and I was steadily rising in the polls as a cinch for the next Republican presidential nomination.

The blackmail threats by Matz and Wolff—that they would implicate me unless I somehow called off the investigation of their cases—were known to Hammerman, and worried him enough to come to me several times, expressing alarm. Once, as I have said, he delivered Wolff's letter pleading for help. Hammerman reported back to his friends that I would do all I could. But I informed him I could not and would not intervene, except to ask the President to make sure the prosecutors did not smear innocent people with trumped-up evidence bought with promises of immunity.

Throughout that time, Hammerman gave me constant reassurances he would never turn against me. He would say, "I never cave in. Count on me."

Judy and I invited the Hammermans to dine with us at our

new home in Kenwood, Maryland, the night of August 20 and they had accepted. We sat around waiting for an hour and a half but they did not show up or call. Another hour later, Bud's lawyer phoned and said, "I have advised him that it wouldn't be wise for him to talk with you any more."

I knew then the prosecutors must have turned on enough pressure to break Hammerman. His lawyer, Sidney Sachs, had advised him he was inextricably caught on the income tax evasion charge and by Wolff's corroboration of the engineers, and the only way to stay out of jail was to make a deal. So he told the "Gang of Four" anything they wanted to hear.

I later learned that Sachs had proposed Hammerman be wired with an electronic listening device and sent to me in hopes of recording some incriminating statements. The mental picture of my old friend seated at the dinner table in my home and secretly trying to trap me with a recording device strapped to his body, is abhorrent. I am told the prosecutors rejected the idea as an unnecessary gamble, because they feared I might contradict Hammerman's story, or that the Secret Service might find the device on him. Then I would have had a clear-cut case of entrapment and violation of my civil rights.

I am aware that the prosecutors claim they gave Hammerman no promises for his testimony. This was a transparent lie, and the Fourth Circuit Court of Appeals proved it so. Hammerman and Allen Green were convicted of income tax evasion and sentenced to prison. Hammerman appealed; Green did not. The higher court reversed Hammerman's conviction on the grounds it had been obtained through the prosecutors' illegal promises that he would not go to jail. He walked away, scot free, just as the Baltimore Four always intended he would.

Yes, as Liebman said in his Justice Department memorandum, when the prosecutors bought a witness, they bought the whole man. They did not care how high a price they had to pay, either, if they could ruin a Vice-President named Spiro T. Agnew.

CHAPTER ELEVEN

GET THE BASTARD

Having failed to make me resign at once, high officials of the Nixon administration launched a campaign to drive me out by leaking anti-Agnew stories to the media. Their whole objective was to force me to step down, and the sooner the better.

The President, while occasionally making an effort to treat me fairly, yearned to get rid of this additional problem on top of all his Watergate worries. He wanted to move the Agnew Story off television and the front pages of the newspapers, appoint a new Vice-President—John Connally was his favorite, I knew—and make a fresh start.

Mr. Nixon did not seem to realize that I was his insurance policy against his own ouster. The left-wingers who despised us both would never push him out of the White House until they were certain I would not be around to take his place. What would be the point of exchanging a weakened Nixon for a President whose ideas seldom meshed with theirs, and who could be stubborn? Therefore, logic dictated that I must be moved aside first, by fair means or foul.

The high-minded Elliot Richardson fretted over my continued presence in the direct line of succession to the presidency. He professed to be horrified by the prospect of my moving into the White House; to him, the signs of an imminent Nixon crack-up were multiplying. In August, the President physically pushed the trustworthy, loyal, helpful, friendly, obedient Ronald Ziegler before the very eyes of the astonished press corps and barked at him. In a speech a little while later, the President muffed several lines, leading to press speculation that he was either "on the sauce" or "off his rocker." Again, the capital heard rumors the "viral pneumonia" that had sent him to the hospital in July was really a stroke, or something worse. Presidential illnesses had been concealed or minimized before—those of Woodrow Wilson and Franklin D. Roosevelt come quickly to mind—and this administration was already notorious for cover-ups.

Through a series of leaks—all damaging to me and depriving me of the most basic and fundamental rights—administration sources arranged to try my case in the media. Richardson himself must take the blame for *The New York Times* story which revealed that he had confronted me with the testimony by certain witnesses linking me to the alleged kickbacks. The article also said the prosecutors had so much evidence they intended to seek an indictment.

The story could have referred to only one meeting, that of August 6. The only people present were Richardson and I and my three lawyers. Obviously, our side could not possibly benefit from such a leak. It is significant that Richardson's memorandum about our conference was dated August 14, and *The New York Times* story appeared exactly two days later. Clearly, a copy of the memo could have been handed to a *Times* man—not necessarily by the Attorney General himself but by some assistant who knew of his keen desire to make me resign before I could reach the presidency.

A Heartbeat Away quotes Richardson as saying to his aides: "My first instincts were to worry about the ability to govern, to function. But now I'm getting the feeling—'Get the bastard!'"

If Richardson really said that, it shows he was not an impartial cabinet officer but a vindictive politician leading a vendetta to "get" me.

Newsweek magazine for August 20 reported that the letter from Beall, informing me I was under criminal investigation, "was cleared in advance by Attorney General Elliot Richardson, who notified both the White House and Watergate Special Prosecutor Archibald Cox . . . The mere fact that the letter was sent had ominous overtones for Agnew."

One of Richardson's aides was quoted by the magazine as saying, "It wasn't sent in jest. You don't send a letter like that to a high-ranking officer of the government unless there is good reason to."

Also on August 20, *The Washington Post* printed a column by Rowland Evans and Robert Novak stating that Melvin Laird, a White House counselor, had been warning some Republican congressmen not to go out on a limb for me. From other sources I have learned that the former Defense Secretary was the man sent to undermine me in Congress. He closed down any chance of my getting a sympathetic hearing, even poisoning the minds of many Republicans.

Time magazine—under a dateline of August 27, but made public a week earlier—said it had "learned that in the view of Justice Department officials in Washington the case against him is growing steadily stronger, and that an indictment appears inevitable . . . 'The department has no choice,' a Justice official in Washington said. 'At least three witnesses have told of delivering cash payoffs to Agnew. The evidence is so strong that the case must be taken to trial.'"

I have seen stories suggesting that the leaks might have come from my own office. But my assistants could not have been responsible; the majority knew nothing at all about my case. Any discussion of the case was closely held by Art Sohmer, Gen. Mike Dunn, and my personal secretary, Mary Ellen Warner. My press secretary, Marsh Thomson, often complained that he was left in the dark. Besides, the damaging information leaked was not about things we knew. How could we leak what was being said and done inside the Justice Department? Furthermore, what earthly motive would we have to leak charges harmful to me? The whole idea is absurd.

No, it is clear to me that, as the stories themselves indicate, they came not only from the Justice Department—where the Attorney General had made clear he wanted me to leave office as soon as possible—but also from the White House. As their actions had shown, General Haig, Laird, and their allies on the Nixon staff wanted me out in a hurry, even though they could not persuade the President to make me resign. It is logical to conclude that they permitted officials to leak all they pleased without fear of censure.* Their campaign amounted to a White House staff war against the Vice-President.

The White House crowd and the Justice Department had shoved me off the team; now they were trying to push me over the side of the seriously listing ship of state. But I stubbornly

* News stories referred to "White House sources," "a White House official," "a White House aide," "high administration sources," among other references.

refused to walk the plank. On August 21, I called reporters to another nationally televised press conference in the auditorium of the Old Executive Office Building.

I read a prepared statement in which I charged that officially-inspired leaks against me had continued unabated ever since the first news story saying I was the target of an investigation. "I can only assume that some Justice Department officials have decided to indict me in the press whether or not the evidence supports their position. This is a clear and outrageous effort to influence the outcome of possible grand jury deliberations."

Recalling that since April I had consistently offered my complete cooperation to U. S. Attorney Beall, I told the press I had that day arranged to have a letter hand-delivered to the Attorney General. Then I read that letter, which said in part:

"I expected that the investigation would be conducted not only thoroughly, but secretly, with the usual safeguards against leaks to the press which might compromise the secrecy of possible grand jury proceedings. Tragically, the safeguards have been virtually nonexistent."

In view of the many stories which liberally quoted unnamed Justice Department officials about my case, I said: "There can be no question that some personnel of your department have regularly released information to the press—when their duty was to maintain silence.*

"There can be no doubt that you now have the obligation to investigate these leaks and to use all the tools at your disposal to expose and discipline those responsible. Only drastic and immediate action will curb this vicious and illegal practice.

"Of course, I am concerned about the impact of these leaks upon me and upon the office I hold. I am equally concerned, however, with the impact which the extensive publicity may have on others—especially private citizens—who may also be subjects of the investigation. It would be a dreadful injustice if their rights were to be prejudiced simply because they are caught in

* Taken directly from the news stories, here are some of the sources referred to: "In the view of the prosecutors"; "prosecutors continued to insist publicly"; "a high official of the Justice Department said"; "Beall told reporters"; "Beall has obtained Wolff's diary"; "Justice Department officials said there is no choice but to seek indictment"; "sources close to the federal investigation said"; "Matz and Wolff given limited immunity, sources say"; "federal court sources said"; "federal investigators have found."

the swirl of publicity created by the charges, rumors, speculations, and leaks involving me.

"Let me dispose of one rumor—that I have encouraged this stream of leaks as part of my 'defense strategy.' This is malicious nonsense. Indeed, in view of the prejudicial character of the leaks and their regular attribution to Justice Department sources, the rumor is inherently absurd.

"I sincerely hope that you will take immediate steps to stop this gross perversion of justice. The American people have a right to insist not only upon determined investigation of criminal charges, but also upon investigatory processes which safeguard the rights of those involved. I, as Vice-President, and you, as Attorney General, share a common responsibility in this regard, a responsibility which I have endeavored to discharge since I first became aware of the investigation."

Richardson soon after held his own press conference and piously replied in a statement:

"I fully share the Vice-President's concern about unfair and inaccurate publicity. I stand by my previous statements that every reasonable step is being taken to assure that the Justice Department has not been and will not be the source of such publicity.

"Any plausible lead implicating the Department of Justice will be pursued vigorously," he said, "and appropriate disciplinary action will be taken against any department employee found to be responsible."

Mr. Nixon, in an August 22 press conference on his San Clemente lawn, said he had ordered Richardson to investigate the leaks and that any Justice Department employee found responsible would be "summarily dismissed." (I do not know of any who were ever fired for leaks against me.)

The President gave me this endorsement: "My confidence in his integrity has not been shaken and in fact has been strengthened by his courageous conduct and his ability, even though he's controversial at times as I am, over the past four and a half years. And so I am confident in the integrity of the Vice-President and particularly in the performance of the duties that he has had as Vice-President, and as a candidate for Vice-President."

He would consider it "improper" to comment on the charges about my conduct as Baltimore County Executive and Governor of Maryland, the President said. As for the idea of my resigning, he added, "The Vice-President has not been indicted. Charges have been thrown out by innuendo and otherwise which he has denied to me personally and which he has denied publicly. And the talk about resignation even now . . . would be inappropriate."

As I indicated earlier, I phoned the President to thank him for his supportive statements and it was then that he delivered his profane and opprobrious characterization of Elliot Richardson, mentioned earlier. His July 3 tirade at Richardson over Archibald Cox's picking at the San Clemente house proved this opinion did not develop overnight.

Richardson said on television that he would make the final decision as to whether or not the evidence against me would go to a grand jury. My attorney, Jay Topkis, sent him a letter August 21 asking to be heard before that decision was made.

"According to the press, you said that the decision would involve two issues: the sufficiency of the evidence and the question of whether an incumbent Vice-President may be indicted," Topkis wrote. "We have no wish to rush you, of course, but may we have your early assurance that at a time you deem appropriate, and before any final action, we may call upon you for this purpose?"

A week later, Richardson replied that he would consider any brief about the indictability of an incumbent Vice-President. "On the issue of the sufficiency of evidence," he added, "I have discussed with United States Attorney George Beall the desire of your client to meet with the prosecutors, and he and members of his staff will accommodate the Vice-President at his earliest convenience in order that the Vice-President may make any statement that he wishes, in any form he chooses, oral or written."

Beall, in a letter to Topkis, asked that I furnish every conceivable personal financial record "from 1 January 1962 to the present," involving "political contributions in the form of cash payments of one hundred dollars or more" delivered to me or to my campaign agents; also cash payments of a hundred dollars or more made to me or to Hammerman or Jones or any other agent of mine; gifts of more than a hundred dollars; checking and savings accounts; stocks and bonds; real estate transactions; loans, mortgages, and inheritances; partnerships; safe-deposit boxes; purchases of personal property worth more than five hundred dollars; insurance policies; "all sources of non-taxable income"; and individual gifts of a hundred dollars or more involving "Lester Matz, Allen Green, I. H. Hammerman, II, J. Walter Jones, and Harry Dundore."

In brief, the prosecutors were asking me to provide all the data for a net-worth examination of myself. Richardson had told his associates they must prove I had actually received cash in person from the men who claimed they had paid it for my benefit. Their statements alone would not be enough to stand up in court. He knew they did not corroborate one another, no matter what his prosecutors might claim.

The government launched a sweeping net-worth investigation, checking on everything of value that my wife and I had ever received or spent during a period of several years. The theory of the net-worth inquiry is that eventually it will show a big bulge in money received or spent and not accurately recorded in the income tax returns. But no big bulge was ever found in our returns, which we had kept meticulously since 1947.

The investigators soon learned that Mrs. Agnew and I were not rich. We owned only a mortgaged house, a few securities, and some personal property. We lived very quietly and conservatively within our income. We paid nearly every bill by check. One of my closest friends, Harry Dundore, had given me money on quite a few occasions since I had become governor and then Vice-President—usually a thousand dollars at a time. He is a retired businessman, very well to do, and he gave it to me out of friendship as a present, because as I have said, it was not easy to live as a Vice-President is expected to live on my salary. He had no business with public works or the government.

The Vice-President's salary of sixty-five thousand dollars was only a little more than a congressman's pay today and did not begin to cover the normal expenses of a large family, plus special expenses such as entertaining politicians and dignitaries at home, or the formal clothing requirements for state dinners at the White House, as well as countless public functions that had to be attended by both me and Judy. I had no income or business on the side.

Nevertheless, the prosecutors got the fixed idea that I had collected well over a hundred thousand dollars in payoffs. They thought I had hidden the money or invested it in land somewhere, perhaps under fictitious names. Swarms of federal agents went forth, snooping into my private affairs. They went to everybody I had ever had any financial contact with, trying to find that imaginary cash. They interviewed merchants, charitable organizations, business associates, the Kiwanis Club.

They checked a store where I had bought two ties for a little over six dollars. They went to a Palm Springs, California, country club where I played golf with Frank Sinatra and asked whether I signed or paid for any tab I ran up. They asked the caddies at several clubs, "Does he tip in cash? How much does he give you? Does he trade in the pro shops?"

They even checked on my five-dollar-a-year membership in a small nonpartisan group, the United Christian Citizens, Inc., of Baltimore. They served a subpoena on the owner of a knitting mill at Asheville, North Carolina, and found that I had received a gift of four yards of homespun cloth, worth four dollars a yard, as a participant in the 1967 Southern Governors' Conference there. (Every other governor got a similar gift.)

The investigators also checked into the twenty-five thousand dollars in royalties which I received from two companies which made the famous Spiro Agnew wristwatches and the T-shirts bearing my picture. The suspicious agents found that I had, indeed, given away every cent of the royalties precisely as my records indicated—half of it to an organization representing families of prisoners of war in Southeast Asia and half to a group improving the education of American Indian children.

Mrs. Donald Shea of Linthicum, Maryland, secretary-treasurer of the National League of Families of American Prisoners and Missing in Southeast Asia, furnished records which proved my $12,500 gift and said, "It was a very generous gesture on his part in 1970. It was the first large donation we had" (*Washington Star*, October 7, 1973).

By combing through the files of my service as governor, the agents came up with a gem of a letter. It indicated that I had complained to the Naval Academy about an overcharge for the use of a golf cart. The amount: three dollars and nine cents!

After my tax returns—which I had kept neatly and accurately for a quarter of a century—had been pawed over by the I.R.S.

strike force, they came back to me in a shambles. They were in horrendous condition with papers all jumbled up into the wrong files.

One agent was quoted as saying I must have hidden my cash away in "a little tin box." But there was no such box. Besides, the idea that I could systematically hide money somewhere is ludicrous. I could not even move out of my house without being accompanied by either a Maryland state trooper when I was Governor, or a Secret Service agent when I was Vice-President. People don't realize how difficult it is to be private when you have security guards. Everything you do is known to them. My own agents would be among the best witnesses to affirm my integrity.

About this time a story was leaked to the press that the prosecutors had been interrogating an old friend of mine, the late Joseph Rash, an executive of Food Fair Stores, Inc., and had learned he had been sending food gifts to the Agnews for years. The media had a field day with this, calling Rash's gifts of hams and turkeys "CARE packages" and the like. According to the media, my accepting these gifts from an old friend whom I was never asked to do anything for amounted to an example of my greediness and venality.

The prosecution put Joe through the wringer but could develop no evidence of impropriety. However, one thing that was not reported should be pointed out here: every time Joe Rash's truck stopped at the Sheraton Park to drop off a food gift for the Agnews, the next scheduled stop for another CARE package was the home of columnist Jack Anderson. I have since learned the Anderson gifts continued long after I left office. So much for sanctimony.

It irritates me to read that the I.R.S. would have developed a big income tax evasion case against me if I had not resigned before the net-worth investigation could be finished. This is sheer fiction. They had plenty of time to develop a case, if it existed, and they just did not have one.

As far as I can determine, by using standards applicable to a private citizen of my income, the I.R.S. thought they had developed a possible net-worth bulge of about seventeen thousand dollars over the entire period 1968–1973. Their evaluations are usually high and this could undoubtedly be knocked down considerably. For example, they estimate that a certain number of dollars are spent normally for meals in restaurants, or for movie tickets or gasoline. A Vice-President, when he goes to a restaurant, almost never picks up the tab; he doesn't go to movies; and the Secret Service provides his transportation. So the guidelines for an ordinary citizen do not fit. Neither was the I.R.S. aware of the gifts I received from Hammerman and Dundore and Jones and Sinatra. These were not income to me and did not have to be reported as such. It seems ridiculous that so much of a furor was created over a few thousand dollars a year in gifts, when Sen. Herman Talmadge successfully explained larger amounts of unaccounted-for cash by saying they were small gifts from appreciative constituents. I am sure I was not the first Vice-President to receive gifts from wealthy friends. I doubt I will be the last.

I was also infuriated to read, even after I had resigned, that George Beall was still telling the press that the agents were "looking for the proverbial 'shoe box' where thousands of dollars in kickbacks may have been stashed." The headline was "I.R.S. seeking Agnew Shoe Box." Asked where he thought the cash went, the prosecutor was quoted as saying wryly, "You mean, does he have a shoe box somewhere? We don't know" (*Washington Star,* October 13, 1973).

CHAPTER TWELVE

A LARGE LUMP TO SWALLOW

On Saturday, September 1, I met with the President again amid wild rumors that he had cut short a San Clemente vacation and flown back to Washington to demand my head on a platter. But it was not a showdown session. Actually the meeting was at my request, to bring him up to date on what was happening. We spent two hours discussing my case, the prosecutors' strong-arm tactics, the unreasonably detailed information they were demanding, and the government's continuing leaks that were destroying my civil rights.

I told Nixon I despaired of finding any court in the Washington area or in Maryland that could possibly treat me fairly, since the minds of most people had been poisoned against me by the outrageous propaganda emanating from the Justice Department and being featured in such sensational fashion in the Washington area and by the national news media. Therefore, I said, I felt obliged to take my case to the House of Representatives. I believed that if a congressional committee would hear the witnesses on both sides, their sessions would be televised across the country. I would make my defense—not to the congressmen alone but to the American people, who would be watching the drama on television, just as they had been staring at their TV sets during the Watergate hearings that summer.

I thought if the people could see and hear cross examination of the chief witnesses against me they would realize that all of them—Matz, Wolff, Green and Hammerman—were free-spending, experienced wheeler-dealers in trouble with the law. Then it would become clear they were engaged in a conspiracy to save themselves at my expense, and that I was being sacrificed on their testimony without independent corroborating evidence.

Also, I reasoned that the House members, all of whom had

experienced the problems of raising campaign funds, would understand the situation much better than a Baltimore jury, which would be heavily influenced by the zealous prosecutors determined to ruin me. In Baltimore, I had made many enemies as governor by publicly criticizing the leaders of the black community for standing idly by, and making excuses for the radicals who were burning down part of the city during the April 1968 riots that followed the murder of Martin Luther King, Jr.

My plan to take my case to the House touched off a commotion in the Nixon inner circle. The President, after listening to me, told General Haig about it; Haig hurried to Buzhardt and Richardson; and they set out immediately to short-circuit my move. They had reasons for extreme concern. First of all, they knew that if I were successful in taking this route, it would close the door on any possibility of my acceding to their continuing demands for my resignation. I would carry on the battle on Capitol Hill for many weeks.

Mr. Nixon's advisers had a second cause for worry. A hearing such as I was seeking ran the risk of resulting in an impeachment. If the Vice-President could be impeached by the House and tried by the Senate, there were plenty of people around who would want to make it a doubleheader.

One thing the Nixon people did not want to do was get the news media and his enemies focused on the exciting subject of impeachment. Already there were vague stirrings in the House; it wouldn't do to encourage them. Worst of all, in the fevered minds of Haig, Buzhardt, Richardson, and company, was the specter of open warfare between the President and the Vice-President. Certainly, any House proceedings would expose not only the concentrated efforts of the prosecutors to wreck me, but also the pressure from the White House to make me resign. The doors of a lot of closets would swing open and the skeletons come marching out!

Haig and Buzhardt determined to intensify the pressure on me so I would give up my idea of appealing to the House. On Monday, September 10, they came into my Executive Office Building suite where I was waiting with my lawyers, Judd Best and Jay Topkis. My recollections of this stormy meeting are substantiated by detailed notes which Best wrote immediately afterward.

Buzhardt began with a cold, clinical, pessimistic analysis of the case against me. He said the Justice Department's top officials considered it strong enough so that I could be indicted, convicted, and sent to prison. Then Haig moved in, saying, "Richardson has a hard case. He wants to throw it to the grand jury, with witnesses testifying under oath. If you dump this on the House, the prosecutors will send the grand jury record to the committee and you'll be playing high-risk ball."

"Richardson is under pressure from the Justice Department and the U.S. Attorneys in Maryland to take the case to the grand jury," Buzhardt said. "Richardson has told me they granted no immunity to witnesses." I knew that was a lie because of what was leaking out of Baltimore, and I said so. The prosecutors' own records later proved me right.

"Yes, all the key witnesses will be indicted—will plead and testify," Haig chimed in.

"I have no confidence in the Justice Department," I said. "This matter is not in the hands of fair-minded people. If people are determined to lie, they will tell anything. They're hostile to me. They've been made to understand that if they don't testify against me, the prosecutors will be angry and take it out on them.

"I am *not* guilty," I insisted. "There is no corroboration for their stories. I can put on the witness stand fifty contractors who did business with the county and state and who will testify that I never directly or indirectly made any improper approach to them."

Informed that Henry Petersen had interviewed several witnesses and believed their stories against me, I said: "I thought Petersen would get all the facts and then render an impartial opinion. He did not . . . now I am fighting for my life.

"Since the House committee hearings in my case would be televised to the nation," I said, "I don't believe the witnesses will stand up before the country." I asked Haig, "Why do you think the congressional process is bad?"

He said Nixon was against it and added, "The President may not back you."

"Won't the President wait until all the evidence is in?" I asked.

"Yes," the General replied. "But you could face both impeachment and indictment, the worst of both worlds. If Elliot Richardson comes up with sworn testimony, he will send it to the grand jury."

"Can't the President tell Richardson to send it to the House instead?" I asked.

"Not until they finish taking testimony under oath," Haig replied.

"They know it will be immediately leaked to the media. The purpose of taking testimony under oath is to pressure me," I asserted. "The President is being emasculated by his own Attorney General."

"Richardson fears that if the evidence presented to the House doesn't stand up, he will be criticized," Buzhardt said.

The truth was still the plain truth—that Richardson had nothing more than the unsworn stories of his four witnesses with no documents to back them up except Wolff's notes, which showed only that payments had been made on certain dates. The notes certainly did not prove the money had gone to me.

As I kept insisting, there was no real corroboration. Petersen virtually admitted as much September 3 when he said, "the case still needs further investigation—*nailing down corroboration, etc. . . .*" (Italics mine). This quotation comes directly from a memorandum in the Justice Department's files. It reports on the prosecutors' strategy session that day at the Rockville, Maryland, home of the Deputy Attorney General, William Ruckelshaus.

The memorandum, by Ronald S. Liebman, quotes Petersen as saying the testimony of four witnesses needed corroboration, but it was enough in its incomplete form to justify sending the case to the grand jury. If the Justice Department did not prosecute and the testimony leaked out, Petersen warned, there would be "a scandal of gargantuan proportions." His chief concern evidently was to avoid a scandal that would further embarrass the Justice Department—already stung by the Watergate blunders—and not to assure fair treatment for me.

I was to be a living demonstration that the President spurned cover-ups, let the chips fall where they might—this was the whole idea behind the White House move to make me quit. Haig kept insisting I must resign at once. I stubbornly refused. So the General and Buzhardt left my office empty-handed, without my resignation.

On September 12, at their own suggestion, I sent Topkis, Lon-

don, and Best to meet with Richardson in his office. My account
of this session is based primarily on a memo which George Beall
wrote the next day; it is in Richardson's files.

Topkis said that, after long research, he and my other lawyers
were ready to advise me that under the Constitution, a Vice-
President is immune to indictment.

"I do not agree," Richardson replied.

Presentation of the evidence to the grand jury is necessary, he
said, and the return of an indictment would also be constitutionally proper. Henry Petersen put in that while he agreed on both
points, "no final decision on the sufficiency of the evidence had
been reached by the department."

This was an extraordinary admission by Petersen, who had interviewed Matz, Wolff, Green, and Hammerman. After their confessions had been trumpeted in the media time and again ad
nauseam, and characterized as making an open-and-shut case
which was bound to result in my indictment and conviction, this
Assistant Attorney General now said his department had reached
"no final decision on the sufficiency of the evidence."

Furthermore, in a September 11 memo to Richardson the Baltimore prosecutors said:

> At this time, this investigation is far from com-
> plete. . . . Documentary and other corroboration must
> still be gathered, analyzed, and compared with the in-
> formation that we now possess. As is inevitably the case
> at this stage of an investigation, there are inconsistencies
> to be reconciled, faulty or absent memories to be refreshed,
> and perhaps some willful misstatements to be disproven.

The prosecutors made this admission of their lack of corroboration, not out of any sense of fairness to me, but in arguing that
no detailed memorandum of their case against me should be
given to the President. They voiced morbid fears that such a
memo "might be disclosed by members of the White House staff
to unauthorized persons, possibly including the Vice-President
himself."

So the Justice Department's own records show that the charges
against me were based upon the testimony of the "bought" witnesses, with no documentary proof.

"We feel it is clear that the grand jury should take testimony and there is no constitutional obstacle to indictment," Richardson said. Then Topkis asked if this view would change if I took my case to the House of Representatives. "No," said Richardson. In that case he would inform the House of his views by "direct communication to the Speaker."

The basic issue, Topkis said, was which procedure—through the House or the grand jury—would be "less likely to incapacitate the Vice-President." He said he would trust the House more because there was no way to prevent leaks from the grand jury; there would be "a circus in Baltimore."

"How could you possibly consider even a leaky grand jury more of a circus than a proceeding on the Hill?" Richardson asked.

"Because we will get our licks in on the Hill, and we cannot do so in a grand jury, which is one-sided," Topkis responded.

"If the impeachment proceedings begin," the Attorney General inquired, "are we to forget about the grand jury?"

"Yes," Topkis replied; he hoped the Justice Department would defer to the House.

Richardson voiced concern about congressional proceedings, which he sought to avoid at almost any cost. The government "would have to think about how it could make its evidence available to the House." It was a strong case, he said, and my lawyers should consider what price they would pay in "getting their licks in" through proceedings in the House.

The conference ended inconclusively after about an hour. Then the White House moved into action again.

At 6:05 P.M. the same day, September 12, Haig and Buzhardt returned to see me. Judd Best was there again, too, and took detailed notes.

"I thought we'd better get together tonight," Haig began. "The President has ordered Richardson and Petersen to go back over the entire case. The President wants to do what's right."

Buzhardt then said, "Richardson has told us he has Hammerman's testimony that he collected money from eight contractors and divided it, fifty percent to Agnew, twenty-five percent to Hammerman, and twenty-five percent to Jerry Wolff. Wolff will confirm that the eight contractors' books show the flow of money. Matz made payments directly and so did Green, they say, and the payments continued even while Agnew was Vice-President."

"Do they have any corroboration?" I demanded.

"Yes, to an extent," Buzhardt claimed. "Wolff confirms Hammerman; Green and Matz will say they paid you while you were Vice-President." *

I became furious. I vehemently denied their charges and declared: "I'll fight this."

"Richardson thinks it's a strong case," Haig said. "It's a hell of a situation. If we go along with the move to the House, Elliot will move concurrently and ask Speaker Albert to hold it up. Albert will want to wait." I wondered how Haig knew, in advance, that Albert would wait. "The President has made some feelers" on Capitol Hill, the General explained. "You won't be supported."

"The President has lost his ability to exercise any power," Haig continued. "The House action will take six months. There will be a clamor for a trial."

Haig went on in his demands for my resignation. He became so rough with me that Judd Best refused to stand by any longer and watch the General's performance. Best proposed that he meet alone with the President's agents.

"I'll leave," I said, and I went out.

Alone with Haig and Buzhardt, my lawyer said: "I'll not have my client lacerated by you any longer. What's the deal? How do you plan to handle it? What will you give me if he resigns? Let's cut out the bullshit and work something out."

After the visitors had departed, Best sat down with me and suggested that we, at least, sound out the administration about arrangements for me to resign, but only with positive guarantees that I would not be prosecuted. I was so worn out and frustrated after seven months in this pressure cooker, and so fearful about the harm which the controversy was causing my wife and family that I said wearily, "Well, let's explore what terms we can get."

---

* It is interesting to note that Allen Green's firm received only one federal contract during the time he claims to have paid me $28,000 in hopes of getting government work, and that was not awarded to Green Associates, Inc., of Towson, Maryland, but to the Pennsylvania branch of the firm headed by his brother, Samuel. I have never met Samuel, nor do I have any idea of what that job might have been. The signature on the documents involved in that transaction is that of another brother, Max Green, who was during that period also under the scrutiny of federal investigators. As part of the Allen Green plea deal, the investigation of Max Green was dropped.

In view of the hostility shown by the White House, I had reason for concern. I was also becoming worried about a trial—wondering whether I, as the former Governor of Maryland who had lectured the black moderates over their failure to speak out against the riots, could ever receive a fair trial in Baltimore. Also, I realized that I was a man who was hated in some areas and loved in others; very few people felt bland about me. I knew, too, how the news media were savaging me with their leaks, and that gave me further concern.

When I look back on my state of mind at this point, it is a wonder that I was able to function at all. Since my trusted friend and attorney, George White, had warned me in February that Matz and Wolff were threatening to implicate me in their troubles, I had been under constant fire from all quarters—the U. S. Attorney's office in Baltimore, the Justice Department, the White House, the news media. Although I knew I had done nothing more than every politician charged with the responsibility for raising campaign funds had done, I was being painted every day by the press as a solicitor of bribes and an extortioner who had violated his public trust for a few dollars. (One Justice Department leader was quoted as being amazed at how cheaply I was allegedly bought.) The quantity of the leaked stories, most of which were so patently ridiculous they were later abandoned, made it appear that I was the most aggressive, crass, and venal individual ever to be sworn into office. The steady stream of accusations—played with eagerness, prominence, and exaggeration by the press—shook the confidence of my staunchest friends. It was impossible to get anything but a gloomy assessment of my chances. Even my own lawyers thought the scales were tilted toward conviction if I had to go to trial in Baltimore. In the final analysis, it would be my word against each of the three witnesses.

Wolff's testimony did not incriminate me in any way. George White, who had been steady and strong as a campaign manager, underwent a strange transformation. Fed a daily ration of horror stories by his friend, Arnold Weiner, George had been reduced over the past few months to a nervous wreck. He would come in frequently to report what he had heard through the legal grapevine and predict disaster. "It's all over, Ted," he would say. "Your career is finished—the President won't support you. You'll be convicted. Go to jail. People will spit on you in the street."

White had been having a series of financial reverses which threatened to bankrupt him. He had gone heavily into property development, overextended himself, and was now threatened with losing everything. I think this affected his judgment and made him morose about everything. Moreover, one of his principal financial backers was under investigation by the same U. S. Attorney in Baltimore and he was worried about that. As the months went by and the news got worse and worse, George continued to deteriorate. He became irrational—not at all like the brilliant, lucid lawyer who had been so dependable in any crisis. He began to confuse my troubles with his.

"Ted, we're all finished—all washed up. We're all going to prison." Here he pulled out his handkerchief and wiped his eyes. "Elnor [his wife] is going to have to go to jail," he mourned, "and they won't even let her take her knitting."

"No, George," I said. "We haven't done anything to justify sending us to jail."

Even in the tragic circumstances, I almost burst out laughing over the comment about Elnor's knitting. But it was no laughing matter. George was genuinely disturbed, terribly depressed, and was hinting at suicide. At one point, I was so worried about him that I sent my old friend, Dr. J. Emmett Queen, down to the White place on the eastern shore of Maryland to check on him. George had mentioned ominously that he had guns there and I was very concerned about his frame of mind.

When things got really acute at the very end of my struggle, George had himself admitted to the hospital. He was on the verge of a nervous breakdown. I am glad to say that he has now completely recovered his health and his problems seem to have been solved. My purpose in relating this history is not to embarrass George but to give the reader some idea of the horrendous pressure that I lived with between February and October, 1973. Except for my family, Frank Sinatra, Art Sohmer, Mike Dunn, and Mary Ellen Warner, encouragement from those who were in a position to know what was happening was in short supply. I deliberately kept most of my staff in the dark because I wanted to have no leaks from my office.

So when Judd Best suggested that maybe we should try to find a way to end the nightmare, I was mentally and physically exhausted enough to agree.

My lawyers looked into what might be done about a compromise. At first, there were indications that my resignation would wipe the whole case out without a trial, a plea, or a penalty. But the prosecutors would never consider that. They had climbed out onto a limb by making the charges public and had done so intentionally, knowing that once the public learned about the leaked accusations, there was no way to call the investigation off without imposing some drastic penalty on me.

The White House was happy about my decision to seek a negotiated solution, and Buzhardt offered a few carrots at this point. I had expressed worries about what would happen to my staff, how I would handle my papers during the transition to private citizen, about finances to cover legal fees, making a living, and the like. Now the White House was ready to make some guarantees if I would get out of the way. First, they promised to place every member of my vice-presidential staff in another federal position of comparable salary. This was a great relief to me as I was worried about the people who had served me so loyally during my years in office. Second, they agreed that I could have a small transition staff and office so that my vice-presidential papers could be catalogued and the business of winding up my nearly five years in the second-highest office could be done in an orderly fashion. Both these requests were ultimately carried out after I resigned.

Third, they promised me that my Secret Service protection would be continued for six months after I resigned. My detail would be cut by at least 75 percent, however. This was done—but only for four months, not for the full six months. I was given twelve agents (whom I jokingly referred to as the "dirty dozen"), but they were withdrawn without warning while I was visiting Frank Sinatra, to attend the late Jack Benny's eightieth birthday party in mid-February 1974. There had been a great furor in the press about my having agents accompany me on that trip. Suddenly one evening, the Secret Service with me received orders to cease my protection at midnight. The White House communications people came in that same evening and pulled out the White House phones, and the agents left at midnight. I had not been notified by anyone until the head of my detail informed me. It was an eerie occasion and a sad one. I had a wonderful relationship with the agents assigned to me. It was like losing part of my family when they left.

There were other promises to help me get some consulting work, to help with the I.R.S. on the civil matters, to help with my pension problems. These were never performed, nor did I even hear another word about them after I left office.

The next morning—Thursday, September 13—Judd Best met with Richardson and told him, "I'll recommend that my client resign. This is only because I think a jury could convict him, even though he is innocent. I don't want my man to go to jail."

"They went crazy at that," Best later reported to me. "Petersen came in; his eyes rolled in his head when I said I could negotiate for the resignation of the Vice-President." Buzhardt had already told Richardson; the scenario was orchestrated by the White House. One reason, I later learned, was that the President was desperately eager to get Archibald Cox out of the job of Special Watergate Prosecutor to stop him from pressing for the secret White House tapes. Nixon could not risk the upheaval at Justice that inevitably would follow the discharging of Cox until he pacified Richardson with my scalp. So again I was treated like a pawn in the game—the game of Watergate cover-up.

On the night of September 13, I told Judy the sad news. I'll never forget the circumstances if I live to be a hundred. We had finished an early dinner with my mother-in-law, Mrs. Judefind, and our daughter, Susan. Judy and I had gone up to our bedroom, where we liked to relax and read in the evening.

As we were getting into our robes, I said, "Honey, there's something I have to tell you. Try to understand this." I said the deck was stacked against me and the chance of winning was slim; that I had already been found guilty by the media on the basis of the leaked accusations. Then I told her I had decided to consider resigning if that proved to be the only way of avoiding a trial that could last for months, further interfering with the President's ability to govern the country.

My wife had been suffering from the strain of the long struggle even more than I. She was standing by the foot of the bed. Suddenly, her knees buckled, her eyes turned up, and she slumped to the floor. I rushed to her and lifted her to the bed. Her skin was waxen, clammy. Fear gripped me.

But before I could move, she came around. Then came the

tears. I tried to comfort her, but I didn't trust myself to talk. It was all I could do to keep myself under control. Finally, she forced a smile.

"It's such a shock," she said in a small voice, "but it's not the end of the world. You still have us, and we believe in you."

In the Congress, I still had a few friends I could rely on. Sen. Barry Goldwater came out to our home in Kenwood at my invitation in mid-September. He was really annoyed when I told him what had been going on—the leaks and the pressure from the White House. He realized that the President's men were doing me in. He had heard reports about Mel Laird being up on Capitol Hill trying to cut my legs off by discouraging Republican congressmen and senators from coming to my defense. Laird's warnings to Illinois Congressman John B. Anderson, for instance, became public knowledge. So did Attorney General Richardson's tip-off to Senate Minority Leader Hugh Scott of Pennsylvania that I would be indicted by the federal grand jury in Baltimore before the end of September (*The Boston Globe*, September 13, 1973). The White House insiders continued to fear that an impeachment hearing in my case would be harmful to Nixon's hopes of holding onto the presidency.

Goldwater was outraged when he heard the whole story. "Hang in there and fight it," he told me. "They're just trying to ride you out. Go to the House, but don't tell the White House—just go on your own."

The senator telephoned Bryce Harlow and complained about the pressure being put on me to get out, then he flew home to Arizona. Buzhardt and Harlow were alarmed at the prospect of Goldwater rushing to my defense. They followed him to Scottsdale and showed him some of the trumped-up evidence against me. Goldwater said he didn't "give a damn if Agnew was as guilty as John Dillinger"; the Vice-President had the right of every American to be presumed innocent unless proved guilty.

Goldwater's recent memoirs confirm my recollection of our meeting at my home, and the subsequent events. In his book he muses about why he instinctively advised me not to tell the White House when I went to Albert. He says he knew Nixon did not really like me; Goldwater had come to that conclusion after a discussion of possible 1976 presidential candidates with Henry Kissinger.

So I gained another clue to the mystery of the President's ambivalent position towards me and my plight.

For a while, I seriously considered closing my suite in the Old Executive Office Building next door to the White House and moving lock, stock, and barrel to my small suite in the Senate Office Building, thus symbolically cutting loose from Nixon and drawing into a tight shell to fight by myself. But I didn't see how I could win that way, in the long run. And I still clung to the hope that somehow the President would see what was happening and come to my defense. So I listened to my lawyers and considered the terms we might get in return for my resignation.

After a weekend of prayerful thought, I told Judd Best on Monday, September 17, that I would contemplate one concession to the prosecutors: I would discuss pleading nolo contendere to a single minor charge of underpaying my income taxes. I would do so even though I did not really believe I owed the government an extra cent. We had to do something to break the deadlock.

But this was not nearly enough to appease the voracious appetites of Richardson and his men. They were out for blood. They wanted me to crawl in surrender, plead guilty to a felony such as bribery or extortion, and admit having received money knowing it had come from engineers for the purpose of influencing state contracts. They prepared a letter to that effect for me to approve. Of course, I had not the remotest idea of ever groveling like that.

At the bottom of the letter from Richardson to Best was a place for my lawyer to sign the statement: "I acknowledge and agree to the terms and conditions set forth in this letter with the full knowledge and authorization of my client, the Vice-President of the United States." But I would not let my attorney sign it. I would never agree to that. Later, the prosecutors insisted that I admit the charges that later made up their famous "forty pages of evidence." That was an insult to my intelligence. It would have amounted to a confession of crimes I did not commit. Only an idiot would have consented to barter away his own rights in such a silly fashion.

I refused to admit any of the allegations, except the single tax count. I rationalized that admission in my mind by thinking that maybe I had retained a political contribution past the end of the year before turning it in; and, therefore, it should have been reported as income for that year. I had to find a point of accommodation. Besides, I wasn't pleading guilty to anything; nolo contendere meant I didn't choose to contest the accusation. I insisted that I be allowed to deny everything else—to say, "This, by God, is all I'm not contesting and the rest is false."

If they were going to say those things against me, I insisted that I must have the right to deny them. Unfortunately for me, very few people are aware that I denied those charges when I resigned. Pages and pages have been written about the charges but hardly anybody ever writes about my denial. Usually the public is left to believe that I remained silent in the face of all those allegations of bribery, extortion, and conspiracy.

A memorandum by George Beall, in the Justice Department's files, shows how Richardson and his men kept insisting upon "the letter" at a meeting with my lawyers on September 18 in the Attorney General's office. Henry Petersen said a full statement must make crystal-clear that at this point in history, the "people's interest" was being fully served. He mentioned "political pressures" which required the prosecutors to be careful to avoid future charges that they had treated my case differently from those of other citizens.

"We want to avoid attacks on this point," Petersen said.

Martin London said that I did not want to be attacked, either.

"Your client could be the attacker six months hence," Petersen said.*

"I can't stop that," London replied.

"We, for the government, are convinced of the need for this letter and its contents," Richardson said. "This is a situation where, whatever else occurs, the stepping down of the Vice-President is a portentous step in the history of this government. The result of that action, and acceptance of a conviction and

* In order to allay Petersen's fear that I might attack the Justice Department, my lawyers had drafted an obsequious statement for me to make. The statement, which Richardson subsequently ridiculed before his Justice Department associates, ascribed to Richardson, the prosecutors and the White House only the loftiest motives for my prosecution. I gagged when the statement was presented to me, but I was told that it was the only way that Richardson might agree to abandon his insistence on the letter admitting my guilt of bribery and extortion. The statement was to insure him against future attack by me should I publicly reject the plea bargaining and claim that the Justice Department was trying to railroad me out by suggesting I plead to a minor charge.

judgment, must be perceived by the public as just.

"There is also the President," Richardson went on. "He should not be perceived as railroading the Vice-President out of his job. It is essential that the Vice-President not be able to walk out of the courtroom, hold a press conference and suggest that, while denying all guilt, he was forced to step down. The only way to avoid that contingency is for him to acknowledge in open court the substance of the government's case."

Petersen said the government wanted a recitation of sufficient "facts" to support the charge of conspiracy to bribe.

"I am sure not going to stand mute to new charges of 'Watergate'," Richardson said. When my lawyers requested the specific charges against me, he responded, "We are not at the stage where the defense is entitled to a bill of particulars or prosecutorial discovery. We must have an eye on the degree of disclosure should negotiations abort."

London asked again why the government was insisting upon "the letter."

It was to avoid "the danger of being trapped," Richardson replied.

"How could the government be trapped?" London inquired.

Richardson said he might be accused of trying "to suck the Vice-President into a modest charge to get him to resign, all contrary to his best interest."

Best said I would be willing to plead nolo contendere to one tax count. But Petersen said the government was not prepared to agree to that because "the investigation was incomplete on this point." He preferred "a bribery or extortion count," but, of course, that was ridiculous. I was innocent of those accusations and would never plead otherwise.

On Wednesday, September 19, my three lawyers met again with Richardson, Petersen and Beall in the Attorney General's office. Topkis reported that I was "just adamant" that I would "never accept the obloquy of a felony—this is a matter of tremendous magnitude."

Richardson said he would "flag that as a potential rock on which the discussions may eventually founder."

Topkis said I would plead nolo contendere to a charge concerning a single payment to me, even though I knew the witnesses were lying when they claimed they had paid me kickbacks, that I would prefer to vindicate myself before a jury, but I did not think it would be in the national interest to have a long, protracted contest.

Richardson replied that he, too, had great concern over a prolonged battle; this would be extremely damaging because the Vice-President is in line of succession, and the whole world is aware that the President is a mortal man, subject constantly to great risks and with responsibilities of "portentous significance." For his successor to be carrying on a fight to prove his innocence on charges brought by the prosecutive arm of the federal government would have "a seriously unsettling effect" on the nation.

So once again, the Attorney General revealed his dread that Mr. Nixon might leave the presidency by one avenue or another at almost any moment, before I could be removed from the line of succession—hence Richardson's frantic rush to make me resign.

Admitting that the American people already had "a profound suspicion" about the Justice Department, the Attorney General feared it could suffer "a damaging scar" if accused of improperly handling this case. "There could be speculation about the pressures on the Vice-President from the President to resign," Richardson said. Indeed, so! And who would know more about those pressures than he, himself—unless it might be General Haig?

Topkis said the first consideration of terrible importance was that I would be forced to resign before entering my plea, and that would be in the public mind "the largest admission imaginable." But Richardson said he would require more than the mere statement, "Once I received money and everything else the government says is a lie."

Richardson was concerned he might be hurt by "a charge of cover-up" and the possible claim that the government granted me too much leniency to induce me to resign. He worried over two things: first, the suggestion that "a weakened President was determined at all costs to cut this albatross from his neck" and that the government accepted my resignation without giving the people a chance to understand the case; second, his personal position.

He knew that friends of the Vice-President desperately wanted to believe in his innocence, and some were saying Richardson himself was motivated by presidential ambitions. He was also aware the prosecutors were being accused of overzealousness in going after the Vice-President. That combination, he said, could create "tremendous doubt about the integrity of the approach" taken by the government in this case.

Topkis insisted I would never authorize him to sign the requested letter "or anything like it"; that I would not agree to such an admission of crimes under any circumstances. Richardson said if I would not acknowledge "the validity of the government's case," he would insist upon a plea of guilty to a felony.

"That is a large lump to swallow," Topkis said.

Richardson said he could not understand that statement; the government had never indicated a willingness to think in terms of a mere misdemeanor.

Topkis replied there was no possibility I would make a guilty plea.

Best said he, too, could not go out of the room leaving the government with the impression his client was "talking about pleading guilty to anything." He said I could conceivably plead nolo contendere to one tax count only, with a firm and clear understanding that "there would be no confinement."

My resignation and plea would be "a great tragedy," Topkis emphasized. He said there was absolutely no chance I would plead guilty or accept a jail sentence; that everyone was wasting his time unless those two possibilities were totally excluded. "My client protests his innocence," Topkis said, "and is not about to do anything inconsistent with that."

Richardson retorted that while he had hoped the allegations would not stand up, he had become convinced I could not make any explanation "consistent with innocence." He said the government could not accept both a nolo contendere plea and my refusal to acknowledge "the substantial validity of the government's case." He refused to see that such an acknowledgment would amount to a confession—which I positively would never make.

So we faced a deadlock. I had offered to resign only on one condition: a nolo contendere plea to a single minor income tax count, in return for an ironclad guarantee of my freedom. Richardson insisted I must plead guilty to a felony and run the risk of prison. I instructed my lawyers to say his price was too high: I would never pay it—never!

CHAPTER THIRTEEN

THE PRESIDENT WILL
CALL FOR YOUR RESIGNATION

On that same day, September 19, General Haig gave me new proof of his determination to drive me out of the vice-presidency. He said the prosecutors would soon seek my indictment by the Baltimore grand jury and make their case public, and immediately after that, "the President will call for your resignation."

This was a threat to strike terror into any man's heart. Although I knew Mr. Nixon would prefer that I resign as a convenience to him, I had been counting on him at least to stand by me publicly or to stay neutral—not to join my enemies openly. This, I thought, would be a rather strange reward for my loyal support of the President in all his troubles over Watergate!

Indignantly I told the General, "The President is not giving me the same presumption of innocence that I gave him on Watergate. I want to talk to the President. I insist upon seeing him now."

In the back of my mind was the question, How much of Nixon's policy toward me was really his own, and how much was dictated by Haig?* The President insulated himself so well it was impossible to find out which orders came from him and which from the people around him.

The next day I met with Mr. Nixon and asked him to support me in my fight for my life. I said, "I have not misused the public trust."

"I believe you," he said.

Then I told him that Richardson was being totally unreasonable and wanted me to admit to multiple crimes I hadn't committed. He wanted me to grovel before the world.

"Will you support me?" I asked. "It is impossible to do anything else but fight."

* According to former White House aide, Charles Colson, Haig, in January 1974, told the Pentagon to ignore Nixon.

157

He hedged. "You must do what is best for you and your family," he replied.

Then I said, "I would be willing to resign and plead nolo contendere to a tax misdemeanor to end this whole miserable business." But I emphatically added I would not step down unless absolutely guaranteed that I would not be prosecuted on any felony charges such as bribery or extortion. I said Richardson was demanding I admit the government's case was valid, but I would never do that. I would defy him, probably be indicted, and I would take my chances on a trial in court, rather than crawl.

The President must have realized that a long, drawn-out trial not only would be ruinous for me, it would also be disastrous for him. His overpowering desire was to save himself in his struggle for survival against the Watergate special prosecutors who were relentlessly closing in on him.

It was hard for me to believe that this President would become my enemy. I was not his enemy; I was just one of the worst complications he could have had. He was trying to consolidate his problems into as small a ball as possible and deal with them head on, and anything on the periphery added trouble. As I left his office, I felt sure I had convinced him that I would fight all the way if Richardson did not come around to my terms for resignation.

After my conference with Mr. Nixon, Richardson was summoned to the White House to receive his new orders. Haig and Buzhardt, under instructions from the President, told the Attorney General he must not force the country into "the nightmare of a trial" by insisting upon unreasonably harsh terms that would cause me to fight it out in court, rather than resign.

Richardson resisted; he had his heart set on making me plead guilty and admit the "validity" of the government's case. The prosecutors in Baltimore put pressure on him to stand firm. They had glorious visions of dragging me into court, convicting me, and sending me off to jail in a sensational case that would inscribe their names in the history books forever, as the brilliant young lawyers who had brought down a villainous Vice-President of the United States.

Meanwhile, my three lawyers were going through another round of verbal punching and counterpunching with Richardson, Petersen, and Beall in the Attorney General's office. Beall's own account of this session shows that Topkis began by saying his client wanted to bring about an end to all the controversy and "to buy peace for himself and his family." He warned that I had been receiving advice to "make a fight of it," to attack the leaks from the Justice Department and to run an all-out campaign for public support. This was true.

Richardson looked over a revised version of the statement which my lawyers had prepared for me. He rejected it, saying he "could not escape the dilemma" of my refusal to make an admission of guilt.

Richardson handed my lawyers his own version of the statement he wanted me to make. They studied it in private and rejected it as "unsatisfactory." The Attorney General said he would accept a plea of nolo contendere but only if coupled with an admission of my "basic complicity" in the offenses alleged by his witnesses against me. The Vice-President, he said, must admit enough so that reasonable persons would conclude that he was "guilty of significant violations of the law."

"I thought it was clear to you," he told my attorneys, "that the points in our letter constituted the irreducible floor of the government's position."

Richardson was determined I not be allowed to walk out of the courtroom, after having entered a plea of nolo contendere, and assert I was an innocent man whose plea was activated only by considerations of the cost to the nation and himself that would arise from a long trial, and that these considerations made it expedient for me to fight for my rights.

Richardson said he "could not leave open for history to question as to whether Mr. Agnew was, or was not, guilty and whether or not he, in resigning, 'bowed to pressures.'"

I can assure him now, as I did in 1973, that I was innocent; and that I "bowed to pressures" in resigning—as the disclosures in this narrative show.

Petersen chimed in that it was "terribly important" for the public to believe the Justice Department was not an "instrumentality of partisan politics" and the only way to avoid that was not "a groveling confession but a sufficient admission of guilt" so it would appear that the government had pressed its case.

Topkis said that in accepting campaign contributions from contractors while I was serving as Governor of Maryland, I had followed the common practice of officials in many other states. In his home state of New York, he said, all contractors made cash payments in return for state work; this was the standard way of raising money for political campaigns, and he did not see why his client was being asked to make an admission that was inconsistent with that premise.

Richardson said it had been his "fervent hope from the beginning" the evidence would sustain a defense that the payments in Maryland had been political contributions, but he believed the evidence did not sustain that conclusion.

"The government witnesses are liars," Topkis said. He noted that Hammerman, for example, even told lies about little things, such as saying he had gone to grade school in Baltimore with me— whereas I had never met the man until many years later. Richardson retorted that Petersen had interviewed the principal government witnesses and analyzed the available proof and could not believe that "the Vice-President did not know what was going on."

Topkis said I was not asserting that the government's case against its witnesses was only "a figment of somebody's imagination," but I was totally unwilling to acknowledge the existence of a criminal scheme that involved my receiving tainted money. Richardson said he could not leave open the question of my "deep involvement in very serious criminal conduct." Topkis said he had never heard of the government insisting on such an admission of guilt by an innocent person in settling a case.

"I have certainly never been involved in settling a case which will be written about forever," the Attorney General replied. He insisted upon my admission of guilt so that after I resigned, there would not be "an endless swirl of debate such as that which surrounded the Dreyfus and Sacco-Vanzetti cases."

It is quite significant that the Attorney General cited these examples as comparable to my case. Captain Dreyfus, a loyal officer in the French Army, was railroaded to Devil's Island for years of unjust imprisonment chiefly because he was a Jew, in a frame-up that involved the Establishment in turn-of-the-century France. Emile Zola, the novelist, eventually achieved Dreyfus' vindication and freedom by exposing the entire corrupt scheme and revealing the identity of the true spy, Major Esterhazy, who had framed the innocent Dreyfus. Zola won international fame with his sensational accusations and his cry, *"J'accuse!"*

Clearly, the Attorney General feared that I, too, could win vindication as Dreyfus did, by showing how an innocent official could be pressured into resignation and disgrace through the relentless efforts of political enemies within his own party's administration. Richardson in effect said, When we force Agnew out of the vice-presidency, we must make sure he cannot convince the people that he was framed, too.

Topkis noted that both of the cases cited by Richardson had resulted in trials and even then they stirred up public debate. He refused to recommend to his client that "he commit suicide or plead guilty." Topkis also pressed hard on one more extremely important point: that I would not go to jail after pleading nolo contendere on the single count of tax evasion. That was an absolute must. Richardson did not want to make a recommendation to the judge against "no jail." If he did so for me, he said, he might have to do it for all the others accused in the case. "If I bite the bullet on 'no jail,'" he said, "it would be understood that we have then renounced any expectation of jail for the others."

Not necessarily, Topkis replied. The government could proceed against the men accused of the payoffs—if the prosecutors had not promised them immunity. As the whole truth emerged in subsequent years, it became clear that the prosecutors had bought the testimony of my accusers by offering them (except Green, who bought his brother's freedom) the highest possible price: their freedom.

John F. Banzhaff, III, a George Washington University professor, filed a brief requesting that a special prosecutor be assigned to my case. He contended that Richardson, being a potential presidential contender against me in 1976, had a clear conflict of interest. The issue, of course, became moot with my resignation.

On September 19, I received some welcome encouragement from an unexpected source. The Governor of Georgia, Jimmy Carter, telephoned me and expressed his sympathy over the abuse I was suffering from the prosecutors and my own administration. Although he is a Democrat and I am a Republican, Carter and I had become friends through my work as a link between the White House and the governors.

I told Carter I felt as if I were "fighting a division with a platoon." He urged me to keep up the battle, and not to resign under fire. When he told the incredulous press corps in Atlanta about his call to me, the governor explained that he and I had become "very close," and he believed I was not receiving fair treatment.

"I felt," Carter said, "he needed to hear a friendly voice."

While I find myself in frequent disagreement with President Carter over both domestic and foreign policy, I still respect his attitude toward the presidency and his fairness to individuals. When I was under heavy fire in 1976 for saying that our attitude toward Israel was affected by the preponderance of Israel's sympathizers in the big news media, the press carried reports that the B'Nai B'Rith Anti-Defamation League had written to both President Ford and candidate Carter soliciting a rebuke of me. Both obliged, and I felt constrained to write a personal letter to each which I had hand-delivered, explaining that my position was not anti-Semitic and that I felt I had a right to comment about a foreign nation, namely Israel. Carter sent me a warm, hand-written reply, although he disagreed on the subject at hand, but Gerald Ford has yet to give me the courtesy of any acknowledgment.

CHAPTER FOURTEEN

PAL, IT'S A DAMN SHAME

On September 22, *The Washington Post* printed a story disclosing that my lawyers and the Justice Department had been plea bargaining for my resignation. CBS News said Henry Petersen claimed he had the evidence to convict me on bribery and kickback charges. Petersen was quoted as saying, "We've got the evidence. We've got it cold."

Naturally, these reports, which were picked up and repeated all across the land throughout the weekend, infuriated me. I had no doubt they were deliberately leaked by the Justice Department to wreck my credibility with the millions of Americans who still believed in me despite the calculated campaign of vilification being carried on by men in my own administration.

"They are out to disgrace and dishonor me," I told Judd Best. I decided to break off the bargaining sessions then and there, and to fight it out—in Congress or in the courts, if necessary. "I'm through with it," I said. "Even if I lose, I'm going through with it rather than capitulate.

"If we have to go to war," I said, "we will blow a lot of people out of the water."

On Tuesday morning, September 25, I met the President again and told him I had decided to wait no longer to take my case to the House of Representatives. I would seek a hearing there in hopes of winning vindication. I would arrange for a meeting that afternoon with the Speaker of the House, Carl Albert.

"I am innocent," I reiterated. I charged that the Attorney General—who with Petersen had left the Oval Office moments before my arrival—was determined to wreck me with tainted testimony. He had informed the President he was taking the case to the grand jury that day. Petersen had repeated his feeling that it was an "open-and-shut case."

"I'm going to take my case to the House leadership early this afternoon," I told Nixon.

"Wait until four o'clock," he said. He wanted to be sure that I would provoke no sudden moves in Baltimore.

He telephoned the Justice Department and made sure the prosecutors had not yet gone to the grand jury. Mr. Nixon wanted to keep the way clear for me to resign. He knew that I had not moved an inch from my refusal to step down unless assured that I could maintain my innocence of the bribery and extortion charges, and be assured that I would keep my freedom.

I suggested the President go on television and tell the people that I could not have a fair trial in view of the countless leaks against me. I was sure that most of them had come from the Justice Department and some from the White House staff.

Instead of a TV appearance, the President issued a statement about our meeting. He said:

> . . . During our discussion, the Vice-President again —as he had done in our previous meetings—denied the charges that have been made against him. He also informed me that he intended to request that the House of Representatives undertake an inquiry into the matter.
>
> I wish to emphasize my strong belief that during these proceedings the Vice-President is entitled to the same presumption of innocence which is the right of any citizen, and which lies at the heart of our system of justice. During these past four and a half years, the Vice-President has served his country with dedication and distinction. He has won the respect of millions of Americans for the candor and courage with which he has addressed the controversial issues of our time. As he moves through this difficult period, I urge all Americans to accord the Vice-President the basic, decent consideration and presumption of innocence that are both his right and his due.

I returned to my office where my attorneys were waiting. The following recitation of events is taken from an *aide memoir* I dictated that same day:

"After consultation with the attorneys, it was determined that we should move quickly to request a hearing in the House under the Calhoun precedent. It was decided that I should hand-deliver a letter to the Speaker and should speak with him alone first, then attempt to have him bring in the Joint Leadership for discussion.

"In order to protect against leaks as far as possible, I telephoned Mr. Albert about 2:30 P.M. and requested to see him at 4:00 P.M. at his office in the Capitol. He seemed curious, but did not press for details after I had indicated that it was a matter of urgency. He asked whether I would prefer to meet him at his private office where the chance of my being seen would be lessened. I stated that the media had me under heavy surveillance and that confidentiality was virtually impossible; that therefore, I preferred to see him at his principal office."

I would take with me a written request to Speaker Albert for a full inquiry by the House of Representatives. In it I cited a similar appeal made by Vice-President John C. Calhoun in 1826, when he was accused of having made profits from an army contract when he was secretary of war in President Monroe's administration. My letter to the Speaker is so important as a clear exposition of my views about the constitutional status of the Vice-President, that I am quoting it here in full:

Dear Mr. Speaker:

I respectfully request that the House of Representatives undertake a full inquiry into the charges which have apparently been made against me in the course of an investigation by the United States Attorney for the District of Maryland.

This request is made in the dual interests of preserving the Constitutional stature of my Office and accomplishing my personal vindication.

After the most careful study, my counsel have advised me that the Constitution bars a criminal proceeding of any kind—federal or state, county, or town—against a President or Vice-President while he holds office.

Accordingly, I cannot acquiesce in any criminal proceeding being lodged against me in Maryland or elsewhere. And I cannot look to any such proceeding for vindication.

In these circumstances, I believe, it is the right and

duty of the Vice-President to turn to the House. A closely parallel precedent so suggests.

Almost a century and a half ago, Vice-President Calhoun was beset with charges of improper participation in the profits of an army contract while he had been Secretary of War. On December 29, 1826, he addressed to your Body a communication whose eloquent language I can better quote than rival:

"An imperious sense of duty, and a sacred regard to the honor of the station which I occupy, compel me to approach your body in its high character of grand inquest of the nation.

"Charges have been made against me of the most serious nature, and which, if true ought to degrade me from the high station in which I have been placed by the choice of my fellow-citizens, and to consign my name to perpetual infamy.

"In claiming the investigation of the House, I am sensible that, under our free and happy institutions, the conduct of public servants is a fair subject of the closest scrutiny and the freest remarks, and that a firm and faithful discharge of duty affords, ordinarily, ample protection against political attacks; but, when such attacks assume the character of impeachable offences, and become, in some degree, official, by being placed among the public records, an officer thus assailed, however base the instrument used, if conscious of innocence, can look for refuge only to the Hall of the immediate Representatives of the People . . ."

Vice-President Calhoun concluded his communication with a "challenge" to "the freest investigation of the House, as the only means effectually to repel this premeditated attack." Your Body responded at once by establishing a. select committee, which subpoenaed witnesses and documents, held exhaustive hearings, and submitted a Report on February 13, 1827. The Report, exonerating the Vice-President of any wrongdoing, was laid on the table (together with minority views even more strongly in his favor) and the accusations were thereby put to rest.

Like my predecessor, Calhoun, I am the subject of public attacks that may "assume the character of impeachable offences," and thus require urgent investigation by the House as the repository of "the sole Power of Impeachment" and the "grand inquest of the nation." No investigation in any other forum could either substitute for the investigation by the House contemplated by Article 1, Section 2, Clause 5 of the Constitution or lay to rest in a timely and definitive manner the unfounded charges whose currency unavoidably jeopardizes the functions of my Office.

The wisdom of the Framers of the Constitution in making the House the only proper agency to investigate the conduct of a President or Vice-President has been borne out by recent events. Since the Maryland investigation became a matter of public knowledge some seven weeks ago, there has been a constant and ever-broadening stream of rumors, accusations and speculations aimed at me. I regret to say that the source, in many instances, can have been only the prosecutors themselves.

The result has been so to foul the atmosphere that no grand or petit jury could fairly consider this matter on the merits.

I therefore respectfully call upon the House to discharge its Constitutional obligation.

I shall, of course, cooperate fully. As I have said before, I have nothing to hide. I have directed my counsel to deliver forthwith to the Clerk of the House all of my original records of which copies have previously been furnished to the United States Attorney. If there is any other way in which I can be of aid, I am wholly at the disposal of the House.

I am confident that, like Vice-President Calhoun, I shall be vindicated by the House.

Respectfully yours,
Spiro T. Agnew

The following description of what transpired in Speaker Albert's office is taken directly from a "recollection of events" I dictated that day:

"Accompanied by Mr. Arthur Sohmer, I arrived at the House side of the Capitol at about 3:57 P.M. Walter Mote [my Senate assistant] had met us on the steps at the Senate side, got into the car and accompanied us to the Speaker's office.

"One of the Speaker's aides took me immediately into his private office, where I waited alone about five minutes while he was summoned from the Chair. Art Sohmer waited in the outer office. The Speaker then entered from a private entrance, not going through his outer office, greeted me cordially, and we sat down to talk. I told him that this was an unprecedented occasion and that I appreciated his courtesy and prompt cooperation about the meeting. I then handed him the letter and asked him to read it. He read the letter very deliberately and slowly, and I could see that he was attempting to make some basic decisions about how to handle the situation.

"When he had finished reading, I explained the difficulties I was having with the prosecutors in Baltimore and with the Department of Justice. I told him that Richardson would probably be in touch with him to request that I not be given a hearing by the Congress at this time because the grand jury was the proper forum. I explained that a fair hearing in Baltimore was impossible.

"Albert seemed sympathetic. At that point he summoned Lew Deschler, the House parliamentarian, for advice. Deschler read the letter. His first reaction did not seem too receptive to the idea, particularly when we began to discuss whether this was properly a matter for consideration by the Judiciary Committee or a Select Committee. Of course, I preferred the Select Committee because the makeup of the Judiciary Committee was rather heavily liberal; and they would probably not be too friendly. Deschler seemed to feel that the Judiciary Committee was the proper forum of consideration, whereas Albert seemed to be leaning toward the idea of a Select Committee. At this point, I fully believe that Albert was inclined to use the power of his office to see that I got a hearing of some kind, or at least an investigation.

"Deschler then suggested that Albert call in the Majority Leader and the Chairman of the Judiciary Committee. Because I had already suggested it to Albert, he decided to call both the Majority and the Minority Leadership and the Chairman of the

Judiciary Committee and the ranking Republican member of that Committee.

"After a short wait, in came 'Tip' O'Neill, Jerry Ford, John McFall, Peter Rodino and Ed Hutchinson.* Copies of the letter were distributed to them, and a general discussion began. It was not until five minutes later that Les Arends, the Assistant Minority Leader, came in.

"There was a great deal of conversation about the letter; and the leadership, with the exception of O'Neill, seemed to approve of the idea of the House doing something about my request. Rodino was immediately and outwardly hostile, and I got the impression that the Judiciary Committee had already begun certain pre-impeachment investigations because of the newspaper accounts and that Rodino preferred that I be summoned before the House to defend myself rather than go there on my own initiative.

"O'Neill kept saying that he didn't see why the House should get involved in the matter and that in his opinion it was certainly a situation that the full House should decide. Ford then said that, as a practical matter, that meant it was for the Democratic members to decide.

"By this time, the situation seemed quite confused; and I suggested that they might wish to discuss it without my being there. Previously there had been talk between Albert, the parliamentarian, and the leaders about how it should be placed before the House. It was decided that Albert should read the letter to the House before I released any copies of it.

"Some thirty minutes after my discussions with the Speaker began, all parties except myself left the office while Albert read the letter to the House."

They then returned to the Speaker's office for private discussions. I had waited until the matter was placed on the public record so that the media would not be informed by me, but by the Speaker's action in reading the letter.

"Just before I left the office, Tip O'Neill came over to me and

---

* Thomas P. (Tip) O'Neill, D-Mass., House Majority Leader, later Speaker; Gerald R. Ford, R-Mich., House Minority Leader, later President; John McFall, D-Calif., House Majority Whip; Peter Rodino, D-N.J., House Judiciary Committee chairman; Edward Hutchinson, R-Mich., senior Republican on the Judiciary Committee.

said he was terribly sorry I was having all the trouble, and his words, as I recall them, were: 'Pal, it's a damn shame.'

"Ed Hutchinson was also very sympathetic and spoke with me personally, saying that he would do everything possible to help. At that point I called in Art Sohmer and told him to release the letter to the press through Walter Mote, Marsh Thomson and himself and to have Mike Dunn deliver copies to the White House press office. Mote hand-delivered copies to the Senate leadership, and a copy was hand-delivered to Attorney General Richardson.

"As I left the office, approximately one hour after entering, there was a tremendous crowd outside in the corridor—mostly members of the media who were pushing, shoving and shouting questions. I told them that the letter spoke for itself and released the letter to them, at which point we returned to the Executive Office Building."

If I had been really guilty, it would not have been logical for me to seek a hearing, which almost certainly would be televised, before the House or one of its committees. I was willing to testify in person and face my accusers. I wanted to see those frightened people testify on national television. I do not believe they would have been credible witnesses. It's very difficult to be a calm liar with the camera recording your every move. I can visualize Matz in the witness chair, fidgeting and wringing his hands; Wolff—so nervous and jumpy he once had threatened to commit suicide—furtive, sweating, voice cracking; Green, oily and unctuous, eyes shifting rapidly; Hammerman, too bluff and hearty to be believed. Under cross-examination, they would have had to reveal all their illegal deals with each other and their understandings with the prosecutors that they would be given light treatment in return for their testimony against me. I believe that I would have survived an impeachment hearing; if not, I would have been acquitted after a trial by the Senate.

Some of my Republican friends in the House had advised me that the Speaker would be heavily pressured by fellow-Democrats to keep his hands off the case and let the administration deal with it. However, Albert was not a total partisan; he had been a hawk on defense and foreign policy, opposed to Communist aggression, under both Democratic and Republican Presidents. He placed national security ahead of politics.

Albert was also aware of this situation: if I should leave the vice-presidency, Mr. Nixon would name my successor. But his nominee must also be confirmed by the House and the Senate, both dominated by the Democrats. Suppose my successor's con- firmation could be stalled for weeks or even months; suppose, also, that Nixon should meanwhile leave the presidency by death or resignation—either of which could happen. Then Albert himself would become President. The Speaker, a man of small stature but great integrity, refused even to think of attaining the presidency by partisan trickery.

I later found out that Tip O'Neill strongly urged the Speaker to keep out of my case and let me stew in my own juice. His sympathy apparently was not genuine.

Albert's own memoirs, tape-recorded by the United States Capitol Historical Society, show that he called the House Judiciary Committee chairman, Peter Rodino, and asked if he would take over the investigation of my case. Rodino, a New Jersey Democrat, replied: "We don't think much of it. It's always been our policy to let the courts carry through with a case." All the Democratic leaders in the House gave similar advice.

Then the Speaker recalled, "I got a call from the Attorney General, Elliot Richardson. He said, 'We're taking Agnew over to the grand jury today, and in my opinion, he will be in- dicted . . . I'm not telling you what to do, I'm just telling you what I think is going to happen.' "

Albert assumed that Richardson was acting on the President's instructions in warning him not to become involved in my case. "I'm sure—knowing Richardson—he would have told the President this before he would have told me," the Speaker said. "He wanted me to know that the civil processes were at work, and that he thought the first step was going to be unfavorable to Agnew; and I imagine he thought that was reason for us to wait before we did anything else."

Albert was puzzled by Richardson's warning. "The whole thing seemed sort of funny to me," the Speaker said. "I thought then that the President was trying to help Agnew. Agnew didn't think so, and certainly it didn't jibe with what the man who had the power was saying—that was Richardson."

Obviously, Richardson moved fast to cut off a House inquiry that could have run for months and prevented my quick resignation. Albert announced the next day, September 26, that since the matter was before the courts, he would not intervene.

Just as Richardson had told the Speaker, the prosecutors started summoning witnesses before the Baltimore grand jury. On September 28, my attorneys filed a motion with the court to "enter a protective order prohibiting the grand jury from conducting any investigation looking to possible indictment of applicant and from issuing indictment, presentment, or other charge or statement pertaining to applicant." We based our pleas on two points: (1) "The Constitution forbids that the Vice-President be indicted or convicted in any criminal court." (2) News leaks by the Justice Department itself had so "grievously abused" my rights that they made it impossible to win "a fair hearing on the merits, by either grand or petit jury."

"We have arrived at a firm conviction that personnel of the Department of Justice have engaged in a steady campaign designed to deprive the Vice-President of the basic right of a free man: the right to be judged fairly, on the merits, without prejudice," my lawyers charged. They said the flood of leaks made it clear that "the Vice-President is the victim of a deliberate campaign, calculated and intended to deprive him of his basic rights to due process and fair hearing."

Not only my attorneys, but much of the world at large was concerned about the effect of the leaks on my civil rights.

Senator Ted Kennedy had this to say: "The White House and the Department of Justice have an obligation of fundamental fairness to let the investigation take its course, free of the pervasive current atmosphere of a kangaroo trial by undisclosed sources. Vice-President Agnew has conducted himself with dignity in recent weeks. He deserves the nation's respect for his demeanor in this unprecedented situation."

Jerry Greene of the New York *Daily News* said, "A lot of faceless bureaucrats have been using the press to convict" Agnew.

Vermont Royster of *The Wall Street Journal* said I contended with Justice that the constant flow of leaks, rumors, and plain errors published in the newspapers and broadcast on the airwaves impaired my right to a fair hearing before the country. Royster questioned whether the people's right to know embraces a right to every rumor, gossip or hearsay conversation regardless of how prejudicial to justice. He quotes an editor from *The Washington*

Post who disagreed with him as saying, "So some guy has trouble getting a fair trial . . . by the pursuit of the First Amendment. So be it."

William Raspberry, writing in *The Washington Post*, said, "Agnew the politician is dead already, and Agnew the human being is close to it. In both cases, the fate may be deserved. The point is, he's been hanged without a trial." "What isn't forgivable, in the name of justice," continued Raspberry, "is that so many unchecked and uncheckable particulars of the allegations against him were made public, primarily through leaks to newsmen. For as a result, there is no longer simply a suspicion of wrongdoing hanging over his head; it has come to the point where many people only wonder how much graft he took, not whether he took it."

In a powerful column that speculates on the outrage that would have resulted had Dr. Spock or antiwar militants been subjected to the treatment I was receiving, John P. Roche had this to say: "In short, with the Attorney General providing the background music, we have Spiro Agnew indicted, convicted, impeached, convicted, and replaced by a nonpolitical figure—all before there has been a single formal legal move against him." Quoting F.D.R.'s famous maxim to define the situation, Roche observes, "It all depends whose child has the measles."

Even my old ideological adversary, the American Civil Liberties Union, agreed that "the government's selected disclosures of prejudicial material . . . marred this investigation."

In the motion, my lawyers cited a series of stories based upon information from Justice Department sources, climaxed by the CBS quotation from Henry Petersen, "We've got the evidence. We've got it cold."

William Safire, writing in *The New York Times* in two separate columns, examines the famous Petersen leak, before and after a defense by William Ruckelshaus, and concludes that the statement is equally damaging whether coming directly from Petersen to reporter Fred Graham, or not. In this regard, *The Boston Globe* report of the Petersen quote, "We've got the evidence. We've got it cold," goes on to state that "Richardson reportedly sat by in approving silence" when Petersen made that statement.

A report in *The Washington Post* September 5 revealed that

Elliot Richardson stated he had been told by the news media that his Justice Department was in fact the source of leaks against me. Notwithstanding that admission, Justice has continued to deny to this day that it was responsible for the leaks.

Without doubt, the most lucid and cogent recounting of the Petersen incident was done by columnist William A. Rusher. It is worth reprinting here.

The Conservative Advocate,
October 10, 1973

WILL NIXON FIRE PETERSEN?
by William A. Rusher

When even Tom Wicker, who holds the leftist portfolio over at *The New York Times*, admits that Vice-President Agnew's rights "obviously have been imperilled by the damaging news leaks about his case," it may fairly be assumed that the stench of injustice is getting pretty bad. And when Wicker's colleague Bill Safire, whom the *Times* hired a few months back to balance Wicker, calls upon his former boss President Nixon to fire Assistant Attorney General Henry Petersen, we are presented, for the first time in this sorry story, with an identified source of at least part of the trouble, and a means of remedying it. The question now is whether Mr. Nixon will do anything about it.

The sequence of events is important:

1. On September 22 CBS news correspondent Fred P. Graham broadcast a report, based on an anonymous "source close to the negotiations" then going on between Agnew's lawyers and various Justice Department officials (including Attorney General Elliot Richardson and his assistant Henry Petersen, head of the Criminal Division), that Petersen had privately told Agnew's lawyers, "We've got the evidence. We've got it cold"—meaning, of course, evidence that the Vice-President was guilty of bribery, extortion, fraud, and conspiracy. (According to Deputy Attorney General Ruckelshaus, however, Mr. Petersen as of October 1 could not remember ever having made such

a statement, nor could Attorney General Richardson remember having heard him make it.)

2. Nevertheless, the next day (September 23) *New York Times* correspondent John M. Crewdson, in a dispatch the *Times* ran as its page 1 lead, picked up the CBS story and repeated it—apparently without bothering to ask either Richardson or Petersen whether it was true. Crewdson neglected to mention that the CBS report was based on an anonymous "source." Instead, his account merely asserted that, according to CBS, Mr. Petersen was confident that the Vice-President could be convicted, and added:

"The network quoted Mr. Petersen as saying:

'We've got the evidence. We've got it cold.' "

That was the form in which the story went around the world. It is hard to imagine anything more damaging to Mr. Agnew. Here was the head of the Criminal Division of the Department of Justice, quoted (falsely, according to his own reported recollection) in America's leading newspaper as proclaiming the irrefutable guilt of the Vice-President of the United States.

3. What do you suppose Mr. Petersen, who can't recall saying any such thing, or Mr. Richardson, who can't remember hearing it, did to correct this deadly impression? Nothing; nothing whatever. For five harrowing days they simply let Spiro Agnew "hang there," in John Erlichman's immortal phrase, twisting "slowly, slowly in the wind." For three more, after James Reston reported Agnew's fury, their press spokesmen were authorized to tell any reporter who asked, that Petersen had never spoken to Graham; but nobody seems to have cared. Finally President Nixon instructed his own counsel to ask Richardson, for the public record, whether Petersen was in fact the source of the CBS story. Why, no, replied Richardson on October 1; no, indeed. On that same day, as we have already seen, Ruckelshaus went further and admitted that neither Petersen nor Richardson could remember the statement ever having been made at all.

Now, it is probably true that such busy men as Petersen cannot be expected to correct every misstatement. It was an all but lethal blow at a Vice-President who hadn't even been indicted, let alone convicted, and who is just as entitled to fair treatment as anybody else. What chance is there, do you suppose, that he will now receive it from the grand jury in Baltimore, under the guidance of Petersen's subordinate George Beall?

There is a well-known principle of law called "estoppel," under which a person to whom a statement is publicly attributed, and who deliberately fails to repudiate it, in legal effect becomes its author by virtue of his silence. Henry Petersen may not have made the statement that so gravely and unjustly injured Agnew, but his deliberate silence in the face of its constant and deadly repetition amounted to the same thing. The question now is whether Richard Nixon is prepared to demonstrate, by firing Mr. Petersen, that justice must be done, even to Spiro Agnew.

My lawyers pointed out that the news stories mentioned in their brief were fairly representative of hundreds of similar stories. "Taken together," my lawyers stated, "they permit only one possible explanation; a number of officials in the prosecutorial arm of our government had misused their offices in an immoral and illegal attempt to drive the Vice-President from the office to which he was elected and to assure his conviction.

"The prosecutors have clearly accomplished their objective," the lawyers went on, because hardly anyone in the United States could not have heard or read "the outrageous statements which the prosecution has leveled at the Vice-President," so it has become impossible to obtain a fair consideration of the case. "Morning, noon, and night, by newspaper, magazine, television and radio—the Vice-President has been ripped and flayed by the prosecution—and all of this before any determination has been even made as to whether any evidence may constitutionally be presented to a grand jury."

Topkis set out to subpoena the newsmen who had written the stories and ask them, first, did they write the story? And, second, did they really get it from Justice Department sources? If the reporters said the answer was "yes" on both points, my lawyer would tell the court that there was clearly a prima facie case showing the government had, indeed, violated my rights and thus had wrecked any chance of a fair trial.

The giants of the media, whose reporters were subpoenaed, struck back with a roar of self-righteous protests. They charged that we were threatening their First Amendment rights of freedom of the press, and the writer's right to keep all of his sources confidential. My chief tormentors—*The Washington Post, The New York Times*, the newsmagazines and the TV networks—saw visions of martyrdom ahead, as some of their star reporters might have to face contempt of court or even prison to maintain the sanctity of their sources, real or fictitious.

They had reason to worry, because of the jurist selected to preside over the case: U.S. District Judge Walter E. Hoffman of Norfolk, Virginia. Judge Hoffman, for good reason, disliked and distrusted reporters. He believed excessive publicity could violate a defendant's right to a fair trial, and he was old-fashioned enough to believe that that superseded the privileges of the media to get the news.

In another move, I granted a background interview to *New York Times* columnist James Reston who wrote on September 27, "Vice-President Agnew has made up his mind about the next phase of what he calls his 'nightmare.' He does not intend to resign, even if he is indicted by the Baltimore grand jury, but to fight for exoneration through the courts, and keep appealing to the House of Representatives for a full and open hearing, no matter how long it takes." Of all the high officials of the *Times*, Reston was the one I knew and I trusted. I found him to be an honorable man, although Mr. Nixon disliked him and repeatedly warned me against trusting him.

Then I took off for Los Angeles to address the National Federation of Republican Women. On the way, I stopped at Palm Springs to visit my friend, Frank Sinatra.

As does every Vice-President, I met a lot of celebrities during my years in office—famous names in the fields of entertainment, sports, and the arts. Most of them were fine people, and I keep in touch with quite a few who have gone out of their way to be supportive and helpful during my difficulties. Francis Albert Sinatra, however, falls in a special bracket, a bracket of one.

When the deluge of adverse publicity began to descend on me

following the leaking of the prosecutors' letter informing me that I was the subject of a criminal investigation, Frank immediately had flown to Washington to offer legal assistance and support. He made his lawyer, Mickey Rudin, available to me for consultation. He spent hours counseling with me, making suggestions and above all doing his best to keep my spirits up. During the rough months preceding my resignation, it was seldom that a day passed without a telephone call from Francis. "I just wanted to check to see how things are going . . . Can I do anything for you?"

We were very close—are still very close—so it was natural that I stopped at his home in Palm Springs before my scheduled speech to the Republican women.

The day before we played golf, although my mind was far away from the game. That evening Frank cooked some pasta for Judy, me, and the few staff members who were accompanying me. Then we all sat around the living room to talk about "the case." Frank was outspokenly in favor of my going on the offensive, and thought I should make it clear to the public that I was being destroyed by the systematic ignoring of my constitutional rights. Everyone wanted me to take off the gloves and fight back, and most thought the Los Angeles rally would be a perfect forum. However, I was depressed about the failure of our attempt to gain a hearing in the House of Representatives and the duplicitous actions of the President; who, it was now clear to see, was not being candid with me. Nevertheless, I feared totally alienating a man who held so much power and who was being driven to the wall by the Watergate prosecutor and the news media.

We retired quite late, and I spent a restless night—confused, angry, and hurt by my inability to do anything about a steadily deteriorating situation.

The next morning we flew to Los Angeles. As I sat in the plane looking over the prepared speech that I would be delivering in less than two hours, it suddenly struck me that it just wouldn't do. Those women, and all my supporters out there, were entitled to know how I felt—what was happening. I began to make some notes on the back of an envelope I found in my pocket. My mind was clear, logical. The ideas flowed. It felt right, very right. I decided to cut down on the prepared speech and "wing" the thoughts I was noting at the end. I didn't say anything to anyone, but suddenly the depression was gone. I felt confident, ready for the battle.

Two thousand Republican women cheered me as I walked out onto the speaker's platform. Some were waving signs that expressed their faith in me: "Agnew for President" and "Spiro My Hero." I knew, in my heart, that I was finished as a candidate for the presidency. But I was determined that I would fight to save my life from ruin.

Gazing directly into the television cameras, I launched my off-the-cuff attack upon the Justice Department and its leaks to the media. "In the past several months I have been living in purgatory," I said. "I have found myself the recipient of undefined, unclear, and unattributed accusations that have surfaced in the largest and most widely circulated organs of our communications media. I want to say at this point—clearly and unequivocally—I am innocent of the charges against me."

This declaration touched off tremendous applause. Raising my voice to be heard above the women's cheers, I pressed on: "I have not used my office, nor abused my public trust as county executive, as governor, or as Vice-President, to enrich myself at the expense of my fellow Americans.

"I say this to you," I declared, "that conduct of high officials in the Department of Justice, particularly the conduct of the chief of the criminal investigation division of that department, is unprofessional and malicious and outrageous, if I am to believe what has been printed in the newsmagazines and said on the television networks of this country, and I have had no denial that this is not the case.

"Now people will say to me: 'Why? You don't make sense. Why should a Republican Department of Justice and Republican prosecutors attempt to get you?' Well, I don't know all the answers, but I will say this—that individuals in the upper professional echelons of the Department of Justice have been severely stung by their ineptness in the prosecution of the Watergate case. They have been severely stung that the President and the Attorney General have found it necessary to appoint a special prosecutor, and they are trying to recoup their reputation at my expense. I'm a big trophy.

"And one of those individuals has made some very severe

mistakes, serious mistakes. In handling his job he considers himself a career professional, in a class by himself, but a recent examination of his record will show not only that he failed to get any of the information about the true dimensions of the Watergate matter, but that he also through ineptness and blunder prevented the successful prosecution of high crime figures because of wiretapping error.

"Those are the reasons why he needs me to reinstate his reputation as a tough and courageous and hard-nosed prosecutor. Well, I'm not going to fall down and be his victim, I assure you."

Insisting that I was the victim of witnesses who told lies against me to save their own skins, I said that was why I had asked the House to make a thorough inquiry into the case. "What I want is not a suppression of the facts but the fullest possible hearing of them, widely publicized before the people of the American nation, so that everyone knows exactly what is going on in this nation," I said. "I'm not trying to hide anything."

Then I brought the women to their feet, cheering, when I declared: "I want to make another thing so clear that it cannot be mistaken in the future. Because of these tactics which have been employed against me, because small and fearful men have been frightened into furnishing evidence against me—they have perjured themselves in many cases, it's my understanding—I will not resign if indicted. *I will not resign if indicted!*"

CHAPTER FIFTEEN

A CANDLE IS ONLY SO LONG

When I made my defiant speech in Los Angeles, I was fully determined to carry my fight all the way to final victory or defeat. My back was to the wall. I was so fired up that I dared the Justice Department to do its worst—take the case to the grand jury, try to get an indictment, and then try to take me to trial. Although I knew it would be virtually impossible to find a jury in Baltimore that would not be prejudiced against me, I still felt in a fighting mood. There was much left in the struggle and quite a few intangibles. First, there was the constitutional question of whether a Vice-President is subject to indictment. Then there was the motion to block testimony before the grand jury because of the prejudicial leaks. Would the House at some point begin impeachment and take the case temporarily away from the court? Would a change of venue be granted to get the matter away from Baltimore? Would the court find I couldn't get a fair trial anywhere in the country because of the swath of national publicity? Or would a six-month or one-year delay be ordered to let the publicity abate? All these questions, and the two levels of appeals from each of them, would take a great deal of time. The fully fought battle could easily consume the better part of three years. My term in office had three years and a half yet to run.

My speech not only evoked roars of enthusiasm from the Republican women and an echoing surge of support from people across the country, it also touched off a wave of anger and fear inside the White House. General Haig telephoned the news to the President, who was at Camp David wrestling with the problems of holding onto his tapes that had been subpoenaed by Watergate Special Prosecutor Archibald Cox.

Mr. Nixon was desperately determined to keep those incriminating tapes out of the prosecutor's hands. Indeed, he was already casting about for some excuse to fire Cox. On the day before my Los Angeles speech, I learned later, the President had confided to Richardson that he was looking forward to getting rid of the Agnew problem so that he could then fire Cox. Nixon was totally obsessed with his own difficulties, and I was an added complication to be removed as quickly as possible without arousing my many friends in Middle America.

General Haig evidently feared that I was declaring war, not only on the Justice Department but on the entire administration. The White House and Justice—probably at his instigation—leaked out a false story that I had a "phased escalation plan for a four-stage assault": first, to attack Henry Petersen; then Beall, then Richardson, and finally the President. Such a thought had never crossed my mind. I was dealing with the immediate problem of Petersen's damaging quotes, which had not been denied. I am convinced that Haig devised this tale in order to persuade the President that he had to get terribly tough with me because he would be my ultimate target; that Nixon, who had thus far specialized in public statements that gave lukewarm support to his Vice-President, had better attack me before he himself was attacked.* Haig must have told Nixon, "Agnew has gone wild—attacking Petersen, saying he will not resign. You may be next. We've got to lower the boom on him *now*."

At this critical flash point, my fledgling press secretary, Marsh Thomson, committed a blunder of horrific dimensions. Without consulting either me or senior staff, on Tuesday, October 2, he hinted to reporters that I would deliver more heavy artillery in a speech scheduled two days later in Chicago. Thomson was trying to whip up press interest in the coming appearance. I guess he thought he was doing me a favor. His remark, seeming to confirm the Haig escalation theory, was widely reported. It hit the White House like a bomb. Haig called my Chief of Staff, Art Sohmer, and told him that the President wanted no more speeches of the Los Angeles type, and that Thomson must be

---

* Columnist Hugh Sidey put it this way: "If the White House had hired Madison Avenue counsel to devise a script to humiliate Agnew and raise rumors that he might not be wanted anymore, they couldn't have done it better."

silenced. I had already told Sohmer that Thomson, who had made earlier blunders, was no match for the hungry Washington press corps, and must be relieved immediately.

The next day, Mr. Nixon said at a rare informal press conference that the charges against me were serious, not frivolous. He went out of his way to defend Henry Petersen, thus signaling the end of White House neutrality. Unable to be unequivocal, he threw a small sop to me to placate my Middle America supporters. He said my decision not to resign was an "altogether proper" one. The President had been assured by Richardson that Petersen had not been the one who leaked his comment, "We've got the evidence. We've got it cold" to the press.

As far as I was concerned, it made no difference whether it was Petersen or someone else in the Justice Department who leaked the remark. It became public, attributed to Petersen, and it was never denied. The damage was done just as effectively as if Henry Petersen had gone on the TV and announced it to the world.

While we are considering the professionalism, restraint, integrity, and impartiality of Henry Petersen, let me relate the following revealing information, taken from my notes in 1973.

I received information from a network TV reporter (who called to see if we knew anything about it). He had learned from sources in the Justice Department that about a week after Petersen had gone to Baltimore to confer with the U. S. Attorney, he held a meeting with three other top people at Justice. The purpose of the meeting was to explain his attitude and outline his approach to my case. The reporter said that Petersen had made it unmistakably clear he was determined to "get me," and used that expression. Petersen, the sources alleged, had stated he intended to resign and make public all of his deep dissatisfaction with the administration as a whole unless he were given full rein in the prosecution of my case.

Petersen had further indicated to the sources that he had demanded to be the one who would go to Baltimore and consult with the U. S. Attorney, and that he intended to continue insisting he should have full charge so there could be no allegations he conducted his business under political influence.

Two of the participants in the meeting corroborated the above to the reporter and indicated that Petersen seemed totally dedicated to ·seeing me convicted. When the reporter approached Petersen, he denied it.

The reporter said the station's policy is not to use such a denied report without a third confirming source which is being actively pursued. Apparently, the reporter was not successful in getting the third confirming source, because the story never surfaced.

Mr. Nixon said the Attorney General had told him again there was no evidence to back up my charges about the leaks from the Justice Department. But my lawyers were pressing in court to get exactly that evidence from the mouths of the reporters involved.

On the same day that Nixon chatted with the press, Judge Walter Hoffman convened the Baltimore grand jury members and sternly admonished them to make their decisions on the evidence given to them in secret session, not on the news reports.

"Unfortunately, in the present-day grab for priority in getting news items, the news media frequently overlook the rights of others, especially where criminal matters are involved," the judge said in his charge to the grand jury. "We are rapidly approaching the day when the perpetual conflict between the news media, operating as they do under freedom of speech and freedom of the press, and the judicial system, charged with protecting the rights of persons under investigation for criminal acts, must be resolved."

Judge Hoffman also disclosed that he had sent Topkis a letter about my charges of unfair publicity and leaks, and dispatched a copy of it to Henry Petersen. He wrote: "Gentlemen: Relating solely to the publicity question raised by the applicant, unless the brief of the Department of Justice persuades me to the contrary, I am presently inclined to the belief that the applicant would at least be entitled to an evidentiary hearing on his charges that the prosecution was responsible for the allegedly prejudicial (leaks)."

Judge Hoffman called my lawyers and the three prosecutors, Beall, Skolnik, and Liebman, to a private meeting in the Baltimore federal courthouse and told them of his plans. He scheduled a closed hearing on Friday, October 12, and since Petersen had told him the statute of limitations was an important issue in the case, said he would make a ruling on the civil suits by October

19. Martin London said I would like to start taking depositions on the leaks at once and the judge agreed. Hoffman said he wanted to be there when the witnesses were questioned, so that he could ask some questions, too. He clearly indicated that any newsman who refused to talk could be held in contempt of court.

Judge Hoffman accepted Topkis's list of witnesses to be deposed, starting with Elliot Richardson, Henry Petersen, and George Beall, and going down the line through reporters for major newspapers, newsmagazines, and television networks.

Beall sent a memorandum to the Justice Department proposing that the government contend I had no standing to interfere with a grand jury proceeding. Assuming that Judge Hoffman would go ahead with his evidentiary hearing, Beall said it must be restricted to the charge by Topkis that "officials of the prosecutorial arm have engaged in the steady campaign of statements to the press."

Furthermore, the U. S. Attorney urged the government to file a counter-suit claiming that "the Vice-President, his staff, and his attorneys are just as likely sources of news media stories, and request that counter-depositions be ordered by the court to explore that assertion." So once again, Beall revived the "red herring" claim that I—or my aides—leaked information terribly damaging to myself. This was ridiculous, and typical of the cheap and sleazy tactics of my oppressors.

Before we could proceed with our battle on the news leaks, however, I had to deal with the most pressing problem of all—the President's attitude toward me in the wake of my Los Angeles speech. I had that very much in mind when I flew to Chicago on October 4 to address a United Republican fund-raising dinner.

As soon as I arrived in Chicago and checked in at the Drake Hotel, I met with W. Clement Stone, the well known Republican fund-raiser who had agreed to be cochairman of the Agnew Defense Fund.

Sometime earlier, it had become obvious that a long and very costly legal struggle was about to ensue. Because I had no assets of this magnitude, my advisers suggested an independent fund be set up to solicit contributions from the public for my defense. Former Democratic Governor of Missouri Warren Hearnes, a highly respected chairman of the National Governors' Conference, along with Senator Barry Goldwater and W. Clement Stone, agreed to serve as cochairmen of the Agnew Defense Fund. The fund operated out of Stone's Chicago office.

There were reports the fund did not do well; that Stone had been disappointed in the response when I met with him in Chicago. Actually, contributions were coming in nicely despite the debilitating leaks to the media. In the three months that it operated, the defense fund raised and disbursed to the lawyers its total assets of $81,725. When I resigned, the fund was closed and the trustees offered to return any contributions that donors might want to request be sent back, but very few requests were made. In fact, money kept coming in that had to be returned because the fund had been dissolved.

When I walked to the lectern at the Chicago rally, my voice and general demeanor revealed that I was a changed person. The reporters were puzzled. They thought I looked sick.

I told them, "Tonight is not going to be an X-rated political show. It's just going to be PG. So if you have to go someplace, go."

Then I said: "A candle is only so long before it burns out."

David Broder, the journeyman political analyst of The Washington Post, said I looked like a man who had been kicked in the groin or had received some terrible news. Broder was right on both counts. I have kept this a secret for over six years but now it must be told.

Not long before our scheduled departure time for Chicago on October 4, I received an indirect threat from The White House that made me fear for my life.

Shortly before 1 P.M., Art Sohmer came into my office and told me that Gen. Mike Dunn, my military aide, wanted to see the two of us in the military office about a matter of extreme urgency. When I expressed surprise that Mike had not come to my office, Sohmer made motions that revealed he feared my office was bugged.

Accompanied by Sohmer, I went immediately to the military suite, where Dunn quickly took us both into the office of my pilot, Lt. Col. Keith Garland, and closed the door. Dunn, nearly always a calm, self-assured individual, was grave and more tense than I had ever seen him. He recounted a shocking story. Here is the memorandum for the record that General Dunn dictated at that time:

At 11:45 A.M. on October 4, I met with General Haig in his office at his suggestion, in response to a telephone call. Peter Malatesta [a special assistant to the Vice-President] was with me in my office at time of call and for that reason knew of visit. Others who know of the occurrence are Haig's [military] secretaries, Major Joulwan and Lt. Colonel Brennan. We met alone, however, so presumably he and I were aware of content. I subsequently debriefed STA [myself] and AJS [Arthur J. Sohmer] privately in Garland's office.

Haig began by stating that he had been briefed on the evidence on STA and it was massive. Buzhardt was absolutely convinced of his guilt—four men would testify that a conspiracy existed headed by STA. The testimony would be interlocking and corroborative. It would not simply be a case of one on one, which was apparently what STA thought. Justice believes that it has an ironclad case for conviction. They feel that they could move successfully with what the IRS alone has produced. The 1968 income tax return by itself would provide a case. Haig indicated "the clock is running—it will be too late once an indictment is obtained to do this gracefully." Money can be dried up—it's the President's men on whom STA must depend. Stone [W. Clement Stone] specifically was awaiting a call from Haig at the very moment. There are many people with one foot in each camp. Haig knows of every phone call made by STA. Conversations were also not unknown. Nixon has been completely supportive to date. Once "facts" are made known to people, further support from Nixon impossible.

In response to a direct question, Haig agreed that it was resignation that was wanted. In response to a further question as to "what was in it for STA," he responded that since this was the patriotic thing to do, this would be recognized. There would be no economic worry for debts or for defense and the like. In return for an admission of guilt on the tax charge, there would be no further trouble with the federal government and no jail sentence.

Haig stated that the NY law firm does not care in the least about STA and how badly he may be bruised by this. They simply are using him to get at Nixon. The local lawyers [Best and Buzhardt] are appalled by the way the case is going. They feel that "he is about to kill himself." In any event, after indictment, we are off to the races and cannot control the situation any longer—anything may be in the offing. It can and will get nasty and dirty. "Don't think that the game cannot be played from here."

I indicated I was personally convinced of STA's essential innocence. I had been close to him throughout and he had repeatedly looked me in the eye and repeated his statement of innocence. I was still unwilling to think of him as guilty of other than minor indiscretions in handling campaign funds. I asked further exactly what Haig wanted of me—did he wish that I leave the staff? He answered "No," that was the last thing he wanted. He said he was seeking someone who had STA's ear to convey a message. I responded that I did have his ear on most matters, but that legal matters had been left largely in the hands of the lawyers. Haig went on to state that both Arends [Congressman Leslie C. Arends] and Ford had been briefed on the case and were strongly against STA going to the House. STA does not enjoy anything like the amount of support on the Hill that he thinks he does. The President recently had remarked that STA seemed to be on a collision course with him despite his frequent reassurances that this was not the case. He made specific reference to the speech in Los Angeles and to Marsh Thomson's remarks quoted in papers regarding the forthcoming Chicago appearance. I responded that Thomson had been fired and the President so informed—the Chicago speech would give him no problems.

Haig went on to say that STA was primarily concerned with economic questions. In earlier negotiations he had asked for economic help and when it was not forthcoming, he withdrew from negotiations. He repeated again that Nixon has been completely supportive to date but—STA should have faith.

With regard to the so-called leaks from WH, Haig said there have been no leaks from the top. They did not get the information from topside, but rather from the old-boy net.

He stated that he would check again with Fred Buzhardt but was convinced that whether STA was guilty or innocent, guilt would be the verdict in court. Conversation concluded on this note and Haig departed to Key Biscayne and promised to get in touch again.

Haig's threat made me realize, with a sickening shock, that I had finally lost the last slim thread of hope that the President would help me in my fight. On the contrary, he had turned against me and become my mortal enemy. Haig insinuated that if I went against the President's wishes and refused to resign, there would be no more help from the White House to prevent a jail sentence and no assistance with the I.R.S., finances, placing my staff, or the other carrots Buzhardt had dangled. I would be on my own and the full penalties would be assessed. Stone would withdraw from the Defense Fund. Nixon would publicly blast me, turn the prosecutors loose, and I would go to jail.

Dunn also informed me that the net-worth investigation of my finances had been stepped up. I was to be warned that "I should not forget that my wife was involved in our joint tax return; if I were found criminally liable, she could be, too." It was the lowest blow of all.

There was no way I could win, now. With the President coming out against me, I was doomed.

General Dunn told me that General Haig also reminded him about the great power of the presidency, saying, "The President has a lot of power—don't forget that."

His remark sent a chill through my body. I interpreted it as an innuendo that anything could happen to me; I might have a convenient "accident." What had Haig meant when he said "anything may be in the offing"?

I was close enough to the presidency to know that the office could exert tremendous power. I had attended secret sessions of the National Security Council and knew something about the functioning of the intelligence community. I knew that men in the White House, professing to speak for the President, could order the C.I.A. to carry out missions that were very unhealthy for people who were considered enemies. Since the revelations have come out about the C.I.A.'s attempts to assassinate Fidel Castro and other foreign leaders, I realize even more than before that I might have been in great danger. Haig's words to Dunn that after indictment "anything may be in the offing" could only be construed as an open-ended threat.

I did not know what might happen to me. But I don't mind admitting I was frightened. This directive was aimed at me like a gun at my head. That is the only way I can describe it. I was told, "Go quietly—or else."

I feared for my life. If a decision had been made to eliminate me—through an automobile accident, a fake suicide, or whatever —the order would not have been traced back to the White House any more than the "get Castro" orders were ever traced to their source.

Perhaps I overreacted, but my mental state after months of constant pressure was hardly conducive to calm and dispassionate evaluation.

The American people should know that in the last hectic year or more of his residence in the White House, Richard Nixon did not actually administer all the powers of the presidency. As I have stated earlier, it was General Haig who was the de facto President. Haig had the power of the bureaucracy at his command, and the Washington insiders knew he was standing there behind Nixon, pulling the strings. Haig had direct connections with the C.I.A. and the F.B.I. and every other agency. For four years he had been Henry Kissinger's chief deputy with clear access to all the government; his power extended into any agency he chose. The very survival of the Nixon presidency was threatened.

Many who are familiar with General Haig's career are convinced that a man does not, in only a few years, climb through the upper echelons of the army—from a one-star to a four-star general's rank—to be the President's top civilian adviser, without being totally self-centered, ambitious, and ruthless. I believe that this man who jumped so easily from general to civilian back to general had placed himself in the position where he took actions far exceeding the proper authority of White House staff personnel. He apparently felt that the President, because of the

Watergate pressures, was incapable of making the right decisions, so the general probably made them in his name. Mr. Nixon did not have the stomach to confront me openly, so it is logical to conclude that Haig took over and determined how to force me to get out. I believe that by using the "escalation theory" after my California speech, he deliberately influenced Nixon to acquiesce in the decisive move against me: the threat to play nasty—and dirty.

I am also convinced that Haig desired not only to move me out, but in due course, after someone else had been brought into the vice-presidency, to move Mr. Nixon out, too. I really think that by this time, Al Haig already knew enough about the discrepancies in the tapes—and the truth about Nixon's involvement in the Watergate cover-up—to be convinced that eventually the President himself must go. And Haig did not want me in the line of succession.

There is another important point: I had no idea how much hot water the President was in. I did not believe the Watergate allegations, and I defended him. If I had known the truth about his involvement and why he was withholding his tapes from the special prosecutor, my actions would not have been as benign as they were. I felt I had no chance to win a fight against the President. If I had known how weak Nixon really was, I might have fought it out.

I regret that I never confronted Mr. Nixon about the threatening message from Haig. I guess it was partly out of fear and partly knowing from experience he wouldn't give me a straight answer that I never asked Nixon if he personally authorized the threat to "get nasty—and dirty." I suppose he would have denied it. At the time, I could not bring myself to believe that the President was not reluctantly being forced into this position by his advisers. I did not have the advantage of hindsight, of knowing for sure how I was being railroaded, until long after I was out. Nixon pretended to help me get a hearing in Congress, yet we now know that he had Mel Laird and others up there on Capitol Hill warning Republicans to steer clear of me. In the end, the President turned out to be nearly as devious as the Nixonphobes claimed.

When he showed his true colors and turned against me, I realized I had no hope of victory. There was one thing and only one thing that brought me back to the bargaining table with the prosecutors: Mr. Nixon's threat, relayed by Haig, that things would "get nasty—and dirty" unless I resigned at once. The White House told Richardson I was driven back to the table by the net-worth investigation, which was supposed to show I had received huge amounts of tainted money. But that is an absolute lie concocted to conceal the ugly truth: that Haig had put the heat on me with his threats.

The net-worth investigation did not develop anything substantial, and what it did develop was in no way illegal. The total "bulge" of income, apparently unreported for taxes over a period of seven or eight years, was calculated by the I.R.S. to be about seventeen thousand dollars. By my estimate of gifts received during that period, I could see they would be unaware of about twelve thousand dollars my friends had given me.

But these gifts were not taxable income and I had no obligation to report them. My actual net worth was less than two hundred thousand dollars. I had what was left of my small inheritance from my father, the cash value of my life insurance—bought many years before, and the comparatively small equity in my mortgaged home. Part of the threat to me was the reminder that my wife could be implicated in the tax charge; they could prosecute her, too, because we filed joint returns.

The prosecutors insisted I had to plead guilty to some felony charge. I told my lawyers, as I had told them before, "I'm not going to plead guilty to bribery or extortion. If I've got to do something to settle this, I'll plead nolo contendere to a tax charge." They asked, "What tax charge?" I said, "Well, say that in late 1967 I collected some contributions for the 1968 campaign, and maybe held the money past the end of the year and didn't use it until the next year so that it was technically 'income' for me."

It was simply a rationalization so that I could tell the judge I had received the money technically as unreported "income." The tax collectors at the I.R.S. later took every bit of testimony of my accusers as being true and billed me for taxes on my fictitious income. When I protested, the I.R.S. officials said, "You want to contest it? Take us into court." That would have meant trying the same issues in a civil hearing and a further circus for the news media, as well as heavy legal fees and a tremendous sacrifice of my precious time needed to start making a living again. Moreover, I wanted to try my hand at international business, because I knew it would be impossible for any U.S. company to hire me without being pestered to death by my enemies. The I.R.S. said they would have to have my passport lifted as I might become an "absconding debtor." That would have made it impossible for me to do business overseas. They billed me for $150,000 in back federal income taxes, including interest and penalties. The irony is that I never got that money; I had to borrow money to pay the taxes on income I never received.

As a condition of the settlement, I had to say in court the tax evasion charge was true. In effect, I had to twist the truth to make it possible for the judge to accept the settlement.

CHAPTER SIXTEEN

GET THAT GUY OUT OF THERE

On Friday, October 5, upon returning from Chicago, I conferred again with Judd Best and instructed him to call Fred Buzhardt and start the bargaining again. "Go speak to Buzhardt," I said dejectedly. "See what can be done."

Best located Buzhardt at the President's retreat in Key Biscayne. In slacks, sport shirt, and sun glasses, my attorney flew to Miami International Airport. Buzhardt met him there after midnight. Best checked into a motel and the two lawyers worked until four o'clock in the morning, drafting the terms of a settlement. Best returned to Washington where Buzhardt, after talking to Nixon, telephoned him and said, "Everything is all right."

On Sunday afternoon, October 7, Richardson called his team together for a conference on their strategy for the last play in the game of "get Agnew." Russell T. Baker, Jr., filed a memorandum which gives the full flavor of the meeting as these hunters moved in on me for the kill. The following is a summary of the Baker memorandum.

Richardson stressed that the war which had erupted in the Middle East the previous day made it doubly imperative to move me out of the vice-presidency. The President faced tremendous new responsibilities as he strove to save Israel from the attack by Egypt and Syria—the Arab forces, having a great advantage from their surprise assault, were pressing forward relentlessly. Nixon was determined to save Israel, but the Soviet Union would also very likely intervene to prevent the defeat of the socialist Arab countries. The world could conceivably be approaching the brink of a nuclear catastrophe. Richardson had been worrying about Nixon's emotional stability—or the lack of it—ever since the President's illness in July; now, more than ever, the Attorney General sought to kick me out and bring in a new Vice-President

194

who might, at any time, have to move into the White House.

The Yom Kippur War demonstrated "how important it was to wind up this matter as promptly as possible," Richardson said. He felt much more strongly about this now than he had two weeks ago.

Richardson wanted someone in the line of succession to the presidency who, like Nixon, would defend Israel, whatever the risk to the United States. My resignation must be obtained immediately.

The Baltimore prosecutors, however, were still not satisfied without the last pound of flesh. Barnet Skolnik insisted that I must sign a statement along the lines of the September 15 letter, which I had spurned—or make admissions of guilt in court, conceding the validity of the bribery charges. Skolnik even threatened to break away from the team in protest. "I personally would find it difficult to be involved in a disposition which I view as wrong in principle," he said. "I might not be able to participate in the court proceedings."

Skolnik said the public would ultimately learn that the Justice Department had backed down from its "nonnegotiable stand" of September 15 and wonder why the retreat came about—perhaps because of Buzhardt's role and the Department's "embarrassment about the leaks." Baker also urged Richardson to insist that I make an admission of guilt. Petersen asked if the prosecutors were not frightened by the prospect of my remaining Vice-President.

Skolnik insisted, "Agnew will ultimately be forced to resign, no later than the date he is indicted. We can indict him by the end of October."

"Agnew's resignation is an important goal," Baker put in, "but it is much more important to handle this matter in a way which will not impair public confidence in the processes and institutions of law enforcement."

"I don't believe I should play Russian roulette with the United States over a few words," Richardson said. "Remember, we failed to get an agreement during the last round. I am reluctant to take a chance that an agreement can be reached later, so I am inclined to make one as soon as possible."

"I don't think Agnew will walk out of the courtroom and immediately launch a new attack on the department," he added.

Skolnik and Baker disagreed, saying: "Agnew's statement in court won't be the last we will hear of him."

Richardson said, "The Vice-President is distraught and not in a position to start any crusade to vindicate himself after the court proceedings. I don't think that keeping Agnew from making some self-serving statements is a sufficient basis for refusing to reach an agreement with him."

Ruckelshaus protested that any public relief over the avoidance of a prolonged constitutional confrontation would be short-lived; he said the settlement of the case must insure long-term public confidence in the Justice Department. Therefore, he opposed a "weak deal" that would give me any benefit.

Richardson told his aides they had not taken the full measure of the damage that would be done to the country if this conflict should run its course through Congress and the courts. The proceedings would be "divisive and traumatic and could seriously affect the capacity to govern," he said, in another reference to the President's problems.

Richardson was gravely concerned that the President would refuse to comply with a Supreme Court order to hand over his tapes to Watergate Special Prosecutor Cox at the same time the Vice-President was under indictment. Again, the Attorney General recalled how frightened he had been by Mr. Nixon's illness in July, when the official report of "viral pneumonia" was suspected of being a mask to conceal some more alarming ailment, perhaps a stroke.

Then Richardson summed up his philosophy in these immortal words: "I want the Justice Department to emerge from this matter in a way that will enhance public confidence, but it is more important to *get that guy out of there*." (Emphasis added)

He assured his eager-beaver prosecutors they should feel free to stay out of the court proceeding if they disagreed with the deal, but he hoped they would not question his "honesty of purpose." He had not come into the department with the idea it would enhance his personal popularity, he said; he would take the heat from the prosecutors. "I don't mind being known as the guy who 'blinked' in the showdown," he said.

The next day, October 8, Judd Best telephoned me in New York and outlined the proposed agreement. Under my instructions he told Haig and Buzhardt, "We will not do anything unless

Richardson and the Department of Justice assure us there will be *no* incarceration." I was determined that unless they guaranteed me "no jail," there would be "no deal." I might just as well take my chances with White House threats and a Baltimore jury, prejudiced and biased as it might be, rather than resign the vice-presidency and be railroaded to prison despite my innocence.

I was deathly afraid of a double cross.

My friends on Capitol Hill were trying to revive my proposal for the House to stage a public investigation so I could confront my accusers and state my case to the American people through television. Two Republican Representatives, Sam Devine of Ohio and Bill Dickinson of Alabama, invited about a hundred congressmen to breakfast on Wednesday morning, October 10— the same morning I was scheduled to be in court—to discuss the plan. Representative Joe D. Waggonner, Jr., a Democrat from Louisiana, was asked to help assemble the band of hard-line Southern Democrats who often backed the administration on national defense issues. David Keene of my staff worked with the congressmen on the breakfast project, but we had to call it off at the last moment. Of course, we could not explain why.

I did see that my congressional friends were notified before they learned from the wire what had prevented my appearance, and why I had been so rude as to make such a late cancellation.

On October 9, Richardson and his aides met again with my three lawyers and finally agreed to recommend that I keep my freedom. That afternoon, the Attorney General told Judge Walter Hoffman, "It is my recommendation that there be no term of imprisonment."

The judge replied, "In the light of the overwhelming national interest, I approve the agreement."

Later in the afternoon, my attorneys informed me that the agreement had been made. I then wrote my letter of resignation and a letter to the President. Arrangements were made to have the resignation delivered to Henry Kissinger, the Secretary of State. In the early evening, I went to the Oval Office to tell Mr. Nixon officially that I was giving up the vice-presidency—that I would resign the following morning. He had won.

The President told me he was grateful for my campaigning and the way I had handled all my assignments. He asked about Judy and others of my family, saying this tragedy must be painful for them. "I know you have made this decision for the good of the country," he said. "And also I believe that you are doing the best thing for yourself and your family."

I looked at the President, his face gaunt and sorrowful. It was hard to believe he was not genuinely sorry about the course of events. Within two days, this consummate actor would be celebrating his appointment of a new Vice-President with never a thought of me. But of course, I didn't know that. My eyes filled at his solicitous words. I was conscious of how tragic the moment was for me and my loved ones. Here I was in the Oval Office for the last time, about to leave in disgrace the office I had fought and worked for so hard. I felt no rancor toward Mr. Nixon, only a heavy, burdening sadness. I was about to let a lot of people down.

I said to the President: "I will make a speech to the nation. It will be lofty in tone. The people's confidence in their government must be restored. I will do all I can to be helpful to you, Mr. President."

As I was leaving, Nixon put his arm around my shoulders, shook his head, and said again how awful it all was. Incongruously, I suddenly had the feeling that he couldn't wait to get me out of there. We shook hands and I walked numbly out of the Oval Office—and out of the White House for what I supposed was the last time.

This is the text of my letter of resignation:

October 10, 1973

Dear Mr. President:

As you are aware, the accusations against me cannot be resolved without a long, divisive and debilitating struggle in the Congress and in the courts. I have concluded that, painful as it is to me and to my family, it is in the best interests of the nation that I relinquish the Vice-Presidency.

Accordingly, I have today resigned the Office of Vice-President of the United States. A copy of the instrument of resignation is enclosed.

It has been a privilege to serve with you. May I express to the American people, through you, my deep gratitude for their confidence in twice electing me to be Vice-President.

Sincerely,
Spiro T. Agnew

One of the questions I have been most frequently asked is, "Why did you agree to the publication of the forty-page 'statement of evidence' submitted by the prosecutors at the hearing in Baltimore on October 10?"

This was a matter that my lawyers and I discussed thoroughly. Fundamentally, there were two reasons why we did not contest the making public of these damaging accusations. We were aware they would be seized upon and referred to as evidence—and of course they are evidence, in the sense that any testimony that bears on a relevant matter is evidence. Yet, we did not anticipate that "evidence," in the eyes of the public and especially the news media, seems to mean something that has been proven conclusively.

The evidence in the forty-page statement—which, as Judge Hoffman pointed out, was totally irrelevant to the case before him—was not proof, it was merely testimony and tainted testimony, at that. It was simply what the prosecutors hoped to prove by the testimony of witnesses who already had been promised they would get off easy, or even scot-free, in return for implicating me. Much of what is in the forty-page "statement of evidence" is so clearly either hearsay or speculation that it would never be admitted in court.

The reasons we did not contest the publication of the statement were twofold. First, we knew it would be leaked and would be much more damaging if it dribbled out piecemeal along with a lot of other accusations that were figments of someone's imagination. Second, and more importantly, we knew that without some definition of which previously leaked accusations were being laid to rest, another prosecutor could say he had discovered new evidence of additional wrongdoing, heating up the possibility of another prosecution in the state courts. So I did not contest their putting into the statement everything they thought they had a chance of presenting in a credible fashion.

It is amazing how many times during the past six years that

forty-page statement has been referred to and quoted from—without the slightest reference to the inadmissability of the hearsay and speculation in it, or to my categorical denial of its contents in open court the day it was presented.

There is another thing that needs to be said here. A plea bargain is a bargain for both sides, not just the prosecution, because the prosecutor isn't sure his witnesses will be believed. My enemies have tried to make it appear that it was just a device to gain me favored treatment.

CHAPTER SEVENTEEN

A JOYOUS PARTY IN THE EAST ROOM

President Nixon reacted with a burst of exhilaration on learning he had finally rid himself of his "Agnew problem." Even as my car was conveying me away from the Baltimore courthouse in the early afternoon of October 10, to join my family in mourning the death of my half-brother, the President was reported to have been eagerly engaged in the delightful game of deciding whom he should name as his new Vice-President. Eyewitnesses said he exuded high spirits as he consulted a host of Republican politicians about their suggestions for the choice.

His favorite, I had long ago known, was John Connally. As early as October 6, four days *before* my resignation, the President had asked the former treasury secretary to accept the vice-presidency. Both men knew it would give Connally a clear track to the White House in 1976. Connally wanted it, but he backed away when his enemies in both parties threatened to block his confirmation by the House and Senate and to drag the hearings on for many months. He was too new a boy in school to muster support from the Republicans in Congress, and his recent defection from the Democratic party did not endear him to those on the other side of the aisle.

By choosing Connally, Nixon would have become embroiled in another vicious partisan dispute, exactly the thing he was trying to avoid. So, with reluctance, he had to drop his favorite. He feared controversy would also rage if he chose Nelson Rockefeller, Ronald Reagan, or Barry Goldwater, all of whom were being strongly recommended by their friends. So he quickly settled on Gerald Ford, the amiable Michigan congressman who had achieved popularity, if not great distinction, as the House minority leader.

Nixon officially introduced Ford on the night of October 12 at

201

a White House party, amid laughter and gaiety that made it seem like the celebration of a great election victory—not the aftermath of a stunning tragedy.*

I had become a nonperson. The Vice-President, who had shared the tremendous victory in the national election less than a year before, was suddenly hurled into outer darkness, into the limbo of forgotten men. Mr. Nixon enthusiastically looked forward to making a new start without me and finally freeing himself from his Watergate entanglement. He hoped soon to be rid of the Special Prosecutor, Archibald Cox, who was pressing for the release of the incriminating tapes. Nixon naïvely believed that by throwing me to the wolves, he had appeased his enemies and they would stop clamoring for his blood. But he had merely whetted their appetite for more.

Within eight days came the so-called "Saturday Night Massacre." Richardson resigned as Attorney General and Bill Ruckelshaus as his deputy, after refusing to obey the President's order to fire Cox. Robert Bork, the Solicitor General, was persuaded to carry out the presidential execution, and the surprised president suddenly found himself in the path of a hurricane. The furious anger which he stirred up by kicking out Cox, led straight toward his inevitable resignation the following August—to avoid impeachment.

It is possible that I lost not only the vice-presidency, but the presidency. For if I had carried on my battle for vindication through the impeachment process and the courts, I would still have been Vice-President at the time Nixon resigned. If he had resigned I would then have become President. This was the one event, as I have stressed, which Richardson was determined to prevent no matter what happened.

Of course, Mr. Nixon could have used my refusal to resign as an argument for his staying in office. This would have been the more likely result. It is ironic that Nixon thought he was helping himself by shoving me out; the truth is that if he had kept me in office, he might have held onto the presidency. His enemies

---

* *Washington Star* columnist Betty Beall wrote, "What other President tossed a joyous party in the East Room to announce a new Vice-President even while the pictures of the former Vice-President were being removed from the walls of the West Wing?"

had to get rid of me first, then move a malleable man into the vice-presidency (Gerald Ford admirably filled the bill), then shove Nixon out and Ford in. They followed the script in one-two-three order with perfect precision.

Too late President Nixon realized he had been suckered by his foes into going along with my ruination, ostensibly to save himself. In his *Memoirs* (page 1004) he says:

"Certainly the first major mistake was the appointment of Richardson as Attorney General. Richardson's weakness, which came to light during the Cox firing, should have been apparent."

He adds: "The Agnew resignation was necessary although a very serious blow, because, while some thought that his stepping aside would take some of the pressure off the effort to get the President, all it did was open the way to put pressure on the President to resign as well. This is something we have to realize; that any accommodation of opponents in this kind of a fight does not satisfy—it only brings on demands for more."

My resignation left me literally destitute. I lost not only my salary but my right to a substantial government pension, and soon thereafter, my means of earning a living as a lawyer. Frank Jamieson, a good friend, offered me a consultancy in his privately owned aerospace firm. When my enemies discovered I was on a retainer there, some stockholders and directors of the Jamieson firm's associated corporation put pressure on him to discharge me. I resigned to save him from embarrassment. This sort of extra punishment was so unfair, it made me furious. They had knocked me down: now they wanted to kick me.

Soon after I satisfied the ten-thousand-dollar maximum fine imposed on me, the I.R.S. contacted me and demanded a hundred and fifty thousand dollars in back taxes, interest, and penalties. I said I had no money. They told my lawyer I should get it out of my "shoe box"—which, of course, did not exist.

The I.R.S. agents said, "If you don't pay this, we will go to court and lift your passport." As I was even then arranging to go overseas to try to develop some international business, I had to have that passport. I was desperate.

So I called Frank Sinatra's lawyer, Mickey Rudin, of Beverly Hills, California, to see if he had any ideas that might let me keep my passport and gain some time. He said he would think about it.

The next day, Mickey called me and said, "Frank thinks you should pay."

"Well, dammit, Mickey," I said, "I don't have the money; I can't pay."

"What is your bank and account number?" Mickey asked. "Frank has directed me to put two hundred thousand dollars in your account."

I couldn't believe my good fortune, or that anyone could be so considerate and generous.

"That's wonderful," I exclaimed. "But where is the promissory note?"

Mickey laughed and said, "Don't insult the man. I wouldn't even dare ask him about that. He knows you will pay him back when you can. That's all he needs."

The day after I resigned, Frank had sent me thirty thousand dollars to pay my ten-thousand-dollar fine and my family expenses until I could find some way to make a living. As time went by and my business improved through my numerous trips overseas, I earned an adequate income and paid back the last of the Sinatra loans in 1978.

Meanwhile, the prosecutors continued to besmirch my name. U.S. Attorney George Beall told the press he had considered charging me with "obstruction of justice" because of my complaints in early 1973 to Richard Kleindienst, then the Attorney General, that the Maryland investigation might have been politically motivated. Beall admitted that his staff disagreed over whether or not these calls were an attempt to obstruct justice, and even the implacable Barnet Skolnik thought the matter was too weak to pursue. Kleindienst himself said (in the *Washington Star-News*, Nov. 1, 1973) he never got the impression I was trying to get him to stop any investigation of myself. Of course, I was not doing any such thing, and the record proves that never—not even when Wolff and Matz were making veiled threats to drag me into their mess—did I use my influence as Vice-President to obstruct the inquiry.

Much has been written about my close relationship with Frank Sinatra. It is not a friendship of very long standing, but from the beginning it was one of those rare meshings of two personalities that create extremely close bonds.

I met Francis during the 1970 Thanksgiving holiday. Judy and

I were staying at a friend's house at Palm Springs. I had just finished playing golf at Canyon Country Club. As I walked off the eighteenth green, Peter Malatesta, one of my staff members, was standing there talking to Mr. Sinatra, and he introduced us. We had a drink in the locker room. Frank said he was sorry he had to leave Palm Springs that evening, but he invited Judy and me to lunch with his family at his home in Rancho Mirage the following day. It was there that we met Nancy, Sr., Nancy, Jr., and her husband-to-be, Hugh Lambert, and Tina Sinatra. We found his family warm and relaxing.

From this casual beginning came many other meetings. Soon it became understood that whenever I was in Palm Springs, the Sinatra house would be home base. We played golf together often, and we spent hours just sitting and talking about our experiences. I recall vividly one night we were sitting in his study talking. Suddenly I said, "What's that?" Everyone was silent and then I laughed. "It's birds," I said. Indeed, it was the chirp of early morning birds greeting the daybreak.

Having both come from Mediterranean stock and similar humble beginnings, we had many attitudes in common. My interest in the popular music of the 1930's and 1940's left me with a good recollection of his work during that period. We felt the same way about this great country that had given us the opportunity to become successful; we were both angry about the cynicism of much of the press; we hated the way the left-wingers were constantly running down the competitive, free-enterprise society that was the real strength of America. In short, we had a lot in common that brought us together.

During the early years of our friendship, certain political allies of mine did everything possible to persuade me that Sinatra was a political liability because of the controversy always surrounding him. They would refer to how the Kennedy family dropped Frank because of hinted ties with the underworld. Some really big people who would normally be in my camp, they said, would shun me unless I put some distance between myself and Sinatra. Of course, I had heard all this garbage that was being circulated about Frank. I didn't believe a word of it. If there had been any substance to it, the decades of effort to destroy him would have borne fruit by then. Also, I knew from discussions with other greats of the entertainment world who revered Sinatra that every entertainer, during those years, began his or her career in nightclubs. Nightclubs were frequented by the underworld big shots: it was impossible for a performer to avoid meeting these people. It was odd, however, that no one pointed out Bing Crosby, Bob Hope, Milton Berle, Joe E. Lewis, Red Skelton, and many others had played the same places and rubbed shoulders with the same people out of necessity. I think I know why Frank is singled out for special attention. Two reasons—he is outspoken and volatile, and he has an Italian name.

In any event, I refused to let politics dictate who my friends were to be, so I rejected that advice. Then in the spring of 1972, something happened that caused me to stand up publicly for Frank.

The House of Representatives Select Committee on Crime had been interrogating a man named Joseph Barbosa, a hardened criminal in the process of "trading up" who had admitted to the murders of twenty-seven people. Barbosa testified that Sinatra had held interests in two hotels as a front for Raymond Patriarca, alleged crime-syndicate head of New England. Patriarca was then in jail on a murder-conspiracy conviction.

The Barbosa statement created quite a sensation in Washington, and several members of the House declared that Sinatra should be brought in to testify. The media were having their usual picnic with the story, with such headlines as "Witness Links Sinatra To Reputed Mafia Figure."

Frank was out of the country at the time. When he heard the reports, he was furious. He returned immediately to confront the committee in a dramatic appearance that quickly put the matter to rest, much to the embarrassment of those who had promoted the credibility of the Barbosa story.

Before Frank testified, the press had been after me to comment on the Barbosa accusations. I strongly defended Frank in spite of the recommendations of most of my political advisers to say nothing. That incident solidified our friendship in the same way his outspoken support of me during my travail has cemented it.

My friend J. Walter Jones suffered a severe penalty for his loyalty to me. As I mentioned previously, he had refused to cooperate with the Baltimore prosecutors by confirming their charges that I had taken illegal money. He said, "I cannot tell a lie to save myself." So this hardworking ex-marine, who had come out of the service to build a highly successful real estate and banking career, was hounded by the "Gang of Four" until they finally landed him on a campaign contribution violation that did not involve me at all. By using the legal bribery of "trading-up," they produced testimony that Jones had solicited an illegal ten-thousand-dollar corporate contribution from The Singer Company for the 1972 Nixon-Agnew campaign. There was no claim that the money was used for anything other than the campaign: it was illegal because it was a corporate contribution.

This is how Jones himself has described the prosecutors' mistreatment of him: "They had literally rooms full of records of every company I was ever involved with. After studying them for six months, the F.B.I. agents decided they had nothing on me and left. But as long as I was alive and saying the prosecutors' charges were not so, I was a threat to them. As chairman of the Nixon-Agnew fund-raising committee for the Eastern region, I was technically at fault for accepting the ten-thousand-dollar contribution from The Singer Company."

Yet why is it that hundreds of similar violations have either been overlooked, or punished with simple fines and probation? The answer is that in Jones's case, they couldn't get him on the "bag man" charges, so they decided to get him on a technicality.

Jones has said: "I was innocent of the nine felony counts which the prosecutors brought against me. Skolnik said that if I won the first case, they would try me on all the other counts. I realized that I was in terrible jeopardy and that I would be harassed for years, so I agreed to plead guilty to the minor charge, expecting that I would draw only probation. Instead, the judge sentenced me to two years and suspended all but ninety days. I went away to the Harford County Detention Center where I served with murderers, rapists, and other kinds of criminals."

Contrast this mistreatment of Jones with the prosecutors' recommendation that there be no jail terms for Hammerman and Green, whose testimony had been so useful to the Baltimore "Gang of Four" in sealing my doom.

District Attorney George Beall told the court that his "extraordinary depth of feeling" had almost led him to bring no charges at all against these two witnesses who were so vital to his case. (Beall's "depth of feeling" for Green might have been linked to the fact that his brother was an employee of Green's company and that Green had been a racetrack crony of his father's.)

As part of their negotiated deal, Hammerman and Green each pleaded guilty to one count of interfering with the administration of the tax laws. All other potential charges against them were dropped. Technically, they faced maximum penalties of three years in prison and five-thousand-dollar fines. But they were smiling on their way to the courtroom because they had their deal with the prosecutors, who would recommend that they be spared any prison sentence.

Skolnik had led Hammerman and Green to believe their guilty pleas would not be followed by jail terms. After a pre-sentence conference with the federal judges in the case on October 11, 1974, Skolnik told Hammerman's lawyer, Sidney Sachs, that the judges appeared ready to receive such a recommendation from the prosecutors. Skolnik said the court had "given the signal," and the two defendants relied upon his assurance that everything was fixed.

However, the three-judge court at Baltimore on November 25, 1974, gave them a stunning surprise—prison terms of eighteen months for Hammerman and a year for Green, and a five-thousand-dollar fine apiece. The judges said "the fact that Agnew did not receive a prison sentence is not a sufficient reason" for letting Hammerman and Green get off with merely a fine.

Green served four months of his term and then was paroled. Hammerman appealed.

The Fourth Circuit Court of Appeals at Richmond, Virginia, October 30, 1975, overturned Hammerman's prison term on the grounds the prosecutors had illegally given him assurances, which he considered a guarantee, that he would never go to prison. The appeals court, referring to Skolnik, said an assistant prosecutor had "most emphatically" assured Hammerman, the judges had given the "signal" they would impose no prison term; and on the basis of that false assurance, Hammerman had pleaded guilty to the one tax charge. The government did not deny that point.

Ruling that these comments had "misled" Hammerman, the

appeals court judges said, "We view the prosecutor's prediction as likely to inculcate belief and reliance and therefore as an essential element of the plea bargain. That the prosecutor lacked power to implement the prediction made it an 'unlawful' promise."

The appeals court sent Hammerman's case back for a new trial. But the prosecutors were so determined to let him off that they never brought him back to trial. The Justice Department formally abandoned the charge on April 22, 1977, a year and a half after the appeals court decree. A department memorandum states that the U.S. Attorney's office in Baltimore desired to dismiss the charge for two reasons. "The first is that the lenient treatment accorded to former Vice-President Spiro Agnew should in effect constitute a 'ceiling' with regard to the disposition of Mr. Hammerman's case, because of the fact that Hammerman's truthful cooperation with law enforcement officials was essential to achieving the primary result in the Agnew prosecution. Second, there is now no assurance whatever that Hammerman would choose again to enter a plea of guilty, and, if he did not, any resulting trial of the matter would present many legal problems which it would be in the interest of justice to avoid. The Assistant U.S. Attorneys most familiar with the case are of the opinion that the government is unlikely to prevail if the matter were to be tried."

Liebman and Skolnik explained to the department that they had several "problems" in any possible retrial: "The problem of pretrial delay, the fact that the case is now quite stale, and finally, but by no means least important, the fact that there are serious witness problems. There are no government witnesses who would be willing to testify voluntarily. According to Mr. Liebman, the principal witnesses would be Spiro Agnew and Jerome Wolff. Mr. Liebman advises that both of these individuals are likely to insist on grants of immunity prior to testifying.* Obviously, immunizng Mr. Agnew creates problems both of substance and appearance. Mr. Liebman advises further that other witnesses have expressed extreme reluctance to testify, and he en-

---

* This reason has no substance because, in accepting my nolo contendere plea to the single tax count, Judge Hoffman extinguished all previous rights of the federal government to proceed against me. Therefore, I would need no grant of immunity.

visions that ultimately their testimony will not be terribly beneficial to the government's case. Mr. Skolnik points out that if the
decision is made to go ahead with the retrial, there will be a bar-
rage of motions from Mr. Hammerman's counsel, Sidney Sachs,
Esquire . . . Mr. Skolnik believes that the government is not
likely to prevail at the motion stage, and believes that the negative public appearance which would be created by any proposed
retrial outweighs whatever possible good could come from Hammerman's conviction . . ."

So the case against Hammerman was dropped. When the appellate court revealed Skolnik's illegal inducements to him to
plead guilty, the prosecutors were so embarrassed that they just
sat on the case and never brought him back to trial. Therefore,
I contend the evidence is clear that his testimony against me
was bought with the coin of the highest price, the assurance of
his freedom.

The prosecutors' fanatical zeal to indict prominent Maryland
politicians, even by using tainted evidence, injured another victim: former Congressman Edward A. Garmatz. This highly
respected Baltimore Democrat was indicted in August 1977, on
charges of having taken a fifteen-thousand-dollar bribe from a
shipping company executive to sponsor a bill favorable to that
firm. But the charges were dismissed in January 1978, at the
Justice Department's request, because Garmatz's lawyer, Arnold
Weiner, proved that important evidence had been faked.

Russell T. Baker, Jr., in moving for the dismissal, admitted that
the government's chief witness, Edward Heine, president of the
United States Line, "created false documentation to corroborate
certain parts of his testimony and had tendered it to the government as genuine."

The Washington Star, editorially deploring the "horrendous"
injustice inflicted upon Garmatz, said he had suffered "six months
of appalling pressure and public indignity, not to mention being
ordered to trial in the federal building named in his honor; and
an indictment will remain, unfortunately, tantamount to guilt in
credulous minds."

The *Star*, on January 11, 1978, commended Weiner's charge
that the prosecutors repeatedly played the game of "trading-up,"
offering immunity to some figures under investigation in exchange for their testimony against officials higher up; and as an

example, the paper specifically mentioned "the case of Spiro T. Agnew."

I am still not free of the aftershocks of the case. Several lawsuits were filed against me in the years that have ensued since I resigned. Although these legal actions are frivolous, they have been well funded by my enemies and have cost me thousands of dollars in legal fees and deposition costs, as well as my time and peace of mind.

The most frivolous but the most costly of these vendetta law actions was filed out of pure malice by a Miami lawyer who is also a member of the New York Bar, one Sam Polur. That case, filed in the federal court in Baltimore by Polur himself, sought to put me in jail for alleged violations of probation including such wild charges as conspiring with OPEC to fix oil prices, giving National Security Council secrets to the Arab countries, and accepting a jeweled dagger for my personal use from the late King Faisal of Saudi Arabia. The suit also sought to recover two million dollars in damages because Polur claimed the value of some oil stocks he held had been adversely affected by my alleged connivance with OPEC. (This despite the fact that the stock had appreciated in value.)

This caricature of a law suit, of which a first-year law student would be ashamed to admit authorship, was highly publicized by the press to the great detriment of my business. Each time Polur filed a paper, he distributed it to the press. He appealed each inevitable reverse he experienced, and the matter dragged on for nearly five years before being finally thrown out by the Circuit Court of Appeals in Richmond on May 3, 1979.

An interesting sidelight of this case is that after having one of his numerous motions rejected by the court, Polur in his appeal accused the court reporter, Judge Rozel Thompson, and me of conspiring to forbid him certain transcripts of the proceedings. This should give the reader an idea of how irresponsible Mr. Polur really was. Naturally, this juvenile accusation was thrown out by the appellate court when the facts revealed that the reason for Polur's delay in getting the transcripts was that the court reporter had been ill.

As of this writing, there is still unresolved a civil class-action lawsuit financed by the left-wing Stewart R. Mott & Associates foundation and filed by a group of activist lawyers. They have boasted that they got the idea while discussing me at a cocktail party. (It seems that cocktail parties cause me trouble even though I do not attend them.)

The theory behind this action is that the alleged payments by the engineers who accused me caused the cost of engineering to the state to rise, and thereby made taxes rise. I expect this case, which is primarily another harassing action by my political enemies, will drag on amid expensive maneuvers and will wind up costing me additional thousands in legal fees and costs, not to mention the cost of precious time. As with the Polur case, this one has been highly publicized, both here and overseas, to the harm of my business.

When I tell my friends about these malevolent attempts to further embarrass and harm me, they wonder why I do not file suit against the perpetrators. In the Polur matter, which is now concluded, I am giving that serious thought. However, I must consider the impact of the publicity on my business. I have become rather cynical about my chances of getting a square deal from the major media. For example, when the Polur case was in the accusation stage, it got headlines. When it was thrown out of court, it got five lines on an inside page.

In the summer of 1978, Hammerman and I were ordered to appear in a lawyer's office in Washington to give depositions in the Mott Foundation-financed lawsuit. He came over to me and said, "How are you, Ted?" and extended his hand. I spurned it and said, "I can't shake hands with you. You've got to be kidding."

Jerry Wolff was there, too. I couldn't bring myself to speak to him. At least, Wolff had the sensitivity to avoid contact with me during the time we were thrown together.

My lawyer said, "Since you have an identity of interest in this case, it would be better if you would be nice to Hammerman."

"I'm sorry," I said. "I just can't be nice to him. It's impossible."

"Well," the lawyer said, "at least shake hands with him."

"No," I said, "I just can't."

J. Walter Jones and his wife have told me of a recent encounter they had with Allen Green in an Annapolis restaurant. Jones said he told Green, "You lied. You know you're a liar."

"I never said I gave Ted Agnew kickbacks," Green retorted, according to Jones. "I gave campaign contributions. If they want to take that and turn it around into a bribe, I can't help it. After all, I went to jail."

Besides these bitter encounters, I have had one that made me laugh. When I was in Washington recently, having dinner with a few of my old Secret Service agents, Jules Witcover came over to my table. He is the author of two obviously biased anti-Agnew books. Witcover knelt alongside me at the table and whispered, "I'm sort of an Agnew student. I've written two books about you. I know more about you than anybody else, and I'd like to write the story from your viewpoint."

I burst out laughing every time I think of that incident. After dipping his pen in poison to write two books about me, Witcover had the nerve to ask me to help him write another!

EPILOGUE

After my brother's funeral on Thursday, October 11, I was sorely tempted to go home, close the door on the outside world, and nurse my wounds. But I knew that hiding from reality would be the worst thing I could do. The few days of isolation might stretch into weeks, then months, and eventually destroy me as a productive human being. Of such beginnings recluses are made.

Two days before, I had told Art Sohmer that my choice was to make the best of the situation that existed. Refusing to face my problems would not make them go away. I told Judy and each of our four children that they must be prepared for some very rough times during the coming months. Their innocence of being even remotely connected with the accusations against me would not protect them from the sneers, slights, and thoughtless actions of many people who would be in frequent contact with them. "Do not avoid the public," I urged them. "Whatever you were going to do today had this not happened, do it. You have nothing to be ashamed of and neither do I."

They followed my recommendation. I know only a little of what they endured, but they never complained. They worried, not about themselves, but about me. They set an example that made it possible for me to survive the abrupt slide from top to bottom. Never doubt the importance of the immediate family in a crisis.

There were many things for me to do. I informed the Secret Service that I intended to spend full days in the E.O.B. office both Friday and Saturday. As they prepared the cars for departure, the press made a concerted rush to get in position where our driveway entered the street. They wanted to talk to me, but I had decided to forego any further discussion of events leading to my resignation. I planned to make an address to the American

people on the coming Monday, and I knew this would be televised live by at least two of the networks. That speech would not
answer the really important questions. There was a good reason.
I did not know the answers myself. It would take time for me to
find out exactly what had happened. I let it be known that I
wanted to write a lucid, complete account of what had transpired;
and, until that had been done, I would not discuss the months
preceding my resignation. What I wanted to avoid at all costs
was a haphazard, disjointed presentation of my story. I knew that
complete information would not be available until the collateral
prosecutions then in progress were ended. Of course, I was aware
that certain things had happened that I would never find out
about.

At the office, I called my staff together and explained why I
had been unable to keep them informed or warn them about the
imminence of my resignation. I explained I had to be certain
that no leaks originated in the Vice-President's office. I told them
that I had, as a condition of resignation, insisted on and been
assured they would all be transferred to other federal positions
at no loss of income. Less than a dozen were asked to form a small
transitional staff to work with me to transfer responsibilities to
the new Vice-President and to put my papers in order. I had already decided to give the historical material from my time in the
vice-presidency to the University of Maryland. This was done the
following year. No tax deduction was taken for the gift.

The staff reaction was one of sadness and sympathy, but there
is no doubt some felt betrayed. Nevertheless, despite intense
media probing in the days that followed, I don't know of any
who took a "cheap shot" at me. I was profoundly grateful for
their loyalty under fire.

After a brief period, I moved from the Vice-President's suite
in the Old Executive Office Building to a townhouse just around
the corner at 716 Jackson Place. The house was used occasionally
by former Presidents as a Washington base, and it would serve
as my transition office for the next six months.

Art Sohmer stayed on as the chief of the small transition staff.
Mike Dunn handled the complex and difficult job of liaison with
Vice-President Designate Ford's staff so that the transfer of responsibility was accomplished smoothly. Dunn also saw to the
placement of former members of my staff in suitable new posi-

tions. Both of these important tasks were accomplished with Dunn's usual efficiency.

Under the direction of Sohmer and Dr. Jean E. Spencer, my research specialist and librarian, the tedious but necessary business of transporting, sorting, evaluating, and packing the tens of thousands of letters, position papers, memoranda, directives, speeches, news conferences, and research papers was begun. It took all of the six months allotted and, when we ran out of space, the papers spilled over into the basement of the adjoining townhouse. The scope of the work far exceeded the capacity of my small staff, but, thanks to some enthusiastic and loyal volunteers who came back day after day, we were able to finish it.

During the transition period, I came to work every day at 8:30 A.M. and seldom left before 5 P.M. Usually I was there half a day on Saturdays. There seemed to be a million details to attend to and plenty of decisions to be made. I immersed myself in the work. It kept me from being constantly depressed.

However, I could not take refuge in the nuts-and-bolts work of the transition twenty-four hours a day, and the last quarter of 1973 dragged by like a bad dream in slow motion. It seemed hardly a day passed without bad news. The media were having a wonderful time airing the opinions of anyone they could find who was interested in jumping on me. They wanted to be sure I was not only down but out. It would never do for me to retain enough credibility to burn them again for their excesses.

Powerful enemies were pressing for my disbarment from the practice of law and doing everything they could to see that I would not be employed by any large corporation. The I.R.S. was claiming back taxes, penalties, and interest based on the uncorroborated testimony of my accusers. The state of Maryland was making concurrent tax claims. Prosecutors in some of the Maryland counties and the city of Baltimore were being urged to indict and try me in the state courts.

Despite a clear statement by the Department of Justice that the forty-page statement filed in court contained the entire case against me, rumors were being circulated and reported that there were other, much worse transgressions that had been suppressed. The prosecutors' records, now available, prove this was just malicious hogwash, but it didn't help matters any at the time.

The disbarment preliminaries were moving ahead rapidly, so I retained counsel to represent me. There was no money left in the defense fund, and little did I then realize that it would take me four years to pay the legal fees connected with the disbarment case. My lawyers were excellent. They did not overcharge. It was just that I did not have the money to pay them right away.

I knew I was facing a certain suspension due to the nolo contendere plea on the single tax count, but I wanted to avoid permanent disbarment if at all possible. Other than the last twelve years, which I had spent in full-time political office, the law had been my livelihood. But more than that, I enjoyed the practice of law, and I felt a deep respect for the profession. I had earned my law degree the hard way—in night school while holding down a full-time day job. Interrupted by nearly five years' active duty during World War II, it had taken me seven years to earn the right to practice law. I decided I would not give up that privilege without a fight.

Toward the end of the year, the State Bar Association brought me before a special panel of judges in Annapolis. Precedent favored a suspension, but my enemies brought great pressure to bear. Although the only charge before the panel was the U.S. District Court's finding of guilt on a single tax count, the opinion of the panel and the appellate opinion that followed it left little doubt that the famous forty pages of allegations had had their effect. Early in 1974 I was disbarred and found myself without any visible means of income.

Between the time the panel heard the matter and released its decision, George Beall committed a shocking indiscretion. Many were surprised that it did not bring him censure from the Maryland Court of Appeals, which still had jurisdiction of the case.

Beall told a reporter that the public could be disappointed if I were not disbarred. *The Baltimore Sun* of January 3, 1974, carried the headlines: "Public held to want Agnew disbarment" and "Beall predicts public dismay." Mr. Beall was quoted as saying, "The public expects disbarment and if disbarment is not forthcoming, I think the public could be justifiably disappointed." Beall in the same article admitted, "I know of lawyers who have been suspended in similar cases," yet he publicly called for my disbarment regardless of the fact that no decision had been reached and the case was being held *sub curia* by the judges at the time. Even a first-year law student should have known that it is highly improper for lawyers to comment on any case that the court is in the process of deciding.

Less than a year later, George Beall's appetite for self-aggrandizement again fuzzed his ethical perception. Shortly after President Nixon resigned in August 1974, Beall was lionized at an American Bar Association convention in Honolulu for his role in bringing about my downfall. He made a speech deploring the Watergate scandals and the Agnew case. Excerpts were reprinted in *The Washington Post* as shining examples of a bright young prosecutor's prose.

Dr. Inis L. Claude, Jr., a University of Virginia professor of government, noted a striking similarity between large parts of the speech and an article which former *Wall Street Journal* editor Vermont C. Royster had earlier published in the *American Scholar* magazine.

"It would be sad, indeed," Dr. Claude said in a letter to the *Post*, "if an article billed as an 'Essay on Ethics' should prove to be a piece of stolen literary property."

Indeed, subsequent examination proved that twelve whole paragraphs of Beall's speech had been lifted, word for word, from Royster's article with no attribution whatever. Royster angrily demanded an explanation.

Beall admitted having copied the article without attribution, but said, "I don't feel I've done anything wrong." He added, "I'm troubled by the conclusion that's been automatically drawn that there is plagiarism."

After a wave of criticism in the press, the pious prosecutor telephoned Royster and apologized, saying: "There was a failure of judgment and an error of scholarship on my part."

Thanks to the Sinatra loan, my lawyers were able to settle my disputed tax liabilities for the years 1966–1972, both federal and state, for a little over $160,000. I did not owe the money, but it would have been useless to fight. The press had already convicted me of the allegations in the famous forty-page statement, and I could not stand the new harassment that would result from a highly publicized trial. I needed one thing, urgently—a way to make a living.

Late in 1973, I had hit on the idea of writing a novel. I knew I was not ready to write the real story of my resignation for the reasons stated earlier, even though I had been offered a substantial advance to do a *mea culpa* and condemn the "system that made me go bad."

Obviously, I was not an experienced novelist, but I had two assets: first, I liked to write and did so with reasonable proficiency; and second, I knew the vice-presidency from the inside. I decided to do a novel about a hypothetical Vice-President who was destroyed by his own ambition. I began the task in early 1974, and it proved to be a formidable one. Since a novel is a creative work, and the author brings nothing to it but his imagination and words, I was determined to do the book without help. It was an arduous job, and I gained a respect for novelists that will be with me forever. *The Canfield Decision* was finally finished and published in 1976. My enemies attacked the book in two inconsistent ways. Some said it was the worst example of prose ever seen. Others said it was too well written for me to have authored it. I challenged the latter group, but they refused the confrontation. The book became a best seller.

The year following my departure from office produced a staggering array of new difficulties for my family and me. Judy's mother, Mrs. R. Elinor Judefind, had been living with us since she became too ill to maintain her own home. Early one morning, just about a month after the death of my brother, she experienced a massive cerebral hemorrhage. She died the following day without regaining consciousness.

We had moved from the Sheraton Park apartment into a new home in the Maryland suburb of Kenwood in June 1973. The Secret Service occupied about 30 percent of the house for the command post of the vice-presidential detail. With their services soon to be curtailed and my mother-in-law no longer with us, we didn't need such a big place. Moreover, we couldn't possibly afford it, heavily mortgaged as it was.

I decided that when the transition office was closed, I would open a small office at Crofton, Maryland. We wanted to get away from the constant scrutiny of the Washington media, so we found a home we liked in Arnold, Maryland—about twenty minutes by car from Crofton.

We were getting ready to move in the spring of 1974 when fate dealt another blow. Judy became ill and had to enter St. Joseph's Hospital in Baltimore County for an operation. Somehow, with the help of friends, we were able to make the move. We were really touched that several members of the Secret Service detail gave up their day off, hired a small truck, and helped with the miscellaneous items that the van couldn't handle.

The Crofton office was opened with the help of my secretary, Mary Ellen Warner, who turned down a much higher paying federal job to help me make a new beginning. Another former member of the transition staff, Stephanie Barry, helped out part-time and was invaluable in assisting with the preparation of the transcript of *The Canfield Decision*. Stephanie later became my secretary when Mary Ellen took another job. About this time Walter Warner, a retired Air Force officer, joined me as an officer of Pathlite, Inc., my small company. All three of these people deserve a great deal of credit for their steadfast loyalty under very difficult circumstances.

Through some old friends in the Washington diplomatic community, I had been quietly investigating the possibility of business ventures overseas. I felt I could be valuable as a consultant to companies interested in developing foreign markets. My travels had gained me many excellent contacts in the Middle East and Asia, and some of these people had shown an interest in helping me. I began to travel and to experience some moderate success.

While I was in the Middle East in May 1974, I received a frightening phone call in the middle of the night. Judy had been taken to the hospital suddenly. The operation she had undergone three weeks before had caused blood clots that had broken loose and lodged in her lung and liver. Had not the clots been small, these embolisms could have been fatal. I grabbed the first available plane and flew home immediately. My wife was hospitalized for fifteen days and did not fully recover her strength until the end of the year.

My business has expanded geographically, and I now find myself traveling frequently to Europe, the Middle East, Asia, and South America. Sometimes I am able to take Judy along on a trip, but usually economics and travel conditions force me to go alone. It is a lonely business, and I hope to reduce the need to move about so much in the future.

The passage of time has diminished, but not eliminated, the efforts of my adversaries to cause me trouble. In 1976, Mr. Polur brought his suit to have me put behind bars and obliterate all my assets. As I said before, he was unsuccessful, but it did cost me valuable time and legal fees. At the time of this writing, the Stewart E. Mott Foundation suit is still open in the Anne Arundel County, Maryland, Circuit Court. It continues to be a source of irritation, but I intend to fight it through to the bitter end.

Since the disaster period, 1973–1976, things have become somewhat better for the Agnews. My business has done quite well, but I hasten to debunk the often promulgated assertion that I am a millionaire. Numerous speculations, mostly inaccurate, about what I am doing have appeared in the media. I have not bothered to correct them, nor will I here. One thing I have learned is that a sure way to destroy your business is to discuss it with curious reporters.

According to published reports, most of the people who framed me are doing very well indeed. In September 1978, Bud Hammerman reentered the mortgage banking and land development field. He will represent, say the news accounts, such prestigious lenders as the New York Bank for Savings, National Life Insurance Company of Vermont, Home Beneficial Life Insurance Company and the Life and Casualty Company of Tennessee.

The Maryland Board of Registration for Professional Engineers, et al, after hearings, suspended the licenses of Lester Matz and Jerome Wolff. However, a Baltimore County Circuit Court judge, Marvin J. Land, reversed the suspensions on a legal technicality. It seemed the Board failed to set hearings on the charges within the six-month period required by law. Land's ruling was not appealable to the Maryland Court of Appeals, so neither Matz nor Wolff lost his right to practice engineering, despite their admissions of far-reaching criminal misconduct. Yet the public impression persists that I, who must live with a criminal record and suffer the permanent loss of my right to practice my profession, got off easy.

And I must live with another, more subtle punishment. I cannot walk through a hotel lobby or down a street and simply be one of the crowd. Although I have none of the benefits of public life—no pension, no former-statesman status, no diplomatic passport to ease my comings and goings in my international business affairs—I have retained a major impediment of public life. I have no privacy because I am recognized all over the world. When people stop and stare at you, you know some are thinking: "There goes Agnew, the guy who was kicked out of the vice-presidency."

I do not want to leave the impression that I have been abused or vilified by the general public. Quite to the contrary, hundreds of people have gone out of their way to reaffirm their confidence in me and say an encouraging word. But I am not so naïve that I don't recognize that there are thousands of others who believe everything bad that has been said against me. It's just something I have to live with—part of the continuing punishment for crimes never committed.

Our first visits to the Palm Springs, California, area in the late 1960's had convinced Judy and me that it was the place to which we'd like to retire. In 1976, we decided not to wait for retirement. My work required no particular situs, so why not live where we enjoyed it most? So we sold our home in Arnold, Maryland, and bought a place in Rancho Mirage, just a few miles from Palm Springs. In October 1977, we became California residents.

We thoroughly enjoy our life here in the Coachella Valley desert. Of course, we retain a great affection for our home state of Maryland, and we look forward to sharing the summer months with family and friends there. However, the above time allocations are not realistic because travel takes me away from both places too frequently.

People ask me, "How is your life now?" That is the most frequent question put to me, in one form or another, since the fateful events of 1973. It is an easy question to avoid but not an easy question to answer—particularly when one faces the unspoken meaning of the question. What they want to know is how it feels to be catapulted suddenly from a position of honor to one of dishonor—to shoot the rapids from fame to notoriety.

The first two years were very painful; the wound was raw and easily inflamed by new irritations. Nights were the worst. There is a vulnerability about waking in a dark room and rediscovering despair.

I did my best to keep my feelings hidden and present a controlled demeanor. I reminded myself that I still had the love of a good wife, family, and loyal friends. Somehow I muddled through those years.

As time went on, it became less acute—more like chronic pain. I adjusted to it, learned to live with it. Things will never be the same, and I have accepted that. I can truthfully say I am happy now, but there is a small black cloud that intrudes on my happiness at unpredictable times.

Writing this book has been wonderful therapy for me. Confronting the prosecutorial records and the contemporary reporting of the media initially brought an emotional reaction that made me physically ill. But continued exposure lessened my sensitivity. Now I can look at the whole thing more objectively.

Yes, there is still a trace of bitterness, but no desire for revenge. Hatred is a dead end street, and I want to continue on down the road.

APPENDIX

Selected letters, memoranda, and statements from the files of the United States Attorney in Baltimore that became available under the Freedom of Information Act. These samples represent no more than a fraction of one percent of the complete Agnew file.

UNITED STATES GOVERNMENT
DEPARTMENT OF JUSTICE

Memorandum

TO: Baltimore County DATE: April 13, 1973

FROM: Russell T. Baker, Jr.
Assistant U. S. Attorney

SUBJECT: ██████████

Less than one minute ago I talked with ████████ ███████████ at Matz, Childs. I placed the call to him. I advised him of my name and title and informed that I knew that he had been served with a subpoena. I said to him in almost exactly the following words: ████████ ███████████ I want to advise you in a formal way that you're in a lot of trouble. What I think you should do is to get yourself a lawyer, if you have not already retained a lawyer, a criminal lawyer, and have him get in touch with me as soon as possible. There was no further discussion. The telephone call took place at approximately 3:20 p.m. on Friday, April 13, 1973.

While reading the draft of the Baker memo of May 18, 1973, on the pages that follow, keep in mind the prosecutors maintained they had never offered Matz and Childs immunity.

Form DJ-150
(Ed. 4-26-65)

F4

UNITED STATES GOVERNMENT   DEPARTMENT OF JUSTICE

Memorandum

TO   :   Baltimore County   DATE: May 18, 1973
                                                   Dictated: 11:20 a.m.
                                                   on May 18, 1973

FROM :   Russell T. Baker, Jr.
          Assistant U. S. Attorney

SUBJECT: Conversation with Joe Kaplan About a Possible Agreement With Mr.
          Matz and Mr. Childs

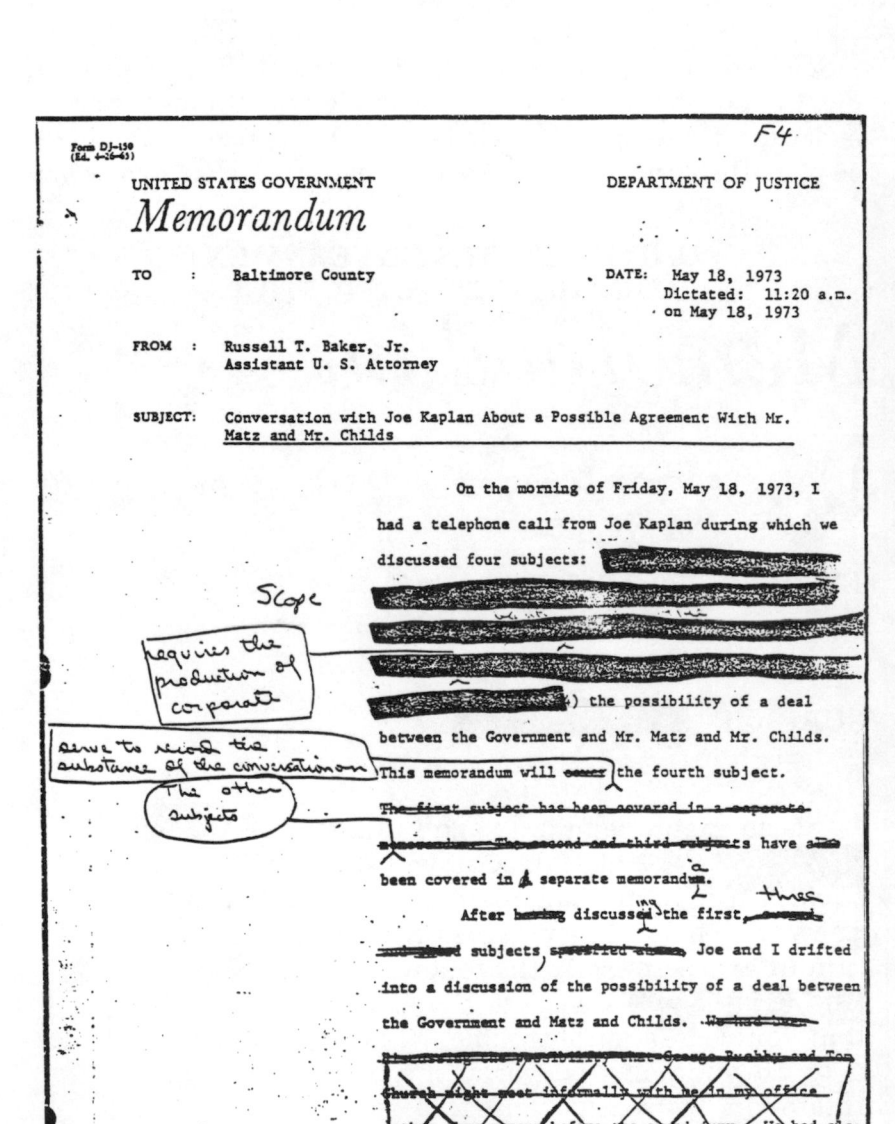

      On the morning of Friday, May 18, 1973, I
had a telephone call from Joe Kaplan during which we
discussed four subjects: ▓▓▓▓▓▓▓▓▓▓▓

Scope

requires the production of corporate

▓▓▓▓▓▓▓▓▓▓▓▓▓▓▓▓▓▓▓▓▓▓▓▓▓▓

▓▓▓▓▓▓▓▓▓▓▓▓▓▓▓▓▓▓▓▓▓▓

▓▓▓▓▓▓▓▓▓▓▓) the possibility of a deal

serve to reach the substance of the conversation on between the Government and Mr. Matz and Mr. Childs.

The other subjects This memorandum will ~~cover~~ the fourth subject.

~~The first subject has been covered in a separate~~
~~memorandum. The second and third subject~~s have a̶l̶s̶o̶
been covered in ⍺ separate memorandu~~m~~.

      After ~~having~~ discuss_ing_ the first, three

~~and third~~ subjects, ~~specified above,~~ Joe and I drifted

into a discussion of the possibility of a deal between

the Government and Matz and Childs. ~~We had been~~

~~discussed the possibility that George Beebly and Tom~~
~~Church might meet informally with he in my office~~
~~rather than appear before the grand jury. We had also~~
~~discussed the fact that Joe Kaplan continued to repre~~

-2-

~~potential defendants and also potential witnesses against those defendants, a situation to which this office has objected. Joe advised me that neither he nor his clients had ever in any way attempted to persuade employees of Matz, Childs to be anything other than completely truthful witnesses with the Government.~~

During ~~this~~ the discussion, _(of the third topic,)_ I advised Joe that ~~his clients~~ _Matz and Childs_ would definitely be indicted at least for several violations of Title 26, and probably for other crimes as well. Joe told me that he and ~~his~~ _Matz, Childs and their_ clients had known for some time that ~~they~~ would probably be indicted. ~~Although his clients were willing to be~~ completely truthful and cooperative with the Government, Joe had made the judgment early in the investigation that ~~his clients~~ _they_ did not possess information in which the Government would be interested. ~~I was surprised at this indication that his clients were interested in cooperating because very early in this investigation I had told Joe that his clients could have immunity if they were willing to cooperate.~~ _and he had_ ~~He had~~ declined that invitation. ~~During my telephone conversation with him I reminded him that he had declined this invitation~~ _Joe then_ explained ~~once more~~ that his ~~clients~~ _were in a position to incriminate_ ~~clients could incriminate against~~ William E. Fornoff, the Administrative Officer of Baltimore County

Matz and Childs

Matz and Childs

He said that Matz and Childs ~~=~~ from an early point in the investigation had indicated to him their willingness to be

This statement surprised me because, as I reminded Joe, I had advised him very early in the investigation that Matz and Childs might be able to earn immunity if they were to cooperate fully and truthfully,

-3-

Joe had

but, ~~he did~~ not offer such testimony to us because
~~he believed that we would not be prepared to give~~
~~immunity to his clients for this testimony because we~~
~~already had sufficient evidence against Fornoff. His~~
~~clients could give no testimony with respect to Dale~~
~~Anderson. Joe then told me that his clients could give~~
~~testimony against~~ Vice-President Agnew but that he
~~did~~ not offer ~~the~~ *ed such* testimony to us because he ~~did not~~
~~believe~~ *this assumed not investigating* we were interested in ~~pursuing persuing~~ Agnew.
I ~~immediately~~ asked Joe what he meant *by that* and he stated
that he had ~~not believed~~ *assumed* that this office would *not* be
interest*ed* in ~~serious~~ investigating the man who is now
the Vice-President of the United States. ~~I told Joe~~
~~that he was wrong then and that he was definitely~~
~~wrong now.~~ I ~~told him~~ *replied* that this office was interested
in doing its job, which is ~~in~~ investigating and ~~in~~ prosecuting ~~any~~ crimes, ~~that~~
~~come~~ within the applicable federal statutes of
limitations. *I stated that had* ~~Since~~ Agnew left Baltimore County *public office* in
1966, all ~~applicable~~ federal statutes of limitations
~~applicable~~ had run by the time this investigation began, ~~but that~~
and that Agnew ha~~d~~ *therefore not* ~~never been~~ a subject of this investigation.
I assured ~~him,~~ however, that we would ~~be interested in~~
Joe
~~investigating and prosecuting Agnew for any crimes~~
~~committed by him within the statutory period. On~~
~~several other occasions during the conversation I~~
~~assured # Joe~~ that this office was prepared to in-

*he had
heard that
we were
saying that
we already
had enough
evidence against
Fornoff, and he
therefore believed
that we would
not be willing
to offer Joe Bailies
immunity for
such evidence. He
had not offered
us testimony
against Dale
Anderson because
his clients had
stated to him
that they were
not in a
position to
incriminate
Anderson. Joe
then mentioned
that his clients
were in a position to incriminate*

-4-   — or anyone else --

vestigate and prosecute Agnew, for any, ~~federal~~ crimes *which may* ~~have been~~ committed within the statutory period.

Joe then indicated that, ~~his client~~ *Matz and Childs* might very well be interested in, *negotiating* ~~reaching an agreement~~ with the Government with respect to, *possible* testimony against Agnew.

I ~~again~~ repeated this office's willingness to pursue any crimes committed within the statutory period.

Joe, *stated* ~~told me~~ that ~~his clients had involvement with the~~ ~~had dealings~~

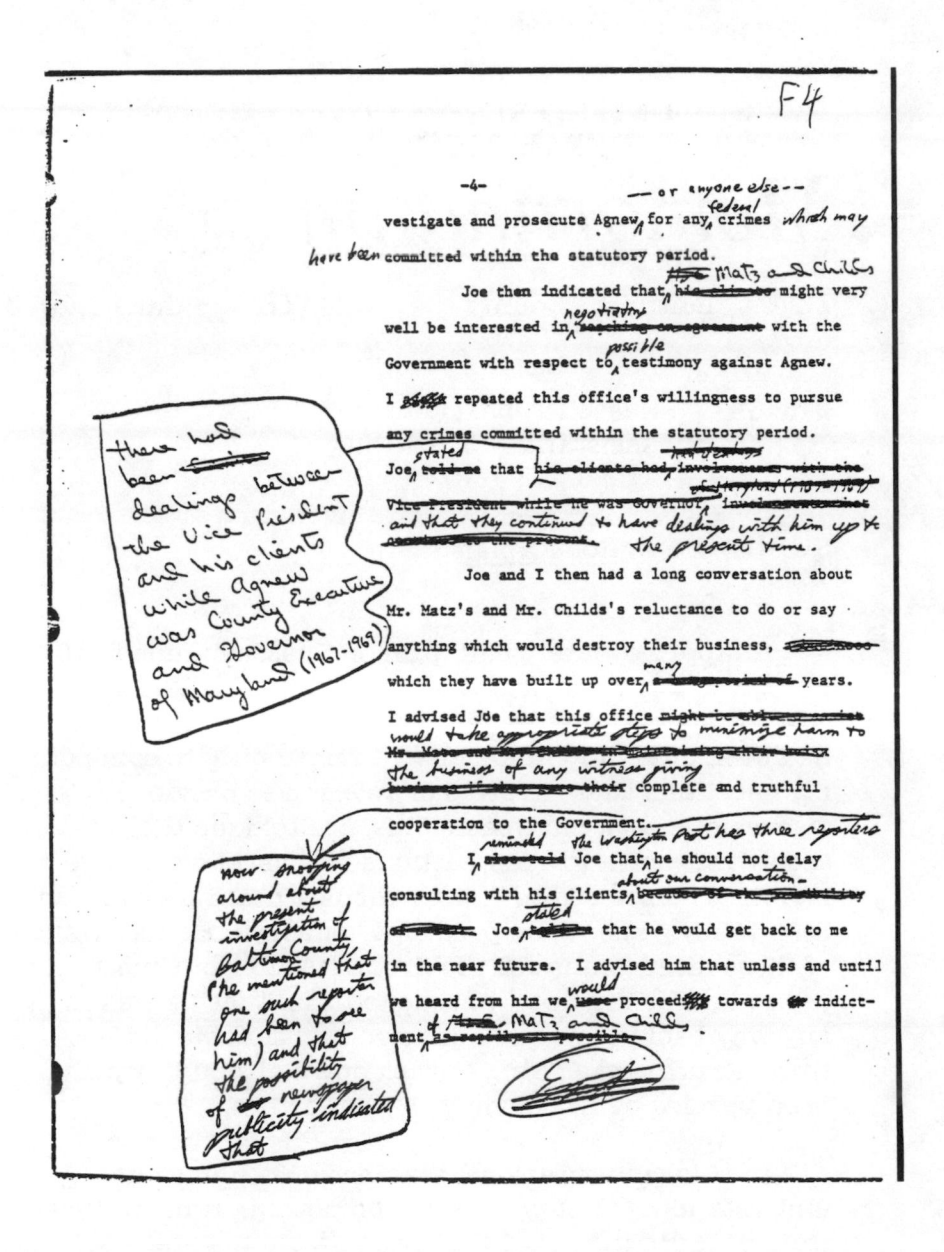

there had been ~~some~~ dealings between the Vice President and his clients while Agnew was County Executive and Governor of Maryland (1967-1969)

~~Vice President while he was Governor~~ ~~involvement that~~ *and that they continued to have dealings with him up to* ~~continues to the present~~ *the present time.*

Joe and I then had a long conversation about Mr. Matz's and Mr. Childs's reluctance to do or say anything which would destroy their business, ~~a business~~ which they have built up over, *many* ~~a period of~~ years.

I advised Joe that this office ~~might to civil contact~~ *would take appropriate steps to minimize harm to* ~~Mr. Matz and Mr. Childs and to protect their long-established business~~ *the business of any witness giving* ~~business if they gave their~~ complete and truthful cooperation to the Government.

now snooping around about the present investigation of Baltimore County (he mentioned that one such reporter had been to see him) and that the possibility of ~~the~~ newspaper publicity indicated that

I, *remarked* ~~also told~~ Joe that, *the Washington Post has three reporters* he should not delay consulting with his clients, *about our conversation.* ~~because of the possibility~~

~~I told~~ Joe, *stated* ~~told me~~ that he would get back to me in the near future. I advised him that unless and until we heard from him we, *would* ~~were~~ proceed ~~ing~~ towards ~~the~~ indictment ~~of~~ *of Matz and Childs.* ~~as rapidly as possible.~~

This memo indicates how eager Joseph H.H. Kaplan was to deliver me to the U.S. Attorney in order to save his clients, Matz and Childs. Kaplan did not even tell Arnold Weiner he was talking to the prosecutors privately.

UNITED STATES GOVERNMENT
DEPARTMENT OF JUSTICE

Memorandum

TO: Baltimore County   DATE: June 6, 1973

FROM: Russell T. Baker, Jr.
Assistant U. S. Attorney

SUBJECT: Joe Kaplan

At approximately 6:45 p.m. on Tuesday, June 5, 1973, I received a telephone call at home from Joe Kaplan. He advised me that during our conference that afternoon he had been quite uncomfortable in responding to some of my questions that involved or referred to previous discussions between Joe and me. Joe told me that in accordance with my instructions of several weeks ago he had never disclosed to Weiner the fact that he and I had been talking about the possibility of a deal. He told Weiner of these discussions for the first time after our meeting yesterday. He did not want me to think that he was in any way backing down. I assured him that we did not think that he was going to back down although we had been puzzled by his obvious discomforture.

In this conversation I reaffirmed with Joe our understanding that we were to do nothing until we heard from him. He indicated that he expected that he would be back to us in a couple of days. He also told me that the reason for the delay was to allow Arnold time that he needed in order to work on Wolff to get him to cooperate.

United States Department of Justice

UNITED STATES ATTORNEY
DISTRICT OF MARYLAND
405 UNITED STATES COURT HOUSE
FAYETTE AND CALVERT STREETS
BALTIMORE, MARYLAND 21202

June 8, 1973

Joseph H. H. Kaplan, Esquire
1800 Mercantile Bank and
   Trust Building
21 Hopkins Plaza
Baltimore, Maryland 21201

         Re: Lester Matz and John C. Childs

Dear Mr. Kaplan:

    At a meeting you had with me and other
representatives of this office on Tuesday, June 5, 1973, we
discussed the possibility that an agreement might be
negotiated under which your clients would furnish to the
Government certain information that they now possess.
You refused, however, to disclose at that time any of the
details of this information other than the identity of one
of the individuals to whom the information relates. On
the basis of this extremely limited disclosure, you have
asked me to indicate if this office would be prepared to
grant your clients total immunity in exchange for their
information.

    I have concluded that I cannot in the proper exercise
of my responsibilities make any representations to you on
the basis of such limited disclosures. As you know, your
clients are presently among the subjects of an
investigation by this office and a federal grand jury. This

investigation has produced evidence of several serious offenses which your clients may have committed, in addition to those offenses about which they may now be prepared to disclose information. In such circumstances this office must refuse as a matter of policy to make representations of potential Government concessions before we have even received hypothetical potential disclosures. Any representation made by this office that was based upon disclosures as limited and general as those made so far by you would, in our judgment and in light of our experience, create an enormous potential for mutual misunderstanding and subsequent dispute.

Therefore, this office is prepared to enter into negotiations with you and your clients only under the terms and conditions detailed in my letters to you of June 7, 1973. I fail to see how the detailed factual disclosures required by those procedures will prejudice your clients in any way, given the protections expressly provided for in paragraph (2) of those letters. Generally, those procedures have been used throughout this investigation and are used routinely in this office. It seems to me important and appropriate for this office not to deviate from such well established procedures.

Sincerely yours,

George Beall
United States Attorney

UNITED STATES GOVERNMENT
DEPARTMENT OF JUSTICE

Memorandum

TO: Grand Jury Investigation   DATE: July 17, 1973
                                              RSL:AC
                             Dictated: July 19, 1973

FROM: Ronald S. Liebman

SUBJECT: ALLAN GREEN

    Tim Baker and I met today with Brendan Sullivan, an associate in Edward Bennett Williams Washington law firm. Mr. Sullivan had advised Baker in a previous telephone conversation that his office represents Allan Green. At this meeting, Sullivan again advised us that his office represents Allan and Max Green. He informed us that the corporation of which the Greens' are principals is represented by the Baltimore law firm of Weinberg and Green.

    Sullivan was advised that we had two matters to discuss. First, he was advised that Allan and Max Green, as well as the corporation, were involved in difficulties with this office for the years 1968, 1969, and possibly 1970. He was also advised that the difficulties were mostly, but not exclusively, criminal tax violations. Second, Sullivan was advised that Allan Green is the subject of an investigation into corrupt activities participated in by him on both the State and Federal level for the years 1969 through 1970.

Sullivan was also informed that no final decisions as to who would be indicted and for what have been made by this office. All of the subjects of the investigation, through their attorneys, are being advised about their status. We are, Baker advised Sullivan, willing to explore whether or not our relationship with people like Green will be a totally adversary one. It was made very clear to Sullivan that we are not offering anything at all at this point in time. If Green is interested in exploring whether or not the relationship between the Government and him will not be a totally adversary one, there are certain procedural steps which must be followed. Baker also advised Sullivan that since Green is not involved alone in these matters we are negotiating with other people. Green, Sullivan was informed, should realize that because of this he does not have a lot of time to agonize over what decision he should make. Baker also advised Sullivan that he would be well advised to inform Green that we are not just fishing with respect to information of corrupt activities performed by his client.

Sullivan informed us that it was always possible to negotiate. He requested that we advise him what we are looking for and what our guidelines are. He was advised that we were looking for information concerning corrupt activities by Green at the State level for the years 1967 and 1968. Sullivan requested us to advise him what people Green allegedly conducted these corrupt activities. Baker advised him that some of the people he participated in these corrupt activities with were Governor Agnew, Jerome Wolf, and I. H. Hammerman.

Baker next advised Sullivan that the Government does not and will not buy half a witness. Therefore, if any relationship does develop between the Government and Green, we would want to know about Green's relationship with Dale Anderson, Joe Alton, Hess, Rogers, Mandel, George Lewis, Dave Fisher, and Joe Jacobs. With respect to Alton and Jacobs, Baker advised Sullivan that we were interested in the years 1966 to the present. The name of Bernie Warner in relation to Baltimore City corruption was also given to Sullivan.

Sullivan was advised by Baker that we are interested in Green's personal tax difficulties.

Baker, upon Sullivan's request, advised him of the guidelines which this office will follow with respect to any negotiations which will be conducted. Specifically, he was advised that the guidelines would be formalized in a letter spelling out the terms and conditions under which negotiations would be conducted with this office. He was advised that the letter must be signed by both the client and the attorney. Following the signing of the letter, the attorney would make substantive disclosures to us. Following that, the client himself would meet with us and convey his information to us and make himself subject to cross-examination. He would also provide any documents or other corroborative materials, including the names of corroborative witnesses to us. After these steps have been followed, Baker advised Sullivan that the Government would then be in a position to commit itself to an agreement, if any, with Green. Sullivan was also advised that the letter states that the disclosures given to the Government would not be used either directly or indirectly against the client. Sullivan was also advised that the Government would make no concessions, if any were to be made at all, up front, before the Government knew what we were buying.

Sullivan was advised that George Beall was not present at this meeting because his brother works with the Green company and it was Mr. Beall's feeling that, out of an abundance of caution, he would not attend the meeting so as to adversely affect either the investigation or, to in any way embarrass either his brother or the Green corporation.

The sensitive problem of publicity was discussed with Sullivan. He was advised that we have had newspaper reporters sniffing around our office. He was also advised that we do not want publicity at this stage of the investigation. Sullivan was very tactfully but firmly advised that he should stay away from newspaper reporters with respect to the information he had gained during the course of this meeting.

Sullivan asked us in terms that he described as "informally" what we would do for his client if his client would give us substantive information. He was advised by Tim that immunity was possible, depending upon what his client would deliver to the Government. Sullivan asked who in this investigation would decide on whether or not someone would receive immunity and he was told that with respect to Green, the decision would be made by Barney Skolnik, Tim Baker and myself. Baker advised Sullivan that it would be possible for his client to earn transactional immunity.

Sullivan next asked if Max Green would fit within the same sort of negotiation pattern described above and mentioned by us with respect to Allan Green. He advised that this was possible, depending upon the corroborative nature of Max Green's testimony, if any. Baker advised Sullivan that because of the familial relationship between Allan and Max Green, some sort of a mutually acceptable deal could be struck. Sullivan next inquired as to the possible negotiated status that the corporation could be placed in and he was advised that the range of possible relationships went from pleading to a criminal offense all the way to being wrapped up in a total deal.

Baker advised Sullivan that at an appropriate point in negotiations, if any negotiation should ensue, Sullivan, or whichever attorney handles this matter for Green, would be told "how it looks".

With respect to the time table and the necessity for quick action, Sullivan was advised that not everyone gets immunity and that time is a factor re: who cooperates, who comes in first and with what.

The meeting concluded by Sullivan advising us that he would talk to his client and contact us after doing this.

The following is an excerpt from an early draft of the Allen Green statement. Most of the last paragraph was deleted from the next draft of the statement.

At some point during 1966, Mr. Agnew first mentioned to me the possibility that he might run for Governor. He told me that he was worried about whether he could raise the substantial amounts of money necessary for a successful campaign because his personal financial resources were severely limited. I understood from my conversations with him that the County Executive's salary was small and that he had very little money.

Shortly before Mr. Agnew's formal announcement of his candidacy, he called me and asked me to have lunch with him. As usual, we met at Thomsen's. There he told me that he had decided to run for Governor if he could raise enough money for the campaign. I recall that he believed that it would be necessary for him to raise approximately $250,000. He asked me if I would be willing to make a substantial campaign contribution. At the end of this luncheon meeting I promised him that I would assume the responsibility to raise between $8,000 and $10,000 for his campaign. I did so in part because I genuinely admired the man and believed that he would make an excellent Governor. I also knew, however, that he would be grateful for my support, and I anticipated that he would express his gratitude by giving my company state work if he were elected.

During the campaign I paid directly to Mr. Agnew somewhere between $5,000 and $6,000 in cash as a part of my commitment to him. Before I was able to fulfill my total commitment, however I was approached by representatives of the Democratic gubernatorial candidate. During the Tawes administration in Annapolis, I had been making illegal cash payments in the amount of approximately $10,000 a year to Joe ████████ in connection with state contracts that my company was receiving from the Maryland State Roads Commission. In return, my company had received substantial state business. I was told by representatives of the Democratic candidate that if he were elected, he would reappoint the man who had been the Chairman Director of the State Roads Commission under the Tawes administration. They demanded, however, a $50,000 cash "campaign contribution" from me. I finally agreed to pay them $10,000 in cash. I simply could not have afforded a larger payment, but I made the $10,000 payment to protect myself in case the Democratic candidate were to win the election and thereafter control state work.

UNITED STATES GOVERNMENT
DEPARTMENT OF JUSTICE

Memorandum

TO: Baltimore County File   DATE: August 8, 1973

FROM: Russell T. Baker, Jr.
          Assistant U. S. Attorney

SUBJECT: Telephone Conversation With George Beall
             on August 7, 1973

At approximately 11:30 a.m. on August 7, 1973, I
received a telephone call from George Beall who was
calling from the Attorney General's office in Washington.
With him were Mr. Ruchelshaus and Mr. Peterson. They
had just completed a meeting with the Attorney General. I
was advised by Beall that on Monday, August 6, 1973, the
Attorney General had met with the Vice-President and his
lawyers in the Vice-President's offices. There the Attorney
General had to some extent disclosed to the Vice-
President the nature of the allegations against him. This
meeting was held as a result of pressure from the White
House (apparently General Haig) that was designed to
force a confrontation which would result in the Vice-
President's resignation. When the meeting did not produce
the desired result, the White House suggested that more
detailed disclosures be made to the Vice-President in the
hopes that he would become convinced that the case
against him was so strong that he should resign.
Apparently the meeting which Beall attended was called
to discuss whether or not Richardson should comply with
these requests. According to Beall, Peterson had
complained about the White House's involvement in this
investigation and had suggested that the White House

was again damaging the Department of Justice. He did
not feel that, according to Beall, Richardson should meet
with the Vice-President again. Instead, he had suggested
that a letter be prepared to the Vice-President advising
him in some detail of the allegations against him.
According to Beall, this letter would summarize the
allegations against the Vice-President with some
specificity including the period of time involved, the
companies involved, and the manner of payment. In part,
Peterson believed that a letter would create a formal
record of the contact and thus have an advantage over an
informal and unrecorded meeting. It would also,
according to Beall, put the ball in the Vice-President's
court and place him in such a position that he could
never claim that he was not given an opportunity to
respond to the charges. Finally, it would have the
advantage of keeping the Attorney General out of it as a
personal matter.

Secondly, George advised me in this telephone call
that the President had requested a full prosecution
memorandum on the case. The discussion at the meeting
had raised all of the obvious risks including leakage to
the press and to the Vice-President. However, George
reported that people at the meeting had felt that the
President was entitled to such a memorandum because
without a full awareness of the facts developed by the
investigation he could not exercise his responsibility to
determine how to handle the matter.

UNITED STATES DEPARTMENT OF JUSTICE

FEDERAL BUREAU OF INVESTIGATION

Baltimore, Maryland
August 15, 1973

RE: JEROME BENJAMIN WOLFF
      LESTER MATZ
      INFORMATION CONCERNING

In the pre-polygraph interview, WOLFF furnished the
following information:

Description:

NAME	JEROME BENJAMIN WOLFF, also known as Jerry
DATE OF BIRTH	March 19, 1918 at Chicago, Illinois
RESIDENCE	Stevenson and Valley Road, Stevenson, Maryland
SEX	Male
RACE	White
HEIGHT	5'9 ¾"
WEIGHT	170 pounds
MARITAL STATUS	Married—wife ELLIE
STEPCHILDREN	JEFFREY, 22½ years of age; KAREN, age 24
EDUCATION	Bachelor of Engineering, Northwestern University, and Doctor of Jurisprudence, Leola University, Chicago. Member of both Maryland and Illinois Bar

WOLFF has been a resident of Maryland for about 25 years.

WOLFF first met SPIRO T. AGNEW in approximately 1958 or 1959 when AGNEW was a member of the Board of Appeals which heard such matters as zoning. During this period WOLFF was Assistant Director of Public Works handling mainly sanitation engineering assignments and later was Chief Engineer in which capacity he testified before the Appeals Board. In approximately 1962 when AGNEW was elected County Executive in Baltimore County, Md., which position is roughly equivalent to being a Mayor, WOLFF was working as Chief Engineer for Public Works, Baltimore County. Approximately six months after AGNEW went in office, WOLFF entered business as a Consulting Engineer. His friendship with AGNEW continued. He said that he knew he would get county engineering consulting jobs but furnished no details. He left his position with the county because of adverse publicity in the press indicating that while he held the county job, he was also doing consulting work for the State of Maryland. Up until March 1, 1967, WOLFF continued to be self-employed as a consulting engineer.

On March 1, 1967, at the behest of SPIRO T. AGNEW, he became Commissioner of the State Road Department for the State of Maryland. WOLFF said that there had never been an extremely close personal relationship between he and AGNEW but they had been friends over the period of time described above. He volunteered that to date AGNEW had never asked him directly for any money. During the period that WOLFF was in private business himself, he gave payments of approximately five percent of the contracts for which he was hired as a consultant and had "an awareness" that some of the kickbacks were going to AGNEW.

In March 1967, while head of the State Road Department in Maryland, which position he held until February of 1969, the following situation existed. Shortly after taking the position of State Road Commissioner, I. H.

"BUD" HAMMERMAN, approached WOLFF and told him that an arrangement was to be made involving him, WOLFF, to work out "patronage" with consultants that were doing business with the State. HAMMERMAN said he would handle the situation himself because it was "delicate", and they could not afford to have anyone else involved. WOLFF knew there was an extremely close relationship between AGNEW and HAMMERMAN. The result was that consulting firms that were to be under contract for consulting projects for the State would kick back five percent of their fee. HAMMERMAN would make the collection, one-third of the amount collected would go to WOLFF, one-third to HAMMERMAN and one-third to AGNEW. However, this was in a very short period changed so that AGNEW was to get 50 percent and 25 percent was to go to HAMMERMAN and 25 percent to WOLFF. There were eight to 10 engineering firms contributing or kicking back in this manner. WOLFF figured that he personally received in kickbacks, approximately $35,000 to $40,000 and said that AGNEW should have gotten about $75,000 during the period. He said when he left the office of State Road Commissioner that this type of situation stopped. He said LESTER MATZ and ALAN GREEN, who are known to him, are people that he knew that were paying kickbacks directly to AGNEW and knew this because HAMMERMAN told him so. WOLFF said that the reason consulting firms were set up to kick back in the above-described manner was because they did not have to submit a bid.

WOLFF advised that he had been the Staff Science Advisor on the Staff of Vice President AGNEW from February 1969 until May of 1970, when he left and returned to again enter in private business. He said that he is currently the president of Greiner Environmental Systems, Inc., Consulting Engineers, One Village Square, Baltimore, Md. 21210, phone 301-323-8100.

On 8/11/73, WOLFF was afforded polygraph examination which was directed towards ascertaining if he had furnished any false information in regards to alleged corruption and kickbacks to date. This was the direction of the inquiry as requested by the U.S. Attorney in Baltimore.

The relevant questions and their answers in the Series were as follows:

3.　Have you intentionally given the Government any false information about the corruption investigation? Answer—No.

5.　Other than what you told me, have you personally ever given AGNEW any money? Answer—No.

6.　Have you ever done anything you are ashamed of? Answer—Yes.

7.　Are you now deliberately trying to protect anyone that you have not told us about? Answer—No.

9.　Are you now withholding any information what-soever about your part in this kickback set up? Answer—No.

11.　Did you deliberately lie to at least one of the questions in this test? Answer—No.

There was an extremely strong emotional reaction to Question 3, showing WOLFF was practicing deception. In the overall verification in Question 11, there is again a strong emotional response. There is also emotional response to Question 9 indicating that WOLFF was withholding information about the kickback set up.

USA BEALL and First Assistant RONALD LIEBMAN were advised that WOLFF was not being truthful in his claim that he has not intentionally given the Government any false information about the corruption investigation that they are heading. It was suggested that the same series of questions be re-run and then other tests continue. When SA PEARCE returned to the room where WOLFF was located, WOLFF was visibly upset. He said that he knew he had not done well. He said he could "feel" the reactions occur. At this point he volunteered that he had not furnished all the details involving monies that he received personally because he feared prosecution for Federal tax violation.

WOLFF was told that the examination, which apparently he and his attorney wanted to have, could continue as quickly as he would allow it. It was pointed out to him that the question could be revised to the effect that other than money, have you deliberately furnished false information about the corruption investigation, and accordingly, if there were other matters that he had not disclosed, he should do so voluntarily. At this point he said there was some information involving LESTER MATZ. At this point the USA, First Assistant, and WOLFF's personal attorney, privately interviewed him further, and, accordingly, SA PEARCE does not know what revelations were made other than that of money and the indications are there was other information regarding LESTER MATZ that needed to be disclosed or that there had been false information furnished regarding MATZ. WOLFF, during the brief period that he was talking to SA PEARCE, was visibly upset and in such an emotional state that it was no longer possible to continue polygraph examination.

On 8/12/73, LESTER MATZ, accompanied by his attorney, ARNOLD M. WEINER, appeared at the offices of the Federal Bureau of Investigation in the presence of his attorney. He signed form FD-328, Consent to Interview with Polygraph. MATZ in pre-polygraph interview furnished the following information and description:

Name: LESTER (NMN) MATZ
Sex: Male
Race: White
Residence: 2811 Marcie Drive, Baltimore, Md.

DOB: 1/30/24 at Baltimore, Md.
Height: 5'10"
Weight: 190 pounds
Education: Bachelor of Science—Civil Engi-
                        neering, 1949—John Hopkins Uni-
                        versity
Marital Status: Married—Wife—Shirley
                        Children: RICHARD EARL MATZ,
                        STEWART ALAN MATZ, HARRY J.
                        MATZ, JONATHAN MATZ
Military Service: 1943-1945, Combat Engineers,
                        rank—Corporal Serial Number 13
                        19 5475 (?)
Employment: Matz, Childs, and Associates, 1020
                        Cromwell Bridge Road, Baltimore,
                        since 1956—Consulting Engineers

MATZ furnished the following background
information:

MATZ first met SPIRO T. AGNEW in around 1961 at
which time AGNEW was a member of an Appeals Board in
Baltimore area, which handled—among other things—
zoning appeals. As a consultant, periodically MATZ
testified before this Board. During the period he also knew
J. WALTER JONES as a social acquaintance. During the
period 1962-1966, MATZ never gave any money as a
direct kickback. He gave a $500 political contribution to
AGNEW when AGNEW was to run for position as County
Executive. Payments were made between 1962 and 1966
to JONES and MATZ has no doubt that part of the money
given JONES during this period was in turn given in part
to AGNEW. He said at a Christmas outing in 1962,
AGNEW made a statement to the effect, "We've got to make
money right after the election." AGNEW in November
1962, was elected County Executive for the County of
Baltimore. During one meeting where he, JONES and
AGNEW were present, AGNEW said, You are not an
engineer, but "the engineer". It is assumed that the
implication being that AGNEW knew that MATZ would

work and make kickbacks to JONES and ultimately to AGNEW.

During the period 1962 to 1966, MATZ said that he gave five percent of his consulting contracts to JONES. He said that he personally was involved in collecting other monies which was delivered to JONES, and accordingly, did not like the idea that he had to make kickbacks on his firm's contracts. He said during the period 1967–68, when AGNEW was Governor, he had to kick back five percent when he was a consultant involving designs. He gave back 2½ percent for survey type of consultation and ⅛ percent of the fee on other types of consultation. He said on June 17, 1968, at 2:00 p.m., he met SPIRO AGNEW in the office of the Governor in Baltimore, Md., and turned over to him $20,000 cash which was the first occasion that he gave AGNEW money directly. He said here that AGNEW never asked for money. He said there was absolutely no doubt that he and AGNEW knew it was kickbacks for State contracts he had taken. He said as a matter of fact all of the kickback money that he personally paid was kickbacks on his fees where he was a consultant. Further, that all of the contracts were federally funded. He said he wanted to pay the $20,000 cash because he wanted to "get the credit myself". He said that the next payment he recalled was in around February 1969, when he personally went to the temporary office of the Vice President in the basement of the White House and turned over to AGNEW what he thought was $11,000, and told AGNEW that this completes my obligation. He then said that his personal notes indicate that the amount was $9,500, however, his personal recollection of the amount was that it was $11,000. He believed that the money consists of all $100 bills. He said AGNEW was appreciative of receiving the money.

MATZ said that in the spring of 1971, he turned over $2,500 to J. WALTER JONES in AGNEW's office. He went on to say that his firm had two $50,000 contracts to advise what was the best way to dispose of a Government installation in Suitland, Md. The $2,500 was a kickback on one $50,000 fee. He never paid the other kickback fee on the remaining $50,000. The plan that he was submitting was for GSA. He said he personally can't recall if he gave JONES the money in AGNEW's office or in an alcove.

In May of 1972 he was asked to make campaign contribution to the Presidential Campaign by one HARRY DUNDORE during a luncheon at the Orchard Inn. He said that at a Bar Mizvah for the son of I. H. "BUD" HAMMERMAN, AGNEW was present and he told him that he wanted to give him the money directly and AGNEW's answer was that MATZ could say, "Tell them you gave at the office". He later went to the Executive Office Building of AGNEW and gave him $1,500 in cash. He said he has no proof but he believes the money went into AGNEW's pocket and added that he has never seen any political contribution list giving him credit for making this contribution. He said that he may have given other smaller amounts in between but he really didn't recall the details. He said one reason he believed that he had given money was because later AGNEW invited him to fly in the Vice President's personal plane to Florida to witness the blast-off of "Moon Shot II".

On 8/12/73, MATZ was asked the following relevant questions in Series I:

3. To date, have you intentionally given the Government any false information about kickbacks? Answer—No.

4. Have you ever done anything that you are ashamed of? Answer—Yes.

5. During June 1968, Did you personally give AGNEW $20,000 cash in his office in Baltimore, Md.? Answer—Yes.

7.   In February 1969, did you give AGNEW at least
$9,500 cash kickback in his office in the White House?
Answer—Yes.

9.   Are you now deliberately withholding any
information whatsoever about your part in a kickback
set-up? Answer—No.

Overall verification of questions:

11.   Have you deliberately lied to at least one question
in this test? Answer—No.

This test was thereafter repeated in the exact same
sequence. In regards to Question 3, there is a very slight
reaction, not necessarily indicating deception. As a matter
of fact there is more reaction to Question 4, a control type
question—Have you ever done anything which you are
ashamed of? answered Yes. There is also a slight reaction
to Question 5 and Question 7, dealing with payments to
AGNEW. Again the reactions are not necessarily
deceptions and may be reactions to the magnitude of the
questions themselves. There is a moderate reaction to
Question 9 which indicates there probably are some
details regarding kickbacks that MATZ has not disclosed
at the present time.

In Series II, the relevant questions with their
answers are as follows:

3.   Other than what you have told the Government,
have you ever committed a crime for which you have not
been arrested? Answer—No.

5.   Did you originate the idea to give cash kickbacks
directly to AGNEW? Answer—Yes.

6.   Are you ashamed of your part in the kickback set-
up? Answer—Yes. (Control type question.)

7.   Do you know for sure of kickback money going to AGNEW that you have not told us about? Answer—No.

9.   Has AGNEW personally ever asked you to give him money? Answer—No.

During this question MATZ began to talk briefly and was later to explain he just remembered something he wanted to bring to the attention of the prosecuting attorney.

11.   Have you answered all of these questions truthfully? Answer—Yes.

There are indications that MATZ is practicing deception in regards to Question 5. There is something specific bothering him that he has not disclosed which deals with the origin of the idea to give cash kickbacks directly to AGNEW. There is a like reaction to Question 7 indicating that MATZ has other information about kickback money going to AGNEW that he has not at this time told about. The overall verification—Question 11— shows a reaction indicating that MATZ knows that he has not necessarily answered truthfully to all of the questions in the test.

In the post-polygraph interview which was very brief, MATZ advised SA PEARCE as follows:

In regards to Question 9, Series I, and Question 3, Series I, he said that he had a thought come into his mind. He stated he and his partner had an envelope in which cash was stored for purposes of having cash available to pay kickbacks. He said that he took about $2,000 on one occasion and that his partner didn't know it and he had the intention to put it back but he never did. He stated that in regards to Question 5 dealing with the payment of $20,000, he said the thought occurred to him that the payment he believed was actually July 1968 rather than June 1968 as he had previously told SA

PEARCE. He was emphatic and stated he actually made the payments and would never change that statement.

The observations indicating possible deception to Questions 5 and 7, Series II, were brought to the attention of the Government attorneys who indicated they will question MATZ further in regards to this.

Both MATZ and WOLFF could logically be interviewed further utilizing polygraph technique to verify certain points that they have furnished information about. Future polygraph examinations will depend on additional briefings by the polygraph operator.

Witness Said to Pass Lie Test

By Bill Richards
Washington Post Staff Writer

A key government witness in the special federal investigation of Vice President Spiro T. Agnew passed an FBI lie detector test concerning his charges that he had passed to Agnew money extorted from Maryland engineering and architectural consultants, according to Time magazine.

The FBI polygraph test, which usually is not considered admissible evidence in court, showed that Agnew associate Jerome Wolff was telling the truth when he told federal investigators he passed money extorted from consultants directly to Agnew when he was Maryland governor, the magazine reports.

Time also said that U.S. Attorney George Beall had asked other prospective witnesses in the Baltimore investigation to take similar tests.

The magazine also reported that federal investigators had obtained a diary from Wolff showing payoffs in 1967 and 1968 that were purportedly turned over to Agnew.

Sources contacted by The Washington Post have confirmed the existence of a businessman's datebook, which listed dates of meetings with Agnew. The sources could not say, however, whether the datebook contained any information other than a list of meeting dates.

Wolff was Agnew's appointed chairman of the Maryland State Roads Commission during that time and was responsible for approving all consulting contracts for state roads.

Wolff subsequently became president of Greiner Environmental Systems, Inc., one of Maryland's largest consulting firms. The same prosecution team probing the Agnew allegations last week secured a 39-count grand jury indictment for bribery and extortion against Dale Anderson, the county executive of Baltimore County.

One of the eight consulting firms listed in the indictment as giving kickbacks to Anderson is Greiner Environmental Systems, Inc.

Wolff could not be reached last night for comment, and both the FBI and the U.S. attorney's office refused to comment on the magazine's report.

Wolff was asked to take the lie detector test, Time said, after a visit to Baltimore 10 days ago by Assistant U.S. Attorney General Henry E. Petersen. Petersen spent two days reviewing the case against Agnew with Beall and questioned at least one of the three government witnesses who have been granted limited immunity.

Attorney General Elliot L. Richardson has said he will make the final decision on whether to seek an indictment from the federal grand jury against Agnew.

It was learned yesterday that Paul Gaudreau, president of a Baltimore architecture firm who has been granted immunity, has not been asked to take a lie detector test.

It is not known whether Lester Matz, a Baltimore engineering consultant who has also been given immunity, has been asked to take a similar test.

During his visit to Baltimore, Petersen went over much of the material that Beall and his investigators have gathered in their nine-month investigation into corruption in Baltimore County. Agnew served as Baltimore County executive from 1963 to 1967, and as Maryland governor from 1967 to 1969.

Petersen also questioned Matz about his allegations that he personally gave money to Agnew. Sources have said that Matz has told investigators that he turned over $2,500 to Agnew.

Agnew has vehemently denied that he accepted kickbacks from consultants for state or federal work, calling the allegations "damned lies."

It is not known whether Petersen also spoke with Wolff and Gaudreau, but both of the consultants have been cooperating fully with the investigators.

Lie detector tests are not ordinarily allowed as courtroom evidence during a trial unless both sides agree to their presentation. However, the same rules do not apply to a grand jury, where no judge sits and the ground rules for evidence are considerably looser.

If Richardson approves, the federal prosecutors are expected to begin presenting their case against Agnew to the grand jury after Labor Day.

UNITED STATES GOVERNMENT

Memorandum

TO: Mr. Gebhardt   DATE: August 27, 1973

FROM: R. E. Long

SUBJECT: DALE ANDERSON, COUNTY EXECUTIVE
BALTIMORE COUNTY, MARYLAND
SPIRO T. AGNEW, VICE PRESIDENT
INFORMATION CONCERNING

    This is to set forth an analysis of an 8/27/73 article
by Bill Richards appearing in "The Washington Post"
captioned "Witness Said to Pass Lie Test." Much of the
data in the article has not been available to the Bureau or
its personnel and in other instances statements in the
article appear to have been made by persons not familiar
with FBI terminology and policy.

    On 8/11 and 12/73 SA J. Robert Pearce of our
Philadelphia office, at the request of the Attorney General,
Assistant Attorney General Petersen, and U. S. Attorney
Beall, Baltimore, appeared in Baltimore and asked
████████ and ████████ a series of questions using the
polygraph technique. The following observations are
made with respect to various comments appearing in the
attached article.

    1. The article states a key Government witness in the
special Federal investigation of Vice President Spiro T.
Agnew passed an FBI lie detector test.

In the use of a polygraph it has been long standing FBI policy that our operators do not make an absolute judgment that a person passed or failed to pass the examination. Our operators must qualify their conclusions to the effect that there was or was no indication of deception on the part of the person afforded the examination. In addition, within the Bureau we refer to it as a polygraph and not a lie detector.

2.   The article states that the FBI polygraph test showed that Agnew associate Jerome Wolff was telling the truth.

3.   This article, based on a "Time" magazine story, reports that U. S. Attorney Beall had asked other prospective witnesses to take similar tests.

The initial request to our Baltimore office on 8/9/73 by Beall was to have SA Pearce afford at least two and possibly four persons* a polygraph examination on the morning of 8/10/73. Other than this, the Bureau has no knowledge of Beall's plans for affording other persons the polygraph. As previously indicated, Pearce afforded only two persons, ███████████ the examination on 8/11 and 12/73. *Identities not disclosed to F.B.I.

4.   The article continues that "Time" reported that Federal investigators had obtained a diary from Wolff showing payoffs in 1967 and 1968 that were reportedly turned over to Agnew and that sources contacted by "The Washington Post" have confirmed the existence of a businessman's date book, which listed dates of meetings with Agnew.

The Bureau has no knowledge of the existence of a diary or businessman's date book. It is noted, however, that an article appearing in the "Evening Star" 8/20/73 carries a comment that "The New York Daily News" said yesterday that Beall reportedly has obtained a diary listing political kickbacks. The News in a story citing unnamed authoritative sources said the diary was kept by former Agnew Aide Jerome Wolff. A UPI release on 8/19/73 states that U. S. Attorney Beall has obtained a diary kept by Jerome Wolff, former Aide to Vice President Agnew listing under-the-table kickbacks to Maryland political figures by contractors and consultants while Agnew was Governor of that State in 1967 and 1968, the New York Daily News reported Sunday.

5.   The article states that Wolff could not be reached last night for comment and that both the FBI and the U. S. Attorney's office refused to comment on the magazine's report.

On the evening of 8/26/73 Inspector J. E. Herington, Press Office, received a call from Bill Richards of "The Washington Post" concerning the "Time" article. Herington advised Richards he had not seen the "Time" article and had no comment.

6.   The article states that Wolff was asked to take the lie detector test after a visit to Baltimore ten days ago by Assistant Attorney General Henry E. Petersen.

Other than this we have no knowledge that Petersen had spent two days with Beall reviewing the case against Agnew and that he had questioned witnesses in this case.

7.   The article states it was learned yesterday that Paul Gaudreau, President of a Baltimore architecture firm who had been granted immunity, had been asked to take the lie detector test.

We have no knowledge concerning this comment.

8.   The article states it was not known whether Lester Matz, the Baltimore engineering consultant, who has been given immunity, has been asked to take a similar test.

9.   The article points out that during his visit to

Baltimore, Petersen went over much of the material that Beall and his investigators have gathered in their nine month investigation into corruption in Baltimore County.

The Bureau has absolutely no knowledge concerning this comment.

10. According to the article Petersen also questioned Matz about his allegations that he personally gave money to Agnew.

We have no knowledge concerning this remark.

11. According to the article, sources have said that Matz has told investigators that he turned over $2,500 to Agnew.

We have no knowledge with reference to this comment.

OBSERVATIONS

The FBI, other than affording the two polygraph examinations noted herein, has conducted no investigation in this matter and has not come into possession of the details of the investigation which has been conducted by the Internal Revenue Service in conjunction with the U. S. Attorney's Office in Baltimore, Maryland. It is quite conceivable that leaks reported by the press may be attributed to the various witnesses and/or their attorneys. The Bureau has afforded the results of the polygraph examination the highest security and has been available to Bureau personnel only on a need to know basis.

UNITED STATES GOVERNMENT
DEPARTMENT OF JUSTICE

Memorandum

TO: File   DATE: August 17, 1973
                                          PTW:mam
                                          51-35-262

FROM: Philip T. White
          Staff Assistant
          Criminal Division

SUBJECT: Agnew Investigation

On Wednesday August 15, 1973, Assistant Attorney
General Petersen and I traveled to Baltimore and met
with United States Attorney George Beall and Asssistant
United States Attorneys Skolnik, Baker and Liebman and
were briefed on the latest developments in the Agnew
Investigation. Thereafter from approximately 10:30 to
3:30 p.m. we met in Mr. Beall's conference room with Mr.
Jerome Wolff and his attorneys Arnold Weiner and Mr.
Albert Figinski. Mr. Beall was present during most of the
conference as were Assistant United States Attorneys
Skolnik, Baker and Liebman, except for short periods of
time.

Mr. Petersen questioned Mr. Wolff at great length
concerning his association with Vice President Agnew
and his knowledge of alleged briberous or extortionate
payments of money to Mr. Agnew in connection with his
official duties as County Executive, Governor of Maryland
and Vice President. Mr. Wolff confirmed that while
serving under Governor Agnew as Chairman of the State
Roads Commission he received substantial payments of

cash money from Mr. I. H. Hammerman in return for awarding state engineering consultant contracts to favored contractors who were making payments to him through Hammerman. According to what Hammerman told him a portion of these payments were also made to Governor Agnew.

Statement of Jerome B. Wolff

The following sworn statement is given by me voluntarily and of my own free will. The purpose of this statement is to set forth my knowledge of illegal activities engaged in by Spiro T. Agnew. This statement has been requested by the Office of the United States Attorney for the District of Maryland. I was advised prior to giving any information that, in the absence of voluntary disclosure, I would be taken before a grand jury, and, after having been given use immunity, I would be compelled to testify truthfully about what I knew concerning corruption in the State of Maryland.

My name is Jerome B. Wolff. My attorney is Arnold M. Weiner. I am an engineer, with principal expertise in the field of sanitary engineering. I am also an attorney. I am the President of Greiner Environmental Systems, Inc., a subsidiary corporation of the Greiner Environmental Systems, Inc., a subsidiary corporation of the Greiner Company, which is in turn owned by the Easco Corporation.

In the late 1950's, while I was Deputy Chief Engineer and later Assistant Director of Public Works for Baltimore County, Mr. Agnew became a member of the Baltimore County Board of Zoning Appeals. He and I became acquainted as a result of my appearances as a witness before the Board.

I left employment with the County approximately six months after Mr. Agnew took office as County Executive, having prepared a master plan for sewer and water improvements for the County. I left because my dual relationship with the State Roads Commission and the County had been brought to the attention of the press in June, 1962, although I was stoutly defended by the ▓▓▓▓▓▓▓▓▓ the County Administration Officer, William E. Fornoff, and ▓▓▓▓▓▓▓▓▓▓▓ Mr. Agnew and I became good friends between 1963 and 1967 while I was in business as a consulting engineer and became an unofficial advisor to him. Mr. Agnew arranged for me to get a substantial number of assignments from the County.

I greatly admired Mr. Agnew. I believed that he was sincerely attempting, with considerable success, to do a good job as County Executive.

Friends in the consulting business asked me, while Mr. Agnew was County Executive, how much I was paying for the engineering work I was getting from Baltimore County. They seemed to assume that I was paying, as it was well known in the business community that engineers generally, and the smaller engineering firms in particular, had to pay either in the guise of political contributions or as direct payments in order to obtain contracts from Baltimore County in those days. Only a few of the larger and well established firms were generally considered to be immune from having to pay.

It is my belief, based upon my experience and understanding of the experience of others, that engineering firms generally have to struggle for 10 to 15 years in order to get established. During their "gestation period" and for some time thereafter they generally make payments—sometimes through middlemen—to public officials at various levels of government throughout Maryland in order to get public work, or they arrange special relationships. Sometimes they reach a point where they are sufficiently established as qualified engineers where they do not generally make illegal payments in order to obtain a fair share of the public work available.

It was my belief that J. Walter Jones was Mr. Agnew's principal middleman in Baltimore County. He courted engineers, developers and others and bragged a great deal about his relationship with Mr. Agnew. Although, as I explained earlier, I was in a favored position with Mr. Agnew, on two or more occasions while Mr. Agnew was County Executive, Jones requested money from me in return for contracts I wanted or had obtained from the County. I paid him $1250 in cash in April, 1966, and in addition made a payment to ▮▮▮▮▮ who at the time was practicing law nearby, ostensibly as legal fees. My present recollection is that I also made one or two other payments to Jones. I felt obligated to cooperate with Jones because of my regard for him as a friend, and because he had helped me by paying me a generous consulting fee when I just started in business in 1963.

In late 1964, Mr. Agnew asked me to go to New York to talk to the late Charles Velze about contributing to the Republican Party as part of an arrangement to obtain a consulting contract for a joint City-County incinerator contract. I met with Velze and had an uncomfortable meeting with him. He indicated he would not pay in cash but would make political contributions by check. We eventually reached an arrangement whereby my firm was named as a subcontractor to his for a County contract. I do not recall if my firm ever did any work under that contract.

It was my belief that ████████████ was another middleman for Mr. Agnew. I learned from others that ████████████ was paying for work through ████ It is my recollection that in his office, Mr. Agnew once remarked to me that ████ was paying 10% for the work he was getting from the County. I inferred from Mr. Agnew's comment that Mr. Agnew was surprised that ████ was paying as much as 10%, in view of the fact that the going rate was generally 5%. Through conversations with ████ an engineer with whom I had several joint ventures, I learned that he was making payments for County work. I am not certain to whom he made these payments, although I thought it was either Jones or ████ or both.

I first met I. H. "Bud" Hammerman, II in the late 1950's while I worked for the County. After I went into business for myself, Mr. Hammerman gave me a substantial amount of private engineering work. I helped him obtain favorable rulings from the County Administration on various aspects of his property developments in Baltimore County. Although I had performed similar work for other developers, by 1966 I was especially well thought of by Hammerman.

Toward the end of Mr. Agnew's tenure as County Executive, I became aware of what might be termed a power struggle between Jones and Hammerman. The two men appeared to be jealous of one another and vied for the favor of Mr. Agnew. At some point in Mr. Agnew's term as County Executive, I formed an impression that Mr. Agnew was to some extent uncomfortable with Jones. Mr. Agnew indicated to friends who in turn reported to me that he did not believe he was getting all of the money which Jones was collecting from various people for Mr. Agnew. As a result of these factors—and perhaps others of which I am not aware—Hammerman seemed to have won the power struggle at or about the time Mr. Agnew became Governor of Maryland. Hammerman then became a dominant figure among those close to Mr. Agnew.

During Mr. Agnew's 1966 campaign for Governor, I offered him and he accepted $1,000 in cash as a campaign contribution. In March of 1966, I was asked by Mr. Agnew to help prepare a list of my clients who might be helpful to his campaign. I gave him a few names. I recall that I called a few of my clients on his behalf. Later, toward election time, he contacted me and indicated he had enough cash. He also asked me for the names of people to whom he might credit portions of my contribution on his official campaign contribution records. I do not recall whether he refunded some of this money to me. I worked in his campaign on his behalf but did no fund raising for him after the primary. I knew that I had a potential personal stake in his election as Governor, as he had sometime earlier indicated to me the possibility that he might appoint me Chairman—Director of the State Roads Commission, if he were elected Governor. Hammerman strenuously resisted my proposed appointment. He advised me that his opposition was no reflection on his regard for me, but that he did not want me to leave my consulting practice. I was handling a project which was important to him at the time. He also stated that he had a good working relationship with

On or about March 1, 1967, I took office as Governor Agnew's appointee as the Chairman—Director of the State Roads Commission. I spent about a month prior to that date working with my predecessor, John B. Funk, on the transition of his administration.

At the beginning of my tenure as Chairman—Director of the State Roads Commission, prior to George Lewis assuming Directorship of the Department of Public Improvements, Governor Agnew had me monitor every consulting engineering and construction contract that came through the State which was slated to be acted upon by the Board of Public Works—the three man board which gave final approval to the Department of Public Improvements contracts, land acquisitions, and the like. (These were not only State Roads Commission contracts, but also the Department of Public Improvement Contracts). It was obvious to me, in view of the provisions of State Roads Commission legislation, that I would in effect control the selection of engineers and architects for work to be contracted for by the State Roads Commission, subject only to the ultimate decision-making authority of Governor Agnew.

At some point, probably in the spring of 1967, not long after I had taken office, Bud Hammerman came to me with a proposition which I believe had been advanced by him to Governor Agnew. It was to the effect that Hammerman would go on "scouting expeditions"—that is, that he would approach engineers, after I had indicated to him which engineers were likely to be getting work from the State Roads Commission, for the purpose of soliciting cash payment to be made through Hammerman for the Governor. At first we agreed that any moneys solicited in that manner should be split three equal ways between Mr. Agnew, Hammerman, and myself. Hammerman later reported to me that Mr. Agnew was dissatisfied with this arrangement and that the arrangement would be 50% for the Governor, 25% for Hammerman, and 25% for me.

Over the course of the subsequent 18 or 20 months that Mr. Agnew remained in Annapolis, there were frequent meetings between Hammerman and myself. I would keep lists of the available contracts, and would notify Hammerman as to which engineers were scheduled to receive work from the State. He would then approach those engineers for cash payments. However, it was my understanding, based upon conversations that I had from time to time with Hammerman, that some engineering firms would not be approached at all by Hammerman. He and I did not believe he knew anyone at those firms with whom he felt safe in soliciting cash payments in return for State work. After receiving cash payments, Hammerman would deliver to me from time to time amounts of cash which he represented to me as constituting 25% of the payments that he was receiving from the engineers. I have supplied to the Office of the United States Attorney for the District of Maryland certain contemporaneous documents and records of mine which indicate in various ways the identity of those engineers whom I understood were making cash payments to Hammerman and the dates and amounts of Hammerman's deliveries to me of my shares of those payments.

All of the money I received was in cash. It was initially kept in my home. It was then transferred to two, and later, three safe deposit boxes, two in Baltimore, and one in Washington. Most of the money was spent on ordinary household expenses over a period of more than 4 years. A small portion of it was used as part of my payments to other Government officials in obtaining work for the two consulting firms which I had sold before I became Chairman, but in which I still had an interest.

As for the 50% of the money which was supposed to be going to Governor Agnew, I always assumed that Hammerman passed it on to the Governor, but I have no personal knowledge that he did so. The only information which I can presently recall as to the disposition of Mr. Agnew's 50% share of the cash payments is that Hammerman on at least one occasion told me, as I recall, that he was holding cash moneys for Mr. Agnew in one or more safe deposit boxes. Mr. Hammerman mentioned to me at one time that he appreciated getting his share of cash because despite his wealth, his needs for tax purposes were so great that the cash helped him meet some of his daily expenses.

During Mr. Agnew's tenure as Governor of Maryland, I met with him from time to time to discuss the status of various projects and the decisions which had to be made with regard to engineering, management, and sometimes architectural contracts. I generally prepared agendas for these meetings in advance. I have turned over to the Office of the United States Attorney for the District of Maryland those agendas which I have thus far been able to find. Mr. Agnew had complete confidence in my technical ability and generally accorded substantial weight to my preliminary decisions with regard to which consulting firms should be given contracts. He would generally concur with my selection. Occasionally where important or unique projects were involved, I would present him with a list of several possible firms from which he would select the one firm to be awarded the contract subject to approval of the Commission. He would also make the final selection for toll facilities, in accordance with the 1967 Toll Bridge and Tunnel Act, subject to the approval of the Board of Public Works. Governor Agnew always had and from time to time exercised the final power to make all decisions.

The selection process for such contracts generally worked as follows: Usually, based upon previous discussions with Governor Agnew, I would make preliminary decisions with regard to consulting engineering, and architectural firms to be given contracts. I would then obtain approval from the State Roads Commission members of my tentative selection. Sometimes I would obtain from them prior approval of a consultant, subject to their final approval of the executed contract. These latter selections would, in due course, also be discussed with the Governor.

Several factors influenced me in my own decision-making in the selection process outlined above. Some of them were as follows:

1. It was a basic premise of my selection process that an engineering firm had to be competent to do the work before it could even be considered for a contract. Any engineering firm which, in my judgment, was competent to perform a certain assignment might be given consideration.

2. Both Governor Agnew and Mr. Hammerman would from time to time ask me to give special consideration to

a particular engineering firm, and I would then try to do so. I remember, for example, that the Governor on one or more occasions asked me to give work to Hsi, Brenner, and Day and the A & B Engineering Co. Hammerman also recommended at least one company that, according to my understanding, had not paid him.

3. My decision-making (and I recall it was something I discussed with Hammerman in particular) was done with an eye toward avoiding substantial and noticeable deviation from general fairness—that is, I tried to avoid having any firm get more or less work than could be justified on a purely legitimate basis. I always viewed the process as one of accomplishing good public work for the State of Maryland, very similar to that which woul have been accomplished if all the selections had been made strictly on their merits, but serving our mutual ends at the same time. I believe Governor Agnew and Hammerman viewed the process in much the same way.

I regarded as important that I not deviate too obviously from the appearance of fairness and even-handedness in my selection of engineers. For example, I became aware I believe initially as a result of a conversation I had with Governor Agnew, that Hammerman had approached an engineer named Ballard to solicit cash payments in connection with potential State work, and that Ballard had complained to Governor Agnew. The Governor was very upset because Hammerman had been excessively heavy-handed with Ballard. I was concerned over Ballard's publicizing his complaint, so I continued to give his firm some work thereafter.

4. The fact that a certain firm was making cash payments was a definite factor in that firm's favor and they were accorded special consideration in the decision-making process. I believe that a comparison of the amounts of work given to certain firms before, during, and after Governor Agnew's administration would confirm this.

On the other hand, there were times when a firm was selected for a specific job totally without regard to whether or not that firm was making cash payments. Some firms had both outstanding expertise in certain fields of engineering and were Maryland firms. This made them obvious choices for certain jobs, whether or not they were making cash payments. Even such firms, however, could never be completely sure that such considerations were decisive so that even some of them were vulnerable to solicitations for cash payments.

    5.   Various other factors worked for or against particular firms or individuals in the selection process. For example, I definitely favored Lester Matz and Allen Green, and their firms, for several reasons, including the fact that I was receiving money from certain illegal dealings that I had with Matz and Green that did not involve Governor Agnew. Conversely, one engineering firm was disfavored by me because in my view they had taken positions contrary to the best interests of the Commission.

    In addition to the cash which I received from Hammerman as my share of payments he was receiving from engineers, I received $4,500 from him as a portion of my share of payments made to Hammerman from the stock brokerage house of Alex Brown & Sons, Inc. in Baltimore. It was my original understanding from Hammerman that a total cash payment of $50,000.00 was expected from Alex Brown, but he later told me that less than one-half of that amount was ever actually given to him. Hammerman indicated that he dealt with a senior member of the Alex Brown firm, but he did not identify him to me.

    The genesis of the events which resulted in cash payments from Alex Brown to Hammerman occurred when I traveled to New York City in the summer of 1967 with Governor Agnew. He and I went to one or more New York bond houses on two different occasions and learned a great deal about the bond business. I specifically remember a meeting with a Vice-President at the firm of Smith Barney. Mr. Joseph D. Buscher, the Special Assistant Attorney General for the State Roads Commission, attended the meeting with Mr. Agnew and

myself. Governor Agnew informed the Vice-President of
Smith Barney that he was interested in learning the basis
of the methods used in syndicating the financing of the
approximately $220,000,000 worth of State bonds that
were required to finance the second Chesapeake Bay
Bridge. The Smith Barney executive informed the
Governor that the local bond house (in this case, Alex
Brown & Sons, Inc.) was not the primary functionary in
such an undertaking. The Smith Barney representative
indicated to Governor Agnew that as in previous bond
issues negotiated in such syndications it would be the
New York house which would do the bulk of the work.
The Governor as well as Mr. Buscher and I were startled
by that information. When Governor Agnew and I got into
a taxicab after leaving Smith Barney, the Governor
slapped his knee and said "we've got 'em!" I understood
him to mean that he was now in a position to put
pressure on Alex Brown to comply with the demands he
would make on them in return for the very substantial
bond work which the Governor was in a position to give.
I remember the Governor commenting with obvious
relish that former Governor Tawes and State Comptroller
Louis Goldstein apparently did not know that the local
bond house did little work in connection with large bond
financings. Bud Hammerman subsequently reported to me
that he had told someone at Alex Brown that the
Governor was thinking of either replacing Alex Brown or
severely limiting their participation in the upcoming
negotiations. Hammerman therefore was able to elicit
from Alex Brown the cash payments out of which
Hammerman subsequently delivered to me $4500.00. In
addition, I recall that the Governor requested that at least
one additional local firm be added to the Alex Brown
group. (In that connection but not necessarily related to
his selection of additional bond firms, I recall that
Governor Agnew told me on one occasion that he had
received valuable advice—I inferred that it was insider
information—on potentially profitable investment
opportunities in the stock market.)

I also remember the following details with regard to

cash moneys paid to Hammerman by the J. E. Greiner Company. I specifically remember a payment of $6,250.00 given to me by Hammerman as my 25% share of a $25,000.00 cash payment which Hammerman said had been given to him by the Greiner Company.

I also recall the following incident, which I believe was related to the $25,000.00 payment from the Greiner Corporation to Hammerman: ███████ was at a certain point "raising hell" about the award to the Greiner Company of the design contract for the second Chesapeake Bay Bridge. Both the Governor and I were eager to answer ██████ complaints. When I complained to Governor Agnew, indicating that I thought it in our interest to have the Greiner Company do something to defuse ████████ Governor Agnew invited █████ then the ███████████, in for breakfast one morning. I specifically remember that I was invited to the meeting but arrived late and I was embarrassed that I missed the earlier part of the conversation. I arrived in time to hear the conclusion of a discussion between the Governor and ███████████ with regard to the possibility of the Greiner Company filing a libel suit against ██████████ after █████ had left, Governor Agnew told me that ██████ had said that if a libel suit were to be filed, ███████ might have to testify and that he would in such a situation have to tell the truth. I immediately understood what that might mean, and believed that the Governor was referring to the threat implicit in ███████ recalling the fact that the Greiner Company had given to Hammerman for the Governor a $25,000.00 cash payment in consideration for the Bay Bridge design contract which had been awarded to the Greiner Company.

I think it necessary to mention that much of my understanding concerning the Governor's actions and reactions to specific situations was inferential, since we seldom discussed any of my relations with Hammerman or others or the fact that we were acting either jointly or individually in a corrupt manner. I have personally believed our relationship flourished because of our mutual sensitivity to our own positions and our mutual respect for one another. I do recall one comment by Mr. Agnew, however. I was in the Governor's office in the State House. Governor Agnew and I were standing in front of the fireplace after a meeting, and he said to me—I paraphrase—"Look after yourself but be careful". . . I understood him to mean that I could personally profit from my activities, but to do it discreetly.

On or about August 11, 1968, I prepared a list, which I have turned over to the Office of the United States Attorney for the District of Maryland, of those engineering firms which, as of that time, I understood to have been making cash payments for Governor Agnew in return for State work being awarded to them. I prepared the list because Mr. Agnew had shortly before that time been nominated to run for Vice-President, and I was interested in knowing to what extent I had profited from the payments we had received from Hammerman and how much I might look forward to receiving if the Governor vacated his office and I terminated my stay with the State. By the use of a certain code on the list, I indicated for my own purposes at that time which firms I then believed to be paying the Governor through Hammerman on the one hand and which firms I then believed to be paying the Governor directly, on the other hand.

At a certain point, which I believe was after Mr. Agnew's election as Vice-President in November, 1968, but prior to his inauguration as Vice-President on January 20, 1969, Mr. Agnew asked me to determine the details of payments which had been made by the State Roads Commission under his administration to the engineering firm owned and operated by Allen Green. I then discussed this request with Allen Green, and asked him to give me his best recollection of these details of the jobs awarded to his company and the fees paid to it. Green subsequently prepared the list and submitted it to me. I used this listing to prepare a list of my own and gave a copy or duplicate of my document to Mr. Agnew. When I handed Mr. Agnew the list, he and I did not discuss it to any extent, according to my present recollection. Mr. Agnew just put it away. It was my belief at that time that he did not need to have the list explained to him in any detail but was able to understand it fully on his own. I have turned over copies of both documents (the original prepared by me and the one prepared by Green) to the Office of the United States Attorney for the District of Maryland.

It is my understanding and belief that both Green and Matz continued to make cash payments directly to Mr. Agnew after he had become Vice President. I say that because of conversations that I have had with both Green and Matz since January 1969, in which each of them indicated to me that he had made payments directly to the Vice President. I believe it was Green who on at least one occasion mentioned to me his fear that his conversations with Mr. Agnew might have been taped or "bugged."

Early in 1973, Matz told me that on one occasion—which I assume to have occurred during the 1970 Congressional Campaign—Matz brought money to Mr. Agnew in the White House and tendered it to him, and that Mr. Agnew's response had been to suggest that Matz give some or all of that money to ███████████ ███████████ Matz told me that he did not wish to do that; I understood that Mr. Agnew ultimately accepted the money from Matz on that occasion.

I went to work for Mr. Agnew on the Vice President's staff on or around March 1969, and remained for about 15 months until May 1970. Thereafter, I continued as part-time consultant to the Vice President until December 1971. My relationship with the Greiner Company, which began in May 1970, eventually caused then White House counsel John Dean to suggest that my relationship with the Vice President's staff be totally severed and that was done.

With regard to Jones, it was my impression that he was "phased out" to a large extent by Mr. Agnew, in favor of Bud Hammerman, after Mr. Agnew became Governor. I believe that was because Mr. Agnew felt that he could not trust and had been embarrassed by Jones, whom he felt to be too crass and too loose in using Mr. Agnew's name. My diaries—which contain a great wealth of information and which I have turned over to the Office of the United States Attorney for the District of Maryland—reveal that I had some 13 contacts with Jones during the period of time that Mr. Agnew was Governor of Maryland. Jones often sought to "romance" me in connection with some potential real estate deals during that period of time, but I finessed him in all of these.

Jones "resurfaced" after Mr. Agnew became Vice President. I am aware of Jones's operating in connection with the General Services Administration after Mr. Agnew became Vice President, but I am aware of few details. I have the definite impression that Jones spent much time and effort cultivating a man named ███████ who was for a time a top official of the GSA.

Some time late in February, or early in March, 1973, I wrote a letter to Mr. Agnew concerning the Baltimore County kickback investigation. The substance of the letter was that my business associates had told the prosecutors that they had paid me money which I in turn had paid to certain officials in Baltimore County and other jurisdictions for the purpose of obtaining engineering work. I pointed out to him that I was deeply concerned that the investigation could create serious problems for the Republican Party.

I was hopeful that he might intercede in my behalf to limit or terminate the investigation of me. I gave the letter to Hammerman and requested that he deliver it personally to Mr. Agnew. I was told by Hammerman that Mr. Agnew was quite upset by the letter but he did not give Hammerman any assurances that anything could be done. Rather, I had the impression that little could be done, but I sent the letter in desperation, realizing I was in serious difficulty.

Hammerman thereafter reported to me from time to time. At one point Hammerman told me that Mr. Agnew had suggested that I hold fast to my position, that no investigation would be made of my tax returns, and that immunity would not be forced on me. At another point, the day after Easter, Hammerman called and told me that he had seen Mr. Agnew and had received assurances that everything would come out fine. I received these assurances with skepticism and without expecting that anything helpful would result.

I conferred with Hammerman from time to time until June. I told him when I was planning to cooperate with the Government because immunity would be forced on me. William Fornoff had just recently entered a guilty plea and was reported to be cooperating with the Government in naming those persons who had made payments to him. Hammerman claimed that Fornoff had assured him that he had not named either of us. I did not believe this. I stopped contact with Hammerman after I began cooperating with the Government.

I told George White of my concern about the investigation on January 30, 1973. I told him I felt desperate. He told me to see him. I met with him in the company of Matz shortly thereafter. Both Matz and I made a spirited presentation of the problems we faced and stated our belief that Mr. Agnew was in imminent danger of being embarrassed, or worse, as a result of the investigation. We both importuned White to intercede with Mr. Agnew on our behalf. I was especially anxious that Mr. Agnew be contacted either by White or Hammerman before I was subpoenaed. Shortly thereafter I sent Mr. Agnew my letter through Hammerman. I later concluded that White had either been unsuccessful if he had tried to help us, or that he had done nothing.

Memorandum

TO: The Files   DATE: August 23, 1973

FROM: Thomas H. Henderson, Jr.
         Deputy Chief, Management and
         Labor Section

SUBJECT:

    At 3:45 p.m., on this date Pamela Higgins, an Assistant District Attorney from Philadelphia who assists Richard Sprague in the Yablonski prosecutions, called me. She stated that she had received a telephone call this morning from a member of the national news media. She stated that this person, who she declined to identify, is a long-time friend of Mr. Sprague. She related that this person said that a colleague of his had received a tip from a Justice Department official in Washington that W. A. Boyle was about to be indicted very soon and that a UMW member from a "Pennsylvania local" had directly implicated Boyle in the murder of Joseph Yablonski. This reporter then stated that the Justice Department official was the same official who had leaked information about the Agnew investigation in Maryland and that while this official was connected with the Agnew investigation he did not know any details of the Boyle information because he had only overheard it in the Justice Department. Mrs. Higgins informed me that she told the reporter that she had no comment on the information, but off the record his information was "lousy." She also stated that, in her opinion, the story would not be printed.

After receiving this phone call from Mrs. Higgins, I then informed Henry Petersen of the above facts. I have been informed that the only two officials in the Criminal Div., Justice Department who are working on the Agnew investigation are Mr. Petersen and Phil White.*

It should be noted that a witness in the Yablonski case has been voluntarily undergoing a polygraph examination in Knoxville, Tennessee, for the past two weeks. The examiner is Special Agent J. R. Pierce, FBI, Philadelphia, Pennsylvania. Mr. Pierce also administered the polygraph examinations in connection with the Agnew investigation in Baltimore last week.

*Mr. Petersen made this known to me as we were discussing this item of information.

INDEX

281